Global Perspectives in the Geography Curriculum

D0207438

Since the early 1990s educational policy makers and some subject leaders have been seeking to fundamentally change teaching geography in UK and US schools, from a subject which encourages students to explore spatial concepts, ideas and skills, to an ethics-based subject concerned with the promotion of environmentalism, cultural diversity and social justice. In this book, new approaches are critically examined, within historical and ideological contexts, addressing a number of fundamental questions:

- Should geography be used as a tool for the delivery of citizenship ideals?
- If the state and teachers are taking more responsibility for the values, attitudes and emotional responses of students, how will they learn to develop these qualities for themselves?
- If global perspectives shift the focus of education from learning about the outside world to learning about the self, what is their vision of social progress and conception of social change?

This book advocates a return to liberal models of education, arguing that new approaches to geography currently being promoted in schools fundamentally undermines the educational value of the subject, and the freedom of young people to shape the world in which they live.

A vital resource for teachers and student teachers alike, *Global Perspectives in the Geography Curriculum* makes a significant contribution to the growing debate about the future direction of the discipline itself.

Alex Standish is Assistant Professor of Geography, Western Connecticut State University, US.

Global Perspectives in the Geography Curriculum

Reviewing the moral case for geography

Alex Standish

Routledge
Taylor & Francis Group

LONDON AND NEW YORK

First published 2009
by Routledge
2 Park Square, Milton Park, Abingdon, Oxon OX14 4RN

Simultaneously published in the USA and Canada
by Routledge
270 Madison Avenue, New York, NY 10016

Routledge is an imprint of the Taylor & Francis Group, an informa business

© 2009 Alex Standish

Typeset in Palatino by
Florence Production Ltd, Stoodleigh, Devon
Printed and bound in Great Britain by
T.J. International, Padstow, Cornwall

British Library Cataloguing in Publication Data
A catalogue record for this book is available from the British Library

Library of Congress Cataloging in Publication Data
Standish, Alex.
  Global perspectives in the geography curriculum: reviewing the moral
  case for geography / Alex Standish.
       p. cm.
    Includes bibliographical references and index.
  1. Geography – Study and teaching – United States.
  2. Geography – Study and teaching – Great Britain.
  3. Curriculum change.   4. Education and globalization.
  I. Title.
  G76.5.U5S73 2008   910.71′073 – dc22
  2008012545

ISBN10: 0–415–46895–7 (hbk)
ISBN10: 0–415–47549–X (pbk)
ISBN10: 0–203–89083–3 (ebk)

ISBN13: 978–0–415–46895–4 (hbk)
ISBN13: 978–0–415–47549–5 (pbk)
ISBN13: 978–0–203–89083–7 (ebk)

Contents

Illustrations

Figures

Tables

Boxes

Foreword

Perceived social, political or environmental crises whether, to take current examples, global warming or the terrorist threat, quickly provoke demands for the schools to do something about them. What should be their contribution to 'the making of good citizens'? Obviously this will include relevant provision in subjects such as geography and history as well as in the plethora of curricular sub-groupings: social education, political education, ethical education and environmental education as well as citizenship education, which is of course increasingly couched in terms of global citizenship. But as Standish points out, a more careful delineation of what citizenship education comprises is essential. In the first place, vital distinctions must be made between education *about* citizenship (the matter or content), education *through* citizenship (the method), and education *for* citizenship (the mission). The former should of course be thought of in terms of the conceptual frameworks of subjects such as geography and history and not merely as a collection of facts. Education through citizenship is not an idea, and can be thought of in terms of a range of activities, for example tending school gardens in the primary area, community activities in the secondary, and collecting for local, national and international charities in both. These focus on practising what is preached.

The great problem arises with the third category. The notion of making good citizens, history tells us in no uncertain terms, has almost always been detached from liberal conceptions of education. Perceptions of a crisis in the physical and moral health of the poor in the late nineteenth century, for example, led to eugenics education and the unimaginable horrors which followed. Imperialists, fascists and communist powers through the last two hundred years and more have similarly fashioned their particular visions of making good citizens. Regrettably, the more draconian they have been the more successful, on their own terms, has been the accomplishment. All have had in common blatant inculcation. Similarly, religious education in faith schools has from time immemorial sought to make good citizens, whether Christian, Jewish or Muslim, but instruction and indoctrination have been the watchwords. We must also scrutinize very carefully latter-day reinventions of the wheel of citizenship education. Geography educators and others must become self-aware of which particular bandwagon they are climbing on. The educational intentions of the evangelical environmentalist and the politicization of any of the social subjects are tarred with the same illiberal brush.

In these circumstances the thrust of Alex Standish's book seems to me to be an absolutely valid challenge to what are euphemistically referred to as the 'reforms' postulated from without as requisites for schooling in the United Kingdom and United States, through seeking to make citizenship some kind of curricular, and one fears instructional, priority. Not least, I agree with his view that ' in terms of education there is much to be valued in the liberal secular model of education as it evolved from the nineteenth century into the twentieth. Reflecting scientific, humanistic and intellectual traditions, this model sought to train young people in the virtues of disciplines such that they gain wisdom and insight into both the outside world and humanity itself.' This is in itself a statement which readers might wish to challenge, but it is a critical issue for addressing the situation of what he and others regard as an illiberalizing slippery slope. While Standish's discussion is in the context of geographical education, equivalent arguments and caveats apply in relation to historical and social education areas in general. His detailed analysis of the issues and general plea for a libertarian approach to geographical education therefore is more than timely and his book should be regarded as essential reading for those involved in geographical education and associated areas. I also welcome most warmly the appearance of what has become an endangered species: a single-authored monograph on geographical education.

William Marsden
Emeritus Professor of Education,
University of Liverpool 2008

Acknowledgements

First, I would like to thank my wife Sarah and my two daughters Olivia (four and a half) and Anna (two) for their patience, understanding and support during the writing of this book. Second, thanks go to Dennis Hayes who has provided intellectual guidance and feedback over the six-year period of researching the geography curriculum in the US and UK. Dennis supervised my master's thesis at Canterbury Christ Church University College and also sat on my doctoral thesis committee. Next, I would like to acknowledge the support and feedback of Briavel Holcomb, Jeffrey Smith, Ken Mitchell and David Robinson, who were all members of my thesis committee at Rutgers University, New Jersey. As co-chair of the committee, Briavel provided much guidance over several years of work. I would like to thank Vanessa Pupavac, Jim Butcher, Kevin Rooney and David Gynn for their feedback on my ideas and writing. Vanessa's insights into the political theory of global citizenship have been especially valuable. A recent lively debate at the Institute of Ideas on *Moralising the Curriculum* produced by Kevin also helped to clarify my thoughts. Finally, I would like to thank Bill Marsden for his foreword, which sets the book in a broader historical context, and Bruce Roberts at Routledge for his editorial comments and for pressing me to finish writing. This book is dedicated to all present and future geography students.

Contributor: Vanessa Pupavac is a lecturer in the School of Politics and International Relations, University of Nottingham, UK. She has written extensively on the topics of human rights (including children), international law, development and post-national politics.

Credits: The author and publishers are grateful to the National Geographic Society Education and Children's Programs, Washington, DC, for permission to reproduce from their Xpeditions Web site the lesson plans in Chapter 7 and to the Humanities Education Centre, London, for permission to reproduce, also in Chapter 7, excerpts from the ecological footprints quiz on the Centre's Web site. The sources of permission to reproduce illustrations are detailed in the captions.

Abbreviations

Applicable to the United States

EETAP	Environmental Education and Training Program
EPA	Environmental Protection Agency
GENIP	Geography Education National Implementation Project
NAEP	National Association for Educational Progress
NCATE	National Council for the Accreditation of Teacher Education
NCGE	National Council for Geographic Education
NCSS	National Council for Social Sciences

Applicable to the United Kingdom

CAFOD	Catholic Agency for Overseas Development
DfES	Department for Education and Skills
GCSE	General Certificate of Secondary Education (usually taken at age sixteen)
GYSL	Geography for the Young School Leaver
ITDG	Intermediate Technology and Development Group
OFSTED	Office for Standards in Education
PSHE	Personal Social and Health Education
QCA	Qualifications and Curriculum Council
SCAA	Schools Curriculum Assessment Authority
SDE	Sustainable Development Education

Other

FAO	Food and Agriculture Organization
NGO	Non-governmental organization
UNESCO	United Nations Educational, Scientific and Cultural Organization
UNEP	United Nations Environment Programme
UNICEF	United Nations Children's Fund

Introduction

Why teach geography? Essentially there are two ways to answer this question. Either, because of something intrinsic to the discipline itself, there is something enlightening about learning geography itself, or because it serves some ulterior or extrinsic purpose. Sometimes it is difficult to separate these two. Knowledge and skills learnt in class may be central to understanding, but also have utility in areas of life beyond the classroom. However, this should not detract from recognition of the intrinsic value of geography as a subject. As teachers it is important to know why you are teaching something, because this will determine how to approach a subject and what you choose to teach. A central premise of this book is that how teachers and other educators answer this question has changed at the dawn of the new millennium. Increasingly, extrinsic rationales are being cited to justify geography's place in US and UK curricula, driven by politicians, policy makers and some leading geographers. These instrumental aims include geography's contribution to citizenship education, values and attitudes education, pre-vocational skills, and learning about global issues and connections. This development rests upon a second premise, that geography as a body of knowledge that contributes to the education of young people is being undermined by the postmodern challenge. This book will show how extrinsic aims are in many cases serving to fill a moral vacuum previously occupied by geographical knowledge and skills. The outcome is that the intrinsic reasons for teaching geography are being lost to many teachers and students. In the instances where this has taken place, what is left is a fundamentally different subject, that goes by the name of geography and may even involve learning about other places and people, but it does not even begin to teach students about the principles and essential ideas behind the subject of geography.

This transition began as part of the educational shake-up that was to follow the counter-cultural movement of the 1960s and 1970s, proceeding more rapidly in the American case. Nevertheless, in both America and the UK, geography was to find additional instrumental purpose with the thawing of the Cold War and the onset of the new global era. Today, geography is looked to by many to offer students a *global perspective* on our fast-changing world. In place of the traditional curriculum, reformists have sought to make geography more 'relevant' to students' lives by focusing on contemporary issues, by teaching about global citizenship and by taking an enquiry approach to teaching, in which the students play a role in determining what they study. As American geographer Joseph Stoltman observed in 1990, 'While citizenship has not been a major goal of geography education, the research and writing on citizenship suggest that the discipline should play a prominent role' (Stoltman 1990: 37). However, advocates for global perspectives in the curriculum fail to acknowledge that the new global era has thus far been characterized by a demoralized political mindset which lacks faith in our ability to know our world and distrusts the moral capacity of the younger generation to shape its future.

In certain respects the 1990s was a decade of opportunity. With the end of the Cold War came the discrediting of the communist alternative to capitalism to which many in the world had clung. In the West, the shallow nature of nationalism was exposed by the fall of its nemesis, against which Western nations had constructed their sense of identity for too long. The evident exhaustion of the ideologies of both Left and Right cleared a path for the new political ideas and possibilities to emerge and gain social purchase. Here, there was the possibility for citizens to build a new international movement for social change that would transcend narrow nationalism and unite people across borders and cultural divides. Such a new political movement could be built upon a shared vision of a better tomorrow, addressing genuine limitations upon people's living circumstances: poverty, unemployment, underdevelopment, restrictive borders, inadequate health care, poor education, inadequate housing, and so forth. The people behind this movement could be united by a political commitment to universal principles of freedom, equality, material advancement, human creativity, not divided by cultural differences. In schools young people could be prepared to inherit this world through the acquisition of knowledge and skills that equip them with insight into the workings of the world and also the role of humans to advance themselves to freedom from the shackles of nationalism.

Unfortunately this did not happen, or at least has yet to happen. Despite initiatives to promote global citizenship and educating young people to develop a global perspective there is no citizen-led movement for international change, and curricula are not transcending cultural differences. Instead, the 1990s were marked by a crisis of social and political meaning and the acceleration of liberalism's demise, as citizens retreated further from the public realm towards their private lives. Politics became less meaningful in people's lives, not more. Despite initial euphoria, globalization has been characterized by an absence of perspectives, lacking a final end goal and the promise of a better future. This situation has arisen from the gap between expectations of change and the discrediting of grand schemes for social transformation (Laïdi 1998).

Surprisingly, the response of many in society has not been to revive political ideas and participation, but instead to promote decidedly illiberal and dehumanizing solutions. The dominant political culture at the turn of the millennium is one that views people as the problem rather than the solution. This culture has set about decentring humanity from most areas of life: people must be subservient to the natural environment, cultures have become objectified as exhibits to be preserved rather than a process of human advancement, developing countries are viewed as inherently backward and unable to advance of their own accord, people (especially youth) cannot be trusted to develop into independent moral citizens, and humanity cannot accurately know its world.

In fact, something approaching the opposite of a progressive movement for democratic change is taking place and education has been at the forefront of this change. The whole curriculum in the US and UK has been influenced by this dehumanized political culture, but geography in particular has experienced rapid change, especially in the UK. This transition is not about the manipulation of curricular content as nation states did in the past to promote patriotism. The very nature and purpose of schools and education are being reformulated in a way that empties them of their inherent moral content. In particular, the postmodern challenge to knowledge and questioning of the 'relevance' of abstract learning to students has undermined the intellectual basis of many subjects. In place of intellectual and humanistic aims, the curriculum has become a vessel for society to fill with pet political and social projects. On both sides of the Atlantic, the 1980s and 1990s gave rise to numerous social, economic and political initiatives heaped on the shoulders of teachers: sex education, drugs awareness, preventing the spread of AIDS, cultural integration, increasing economic competitiveness through skills education, crime prevention, to name but a few. In effect, the political crisis has been exported into schools under the misguided assumption that nurturing the moral and emotional well-being of youth will solve society's problems tomorrow. This is by no means the first time education has been looked to for a social fix. For one, Hannah Arendt cautioned that schools need to be reminded 'to teach children what the world is like and not to instruct them in the art of living' and of the authoritarian consequences of the latter (Arendt 1968: 192). But when social, economic and political objectives are brought into schools at the same time as the intellectual basis of the subject is being undermined, there is a danger that they can become the curriculum.

In some geography curricula today, a global perspective is precisely one of these political initiatives being offered as a way to engage young people socially. However, global perspectives fail to provide meaning to people's lives in the way that national perspectives did in the past. This is because it lacks a positive vision of a better tomorrow, faith in collective action for social change, a final goal and distrusts the moral autonomy of individuals to bring about such change. As such, it is more of a project in shaping individuals than society. This 'global' model of citizenship emphasizes personal and local actions tied to 'global issues', including environmental problems like climate change, inequality, disease and ill health, cultural conflict, poverty and natural disasters. Underpinning global citizenship are several socio-political values or 'global ethics'. These include respect for the environment, respect for cultural diversity, tolerance of other viewpoints, concern for social justice and empathy towards those in need or different. Here, society's problems have been relocated from the wider political realm to the internal psychology and the skills of individuals themselves.

Yet few have stopped to ask how geography's ethical turn impacts the nature of geographical education itself and whether it enhances or hinders the education of young people. This is the objective of this book. Should teachers include ethical objectives in the curriculum and, where they do, how do they affect learning about geographical phenomena? Are ethical and intellectual objectives mutually compatible or do they interfere with one another? Which issues should be included in the curriculum? Do geography curricula focus on genuine problems people are facing in the developing world or are we projecting Western concerns overseas? Can children really be treated as citizens when they have yet to reach the intellectual and emotional level of adults? What is the relationship between individual psychological change and widespread social and political change? Can the former lead to the latter? How should geographers decide which values to emphasize in their teaching? If geography becomes akin to global citizenship, is it still geography or will it be an entirely different subject?

The conclusion drawn here is that geography's ethical turn with a focus on global perspectives itself serves to directly undermine the moral case for geography. It does this through its retreat from geography as an objective body of knowledge and seeker of truth and its replacement with personal geographies and truths. The outcome is to deny students the geographical knowledge and skills they need to make sense of the world around them. Moreover, its ethical agenda is a direct intrusion into the private conscience of young people themselves, driven by the contemporary misanthropic mindset reinforcing a negative view of our potential to shape the world for the better.

However, this does not mean that all school geography has become subsumed by the themes of global citizenship. In talking to teachers and textbook authors it is clear that there are many excellent geography teachers in American and British classrooms who were well trained in their subject and know what a good geography lesson looks like. Similarly, there are some who resist the moral erosion of geography and its replacement with values education. Some teachers report that they have a strong understanding of their subject, but they feel that young people need something different today, that somehow they have lost confidence in the value of their discipline for the up-and-coming generation. Without a widespread debate about the educational value of geography versus global citizenship many educators will be swept along by the global ethics bandwagon.

To grasp the stature and nature of this change it is perhaps best to begin with some questions of a fundamental nature such as: what is geographical education? And, why study geography? Of course in today's disorientated political climate there are multiple opinions on the answers to these questions, but not all equally valid. In order to advance society and its education system it is necessary for some consensus to be built about the nature of education and its purpose. Or, to put it another way, the moral case for geographical education needs to be remade. To do this it will be necessary to look back at the history of geographical education and how it evolved into an intellectually credible discipline. This is the topic of Chapter 1.

Of course the world changes and so should curricula. However, in order to capture the nature and purpose of education itself it is not necessary to reinvent the wheel. It is the contention of this book that in terms of education there is much to be valued in the liberal, secular model of education as it evolved from the nineteenth century into the twentieth. Reflecting scientific, humanistic and intellectual traditions, this model sought to train young people in the virtues of disciplines such that they gain wisdom and insight into both the outside world and humanity itself. Through education young people can inherit the wisdom of their forebears, opening the possibility for the new generation to see deeper and further. In this sense, education makes us human. It is through education that we gain an understanding both of our world and our place within it.

Within the liberal education model, geography's role has developed as one of mapping and comprehending spatially related phenomena. Learning about the physical and human variance upon the planet helps students to understand the world around them. In order to play this role geography has a number of fundamental qualities: mapping of spatially related phenomena, examining spatial relationships between different phenomena, comparing distant places and people, identifying interactions and relationships between people and the natural environment. In addition to this role there are times when geography crosses over from being a social science into the humanities. Here, geography offers insight into how the human condition varies across the planet through an exploration of culture and human–environment interactions. Whether as a social science or as part of the humanities, geography brings a vision of natural and human diversity and the wonders of the world into the classroom. Learning to comprehend and appreciate the physical creations of both nature and humanity again makes us a more complete person.

Research and methodology

The demoralization of geography first became apparent to myself and some of my colleagues while teaching the subject in schools in the south of England in the late 1990s and early 2000s. This insight was pursued as a master's thesis on the changing nature of geographical education in England and Wales at Canterbury Christ Church University College (Standish 2002). This study traced child-centred thought in geography from the 1960s to its inclusion in mainstream national documentation in the 1990s as well as the growing prominence of issues in geography curricula. Analysis was conducted on government and geographical associations' documentation, examination syllabi and geography textbooks. Additionally, a small survey of geography teachers was conducted to ascertain their views about the nature of the geography and the inclusion of global ethics.

This was followed up with an historical study of geography's relation to citizenship education in American schools as a requirement for a doctoral degree at Rutgers, the State University of New Jersey (Standish 2006). Content analysis was conducted on high-school world geography textbooks from 1950 to 2005, state geography standards were analysed and interviews were conducted with social studies teachers and authors of geography textbooks. This international research has been expanded to include further content analysis of geography textbooks used in England and Wales, analysis of online curricular materials and documentation, and new developments within the subject, such as the new pilot geography General Certificate in Secondary Education (GCSE) in England and Wales. The results of this work inform the analysis presented in this text.

Kincheloe (1991) correctly highlights the importance of place to curricular evolution. In an international study such as this, there is a danger that generalizations are elevated over specifics. Nevertheless, this text aims to work from geographical and historical specifics in order to identify some common trends. This is not to belittle the specifics of different localities. The curriculum in Washington, DC, is indeed different from that in Wisconsin or Wales. However, on both sides of the Atlantic the standardization movement has given rise to homogenizing trends. In England and Wales this took place through the introduction of the national curriculum. In the US individual states have centralized their own curricula and just four, highly similar, textbooks dominate the high-school geography curriculum across the country. This does not mean that locally teachers are not doing their own thing. They probably are. The objective of this text is not to analyse these local differences, it is to identify some common threads to geography emerging from very different localities: the US and England and Wales. England and Wales are taken as a geographical entity to study because Scotland and Northern Ireland have their own education systems. In England and Wales they are combined, albeit with some local differences in the Welsh curriculum. The book is mostly orientated towards secondary education as this was the focus of the research studies that inform its content.

Outline of the book

Chapter 1 recounts the historical evolution of geographical education with a view to ascertaining its moral worth. Students are asked to consider what geography is and why it should be studied. This chapter shows how the content and nature of geographical education have varied over time, but from this seeks to draw out the fundamental qualities of the subject that need to be retained in any modernization process. The chapter will elaborate on the question of how geography contributes to our humanity. In Chapter 2 geography's ethical turn is described and also how it challenges geography as an objective body of knowledge. In Chapters 3 and 4 the impact of this ethical turn on the geography curriculum in the US and England/Wales is documented, showing how this has given rise to global ethics in geography and its preoccupation with 'citizenship'. Chapters 5, 6 and 7 take a closer look at the meaning of global perspectives in the curriculum. Chapter 5 shows how teaching students to respect cultural diversity and faith in multiculturalism are frequently presented as the aims of cultural geography today. In Chapter 6 the methods used to teach about global issues and perspectives are reviewed, while Chapter 7 provides some examples of prominent global issues which feature in American, English and Welsh curricula. Chapter 8 is concerned with scrutinizing geography's new-found citizenship role. While national citizenship was about political rights and responsibilities, the chapter shows how global citizenship is focused on the personal ethics of young people themselves. The conclusion will discuss some of the implications of global perspectives in the geography curriculum and restate the moral case for the value of geography itself.

Key terms used in the book

To assist comprehension of the text the basic meaning of a few terms will be clarified, although there may be different nuances of meaning depending upon the context in which the terms are used. This will be addressed in the relevant chapters.

Central to this study are *values*. Hill (1991) describes values as beliefs that individuals attach special priority to, which subsequently determine how they live their lives (Hill, cited in Edwards 2002). Hence, all values are beliefs, but not all beliefs are values. Values suggest that some sort of action is judged as desirable or undesirable. Attitudes differ from values because they tend to be situational and less concrete (Roheah, cited in Edwards 2002). Roheah suggests that values are more central to our personality, transcending and guiding actions, attitudes and judgements. They provide the scaffolding for evaluating norms.

Moral values are a specific category in that they describe positive or negative social behaviour. Most values have a moral character to them, such as materialism or marriage, in that individuals or society deem them to be good or bad for society or individual character in certain circumstances. To moralize means to give a moral quality to something. To demoralize means to take this moral quality away (see Fevre 2000). *Ethics* is usually defined as moral philosophy or thinking about moral issues.

Values are an inherent part of education. Consciously or unconsciously, explicitly or implicitly, teachers will communicate to students that which is held in esteem, and that which is not. Different societies at different historical times held different values, which were passed on to the next generation through education, other social institutions or even informally.

Citizenship has several meanings, depending upon the context, including political, legal, moral, and membership of some organization (Smith 2002). These meanings will be explored in Chapter 8. *Citizenship education* is generally taken to mean the knowledge, values and skills that young people need to acquire to become rounded citizens. A useful distinction to make is between education *about* citizenship (the matter), education *in* or *through* citizenship (the method) and education *for* citizenship (the mission) (Marsden 2001a). Education *about* citizenship involves learning about political systems, rights and responsibilities in an abstract sense; education *in* or *through* citizenship means involving students in citizenship activity such as service-learning; while education *for* citizenship may or may not include the other two definitions, but also includes a moral commitment to a community or idea.

Developing multiple or global perspectives. One of the central themes of the new geography is that students, and teachers, should see the world as interconnected and develop a global perspective. In general, taking a global perspective, or multiple perspectives, means respecting the contributions of other cultures, viewing one's culture as an equal among others, and learning about global issues and viewing these from the perspective of others.

Chapter 1

The evolution of a discipline and its instrumental applications

KEY QUESTIONS

1 What is geography?
2 Why study geography?
3 What is the relationship between geography as a subject and social change?

Geography's recent ethical turn and the inclusion of global issues in the curriculum are by no means the first time that the subject has been utilized for political objectives and imbued with extraneous morals. Indeed it was not until the end of the nineteenth century that education was first understood as an intellectual activity distinct from moral indoctrination. The purpose of this chapter is twofold. First, it will chart the evolution of geography as a discipline, highlighting its fundamental humanizing qualities and how these emerged in different historical periods. Second, it will demonstrate the ways in which the subject has been seized upon for instrumental purpose. At different periods these external moral agendas have been religious, political and social reformist in nature. What is common to each is the conscious attempt to use geography as a vehicle to provide students with a predetermined set of socio-political values or to induce a type of desired behaviour. Indeed, geography's very evolution as an institutionalized discipline towards the end of the nineteenth century was not unconnected with its role in supporting imperialistic tendencies of European nations and instilling in children a sense of pride in nation, and empire in the case of Britain. Whether these extrinsic moral campaigns have been successful or not is not the prerogative of this chapter. At other times, such as during the Enlightenment and in the mid-twentieth century, there have been demands for greater scientific rigour from the subject.

During these periods, many geographers resisted the prevailing political orthodoxy and sought, as far as possible, to isolate their subject from political and instrumental moral pressures. Here the emphasis was on the value of geography itself and how it helped young people to become more complete human beings.

The evolution of geography will be explored in four distinct periods: the Age of Exploration, the Enlightenment period, the end of the nineteenth/ beginning of the twentieth century and the mid-twentieth century. In each period important contributions were made to the foundations of the subject, enhancing its intellectual and social credibility, but also its ulterior aims for geography are considered. It is evident from this brief sortie into geography's past that it is not a coherent discipline with clearly defined parameters. Hirst (1974) described geography as an area of knowledge rather than a distinctive field such as biology or mathematics. This has made the subject more sensitive than others to cultural and political pressures of the moment. Over the course of the twentieth century geographers branched out in several different directions. This is why geographers today refer to the subject's different traditions rather than providing an all-encompassing definition.

Geography in the Age of Exploration

From the Ancient Greeks to the first circumnavigation of the global by Magellan, geography became synonymous with the pursuit of spatial data, knowledge of distant places and mapping. It is well established that the roots of geographical enquiry lie in Ancient Greece and Rome. The Greeks coined the term *geographie*, meaning 'earth writing' or 'earth describing'. Ptolomy and Strabo were two of the founders of the discipline. In *Geographia* Ptolomy calculated locations using lines of latitude and longitude. The task for Greek geographers, and the Romans' thereafter, was to intellectually conquer the world: to find the geographical configuration and limitation of the world about which the Europeans knew little. Of course this 'world' was geographically restricted to Europe, North African and parts of Asia, but over time the coastline and some interior features of continents were mapped. These early geographers also kept records of climate, vegetation, landscape and people they encountered. As Europe entered its Dark Ages it was left to the Muslim world to take up the pursuit of geography. The work of ancient Greeks and Romans was translated into Arabic. Muslim geographers theorized that the world was a sphere and estimated its dimensions. They calculated the precession of the equinoxes, observed weathering and the hydrological cycle, and correlated human activity with different climates. Much of their work concerned observation and classification, given the limited knowledge of science at the time. Two prominent geographers of the time were al-Mas'udi and al-Idrisi.

The Europeans returned to geographical conquest following the scientific revolution. Geographical pursuits were held in high regard during the age of European exploration. This period included the explorers of the sixteenth, seventeenth and the early eighteenth centuries. The Europeans returned to the task of geographically knowing the world, but now on a global scale. To do this meant mapping the land and oceans in significant detail, identifying distant people and learning about distant lands. Given the centrality of this task to humanity at this time, geography is sometimes known as the Mother of All Sciences and, given its preoccupation with the mathematics of the globe, it was closely associated with mathematics and astrology at this time. It was the work of Copernicus that led to the identification of the spherical world. Constructing an intellectual map of the world necessitated recording all manner of detail about foreign lands: flora and fauna, people, culture, economic activity, politics, architecture, food and of course measurement of coastlines, hence geography developed early on with a strong empirical tradition. Early geographers frequently depended upon the work of travel writers for their material. Explorers returned to European shores with elaborate, and sometimes embellished, stories as well as specimens and images from their travels. In Europe, and later America, there was a hunger to learn about all things foreign and taste new exotic foods and drink.

Of course at this time science was intimately tied to ideas of divine creation. While scientists were seeking to understand natural processes, many thought that this would reveal the work of God in nature and hence there was no distinction between knowing the world and knowing God. Another external moral framework that influenced the development of knowledge at this time was the forging of national sentiment. As this was a period of colonial conquest and expansion, geography in particular was concerned with statecraft.

Hence it should come as no surprise that in the seventeenth century and for most of the eighteenth geography was imbued with religious and state doctrine. Earthquakes, for example, were seen as a punishment from God for the moral failings of people. Peter Heylyn's (1599–1662) geography texts included strong 'defences of church ornament, attacks on Presbyterianism and distancing of the English Reformation from European Calvinism' (Mayhew 2000: 53). Geographical facts were used to validate British exceptionalism and independence as well as the hand of God. Heylyn's text *Microcosmus* was subtitled 'a treatise historicall, geographicall, politicall, theologicall', emphasizing the interrelated nature of these topics to the author. Many early geography texts depended upon the work of travel writers such as Richard Hakluyt, John Wesley and Walter Raleigh. Again, there was an emphasis on the benefits of overseas conquests and the need to strengthen faith in the British Empire.

Two traditions for geographical education were evident at this time. The first was as part of the liberal sciences, which were necessary for the training of young minds for their coming civic duties. In geography, students (mostly boys of wealthy families) would learn about mathematics, geometry, astronomy and general knowledge of the earth. The second tradition viewed geography as a practical subject for merchants, statesmen and soldiers. This latter tradition dates back to the Greek geographer Strabo. With both of these traditions geography played a role in shaping attitudes and values towards the nation state and God.

Geography in the Enlightenment (approximately 1750–early 1800s)

The Enlightenment period gave rise to a profound sense of optimism and possibilities for humankind. Geography made several significant advances during this period, but in general sought to make the subject more scientific. Through the work of prominent geographers it gained scientific rigour: with greater attention to accuracy and methodology, geographical knowledge was organized into a more meaningful form, large-scale studies were undertaken to map unknown lands and oceans, first attempts were made to study people of other cultures and some geographers began to recognize how cultural and political ideas influenced human interpretation of reality.

Most geographers before the Enlightenment did not conduct their own fieldwork (Mayhew 2000). The advance of science and better understanding of the role of people in knowing and shaping their world changed the way geographers set about their work. Leading geographers sought to make their work more scientific by basing their studies on principles of accuracy and evidence. Major James Rennell (1742–1830) was one of the first geographers to represents the 'formal empire of professional knowledge' (Mayhew 2000: 194). As surveyor-general for the East India Company's dominions in Bengal he successfully completed the surveying of that region in 1776.

Similarly, James Cook (1728–1779) was a pioneer of scientific geography, undertaking a methodical approach to analysis of foreign lands and people. For each of his three Pacific voyages his crew were made up of scientifically trained officers, painters, astronomers, naturalists and surgeons. His observations, record keeping and collections of thousands of different species were informed by his commitment to scientific principles. His particular achievements included mapping the Islands of New Zealand, the first European contact with the aborigines of Australia, a circumnavigation of the globe, charting the location of several Pacific islands such as Hawaii, the first crossing of the Antarctic Circle and charting the majority of the North American north-west coastline, including Alaska.

Among his crew was the botanist Joseph Banks (1743–1820). Banks was to record and collect the numerous different species encountered on their travels, a significant complement to Cook's more general geographical observations. Upon returning to Britain Cook and Banks brought with them thousands of these species, many of which were kept at sites such as Kew Gardens. Cook himself developed his skills as an ethnographer, observing and interacting with people of other cultures. In Tahiti he spent some three months studying the people and their environment. This methodical approach sets Cook apart from pre-Enlightenment explorers, whose observations were more general and erratic, and most of whom were dismissive of other cultures. This is not to say that Cook was free from political influence. Livingstone posits that Cook was under orders from the British Crown to chart territory for potential imperial conquest. Most probably this drove his quest for the southern continent. However, it is also clear to see in his work a commitment to the intrinsic values of science and knowledge.

A significant contribution to the advancement of geography, and science more generally, was made by Prussian philosopher and geographer Immanuel Kant (1724–1804). Not only did Kant lecture for many years on the nature of physical geography, but his philosophical analysis gave insight into how we make sense of the world. Prior to Kant, scientists mistakenly believed that people directly interpret reality as it exists; that there was no role for human mediation. In contrast, Kant made a distinction between noumena (external reality) and phenomena (our perception of that reality). Kant separated our ideas from the natural world itself. This opened up the possibility for scientists to become aware of how cultural and political context can shape their interpretation of the world. This does not mean that scientists can necessarily separate themselves from these influences. The prevailing cultural and political outlook of the time will always influence questions asked by scientists and how they interpret their results. However, at least awareness of them provides for the possibility to minimize this process. Individuals are not machines that automatically regurgitate every idea that pops into their heads. Humans have the capacity to reason and therefore can support or reject the prevailing cultural and political perspective.

William Guthrie was one of the few geographers to challenge the prevailing orthodoxy of his time. Robert Mayhew, in his review of British geographers during the Enlightenment, notes that Guthrie's *Geographical Grammar* was informed by the Scottish Enlightenment thinkers more than the Oxbridge–London axis. As such, 'he gave a distanced perspective on the political issues which had previously been central to the Anglo-centric geographic tradition', with the effect that the text 'undercuts the English exceptionalism and patriotism upon which geography books had been grounded since Camden' (Mayhew 2000: 179). Mayhew is quick to point out that this does not mean that Guthrie's geography was value-free. His political outlook included 'a moderate and Protestant form of Christianity, supporting the liberties of the people (albeit not the "mob") and working for toleration within the established structures of church and state' (*ibid*. 2000: 179). The point is that people are born into a society with a given cultural and political outlook that is not of their own choosing, but ideas are mediated through the minds of these very same people who can accept, reject or even modify them, and ultimately shape society in a new way.

Kant's revolutionary step was necessary for science to be able to advance beyond many extraneous social and political demands. In the words of Livingstone he 'de-theologised the scientific study of the natural world' (Livingstone 1992: 116). Nevertheless, many scientists continued to take a teleological view of the natural world. Ritter (1779–1859) is one such example. Ritter took significant strides towards a more meaningful organization of geographical knowledge. His areal differentiation approach led him to make regional classifications. His objective was to:

> [P]resent a living picture of the whole land, its natural and cultivated products, its natural and human features, and to present these in a coherent whole in such a way that the most significant inferences about man and nature will be self evident, especially when they are compared side by side.
>
> (Tatham 1951: 43)

Yet in this picture of Ritter's he was searching for evidence of God's design. Likewise, it was not until the end of the nineteenth century that education would begin to be separated from religious moral instruction.

Drawing upon the empirical approach of Cook and the philosophy of Kant, Alexander von Humboldt (1769–1859) advanced the scope and meaning of geographical knowledge and contributed to the synthesizing tradition of the subject. His work took him across Europe, Asia and the Americas. In 1799 Humboldt led an expedition to the Spanish colonies in South America. Over the five-year period of their stay Humboldt and his crew visited Venezuela, Columbia, Cuba, Peru, Ecuador and Mexico. Livingstone (1992) reports that Humboldt's work was characterized by precise measurement (he took with him some fifty measuring devices), regional classification and the mapping of spatially distributed data. Livingstone also comments on how Humboldt searched for 'the universal behind the particular, for underlying patterns and unities that tied nature together as a beautiful, functioning system' (Livingstone 1992: 135). This demonstrates Humboldt's quest for causal relationships and laws of nature and also his sensitivity to ecological harmony and the relationships between species. His work, like that of other Enlightenment thinkers, also conveyed his aesthetic appreciation of the beauty of nature itself. As scientists began to comprehend the natural environment was produced by its own forces of nature, for many there was a sense of awe and amazement at its inner workings and interconnectivity. Hence Humboldt, like others, was driven by a desire to gain an appreciation of the whole: that is, how natural and human systems all fit together on the planet. From this standpoint it is apparent how geography grew as a synthesizing discipline. For Humboldt it brought into relation knowledge that other subjects studied independently.

This holistic approach of Humboldt's culminated in his attempt to write a book that depicted the entire universe.

> I have this crazy notion to depict in a single work the entire material universe, all that we know of phenomena of heaven and earth, from the nebulae of stars to the geography of mosses and granite rocks – and in a vivid style that will stimulate and elicit feeling. Every great and important idea in my writing should be registered side by side with facts. It should portray an epoch in the spiritual genesis of mankind – in the knowledge of nature . . . My title is *Cosmos*.
>
> (Humboldt, cited in Livingstone 1992: 136)

This manuscript was not surprisingly unfinished, yet it demonstrated his view of geography as a universal science and quest to expand scientific enquiry and the frontiers of knowledge such that humanity could more completely understand its world.

Like Ritter, Humboldt sought to distinguish his work from the 'geography' of travel writing. In his eyes geography was more than the careful collection of detailed and accurate factual material. For him the scientific organization of knowledge demanded that 'the material was given coherence and made intelligible by being subsumed under a number of laws which should express the relationships of cause and effect to be found in phenomena as simply and concisely as possible' (Chorley and Haggett 1965: 4). This approach to the subject is sometimes referred to as classical or systematic geography. His goal was to arrange geographical knowledge in such a way that it could be made intelligible and meaningful to students of geography. However, at this time a distinction had yet to be made between the methods used to approach the physical and social sciences, which limited potential insight into social systems.

Upon his return from South America Humboldt visited Philadelphia, where he lectured about his work and met President Jefferson, himself a scientific advocate with personal surveying experience. The scientific pursuit of geography rapidly expanded in the States during the Jefferson era, although this is not to belittle the work of earlier American geographers such as Thomas Hutchins. Inaugurated as President in 1801, Thomas Jefferson understood the importance of science and the need to accurately map the largely uncharted American continent to facilitate the safe movement of people and goods. For this reason he has occasionally been referred to as a pioneer of American geography (see Surface 1909). Jefferson's ambition epitomized the American spirit of the time, demonstrating enthusiasm for the vastness and richness of the continent. His aim was no less than to 'enlarge our knowledge of the geography of our continent . . . and to give us a general view of its population, natural history, productions, soil and climate' (Greene 1984: 196–7). To this end he set in motion explorations and surveys of the continental interior and the coastline. One of the first of these was led by Meriweather Lewis and William Clarke. In 1804, travelling from St Louis to Missouri, they led an expedition to gather geographical data on the West.

In 1807 Jefferson convinced Congress to pass an Act authorizing the Survey of the Coasts. Thus began the task of mapping out some 95,000 miles of coastline, setting up hundreds of thousands of survey markers and installing tide and current measuring stations. Under the supervision of Ferdinand Hassler, Alexander Dallas Bache and George Davidson the Survey expanded its remit to include the interior of the continent, taking much of the century to complete. However, Jefferson was also a patriot and a utilitarian. Undoubtedly, he wanted to use this geographical knowledge to advance the economic standing and the security of the nation.

The Enlightenment period for geography can be summarized as one in which humanity sought to bring *terrae incognitae* into the realm of human knowledge for intellectual, spiritual, economic and political ends. This was done with greater precision, purpose and conceptual understanding than in previous periods, enhancing the scientific credentials of geography.

End of the nineteenth/early twentieth centuries (1880s–1920s)

The Enlightenment period gave way to the moralistic Victorian era with its dominant ideologies of race and class. However, significant in this time period was the growing movement for common schooling on both sides of the Atlantic. Initially, the movement continued to view education as synonymous with induction into religious orthodoxy, but also the school curriculum was increasingly being viewed as a means to induct the population in the virtues of national interest. Goodman and Lesnick (2001) correctly note that the notion of moral education at this time would have been redundant: since morality was seen as integral to education, it would not have needed a separate category. Similarly, Hunter comments of the common schools movement in America; schools were 'permeated with religious, and specifically nondenominational, protestant content' (Hunter 2001: 40).

The important change here came during the second half of the nineteenth century as a distinction began to open up between intellectual and moral education. For the first time knowledge could be viewed as something with intrinsic value rather than as a means to some external end. This knowledge was also being subdivided into disciplines as the curriculum was modernized and institutionalized, with geography gaining its place as an independent subject.

The second half of the nineteenth century witnessed increasing challenges to the classical curriculum, in both North America and Europe, through calls for a more modernized curriculum, particularly from a middle class growing in political significance who wanted their children to acquire knowledge that had more relevance to the nineteenth century. While classical education appealed to many because it offered tradition and the potential continuity of the social order, others sought a more modern curriculum based in scientific thought. Education itself was for the first time seen as a science. For instance, Froebel (1826) in *The Education of Man* described how child's play led to new mental constructions. And Herbart's ideas of knowledge as a taxonomy of external relationships in an objective world were popularized. He saw education in four steps: clarity, association, system and method.

In the latter decades of the century religious orthodoxy declined under the weight of natural science and modernization. As the liberal modernist perspective grew in popularity values of industry, hard work, loyalty, thrift, self-reliance and individualism came to replace Protestant morality. In America this transition reflected the rapid industrialization, substantial immigration and general influence of corporate America on social life in the late nineteenth century (Bohan 2004). For most natural scientists the teleological approach of natural theology gave way to evolutionary ideas, following Darwin's line of thought. This new outlook upon the world and the role of humanity within it gave rise to three philosophical positions: liberal humanism, progressivism and conservatism. None of these approaches would win out in this period. Rather, all three existed simultaneously, although each was more or less significant in given decades. However, all three placed their faith in science to a greater or lesser degree. Here the influence of each upon advancing geography and its role in the curriculum will be briefly reviewed.

The separation of knowledge and subsequently subjects from religion was a product of scientific and liberal thought. This perspective placed emphasis upon the individual to rationalize, both intellectually and morally. This changed the nature of education, in which subject areas had now to justify their moral worth to individuals and society on intrinsic scientific grounds, and education was viewed as a process of learning (Bohan 2004). During the 1880s and 1890s intellectual liberalism became virtually synonymous with a faith in scientific ideas and method. Philosopher Herbert Spencer and natural scientist Thomas Huxley were two of the most influential thinkers of the time. Spencer argued that education necessitated both useful knowledge and knowledge for training the mind through subjects like physiology, biology, chemistry, mathematics and sociology. He downplayed moral education and rigid discipline in favour of freedom and kindliness. Spencer thought the goal of education was to produce not ideal people but good citizens, downplaying the role of moral education in favour of greater freedom of thought.

Huxley was a strong advocate of freedom of conscience and education in the laws of nature, in which he included the study of people. He saw liberal education as creating a person whose:

> [B]ody is the ready servant of his will . . . whose intellect is a clear, cold, logic engine . . . whose mind is stored with knowledge of the great and fundamental truths of Nature and the laws of her operations . . . who, no stunted ascetic, is full of life and fire, but whose passions are trained to come to heel by a vigorous will . . . who has learned to love all beauty . . . and to respect others as himself.
>
> (cited in Bowen 1981: 86)

Emerging subject disciplines fell into three categories: natural sciences, social sciences and humanities, with some scientists beginning to treat social phenomena differently from those of nature. The job of natural sciences was to investigate the laws of nature that governed natural phenomena. Humanities continued to investigate questions regarding the nature of humanity and its cultural expressions. Social sciences sought to remove themselves, as far as possible, from the realm of non-academic values so that they could study social phenomena from a distance.

What would be geography's contribution to the development of individuals in the new curriculum? Clearly it could no longer claim to be the Mother of All Subjects. Forcing geographers to account for the intrinsic and scientific rationale for their subject was the outcome of liberal scientific thought. The Royal Geographical Society, established in 1930, played an important role in professionalizing geography, acting as a focal point for leading geographers and sponsoring overseas expeditions. The society also acted as an advocate for the subject during curricula modernization. Leading geographers of the time settled on human–nature interactions as the core of the subject. Halford Mackinder (1861–1947) was instrumental in shaping a new geography more suited to the post-Darwinian times. Mackinder sought a geography more organized as a discipline, but also one in keeping with the intellectual and political ideas of the time. In 1887

Mackinder delivered a seminar paper 'On the Scope and Methods of Geography' to the Royal Geographical Society, outlining his vision of geography as a 'science of distribution' (Mackinder, 1887: 174). Mackinder and others defended the notion of geography as a discipline that addressed the interaction of the human and natural worlds. This was precisely the approach taken by William Morris Davis (1850–1934), one of the founders of academic geography in America. Morris Davis was instrumental in establishing geography's place in higher education as he fought to distinguish it from geology. His cyclical theory of uplift and erosion of land applied evolutionary thought to geomorphology. Although Morris Davis's subject was physical geography, he, like Mackinder, depicted a role for humans within that. Both were heavily influenced by an ideology of environmental determinism, imperial ambitions and the prevailing racial political climate of the era, but their attaching of some significance to human conscience was indicative that change was afoot.

At the turn of the century some geographers were beginning to react against environmental determinism, paying greater attention to the role of people in shaping their world. In France, Paul Vidal de la Blache (1845–1919) transformed geography through his methodical depiction of French regions. His work emphasized the role people play in transforming the landscape, with the physical and the human being intimately connected; the one was not possible to comprehend without the other. In America Carl Saur (1889–1975) would continue this line of thought later in the twentieth century with his descriptions of cultural landscapes. This was the beginning of regional geography, which has remained a significant approach to the subject to this day.

Mackinder's contribution to geography went beyond clarifying its disciplinary boundaries. He also discussed the different methods by which he believed geography could best be taught. In particular, he felt that at elementary level it was important to combine the teaching of facts and principles (Mackinder 1887: 174). Mackinder's philosophy of geographical education was clearly informed by the scientific educational theories of the time.

Progressivism was the second strand of thought on education to emerge with the decline of the Victorian era, reaching its heyday in the 1920s and 1930s. Progressives focused on the process of education, and the needs of the learner in particular, and hence actively promoted curricular experimentation. With its interest located in the workings of students' minds, progressive thought depended upon the contribution of psychologists. John Dewey, and other progressive educators, stressed the need for young minds to have the freedom to find their own lines of enquiry. Hunter reports that this period led to a 'new-found emphasis on the independence of the child for the purposes of liberating children to develop socially, intellectually, and morally' (Hunter 2001: 62). In seeking to separate education from previous moral doctrine, progressives shared some common ground with the liberal approach. Where they differed was in the roles ascribed to process and content: progressivism elevated process over content, while the liberal educational model saw process as secondary to content.

However, progressives went further than the science of education; they frequently also advocated a social role for education, that of preparing future citizens. This trend was especially apparent in America, where citizenship became a major curricular objective. Yet the idea of citizenship was at this time also changing, to be expanded beyond its traditional political meaning. Preparation for participation in democracy did not just mean learning abstract concepts and principles of government and political systems, but emphasized participation in community activity and character formation. In essence it was about nurturing a certain type of individual for participation in the republic. This model of citizenship education is explored in greater depth in Chapter 8.

Progressive thought heavily influenced the direction of American curriculum reform in the 1910s and 1920s. In 1916 the Committee for the Social Studies published a report that laid down the foundations for the general subject of social studies (including history, geography, politics, civics, economics, psychology, sociology and anthropology). Embodying progressive social and personal goals for education, the social studies curriculum was introduced to American schools in 1926. Woyshner et al. (2004) suggest that the committee 'conceived of social studies as a school subject intended to increase students' affection for and understanding of democracy' as well as personal relationships (Woyshner et al. 2004: xii). In this respect progressivism led to a focus on psychological and social objectives in the US curriculum in addition to academic ones. In this matter one instrumental aim of education, induction into a religion-based moral order, had been replaced by another, induction of citizens into a republican liberal democracy. The outcome for geography was that its place in the curriculum was marginalized as a cross-curricular subject dominated by history.

In Europe progressive thought during this period was more marginal to mainstream education. There were many schools that individually experimented with the curriculum. Montessori schools in particular developed on a basis of progressive ideals. In England and Wales, progressivism would come to play a significant role in geography projects of the 1960s and 1970s.

Therefore, moral education was not expunged from schools at the end of the nineteenth century. Rather it was resurrected in the form of character education (or even moral reasoning), being more focused on desirable individual traits than a religiously prescribed morality, and nationalism.

In the words of Wilhelm Rein, 'The aim of instruction . . . coincides directly with the aim of the formation of character' (cited in Bowen 1981: 363). Highlighting the prominence of conservative thought, in some instances this still amounted to adherence to Protestant ideals of piety, righteous living and salvation, although by the end of the century in the US at least forty-one out of forty-six states had banned sectarian influence in public schools. In place of religious aims for education, national allegiance was emerging as a new extraneous moral rationale for subjects such as geography, and especially history. While in the US this was conducted explicitly through the social studies curriculum, in England and Wales citizenship was only occasionally taught as a school subject. Instead, history played the role of generating a sense of national belonging and geography was used to teach about the British Empire.

Geography's place in the school and university curriculum was undoubtedly linked with its growing role with respect to statecraft and the promotion of nationalist causes. This was especially the case in Britain, where geography was used to teach about the positive virtues of its empire. This was the approach taken by Mackinder, frequently cited as the founder of political geography. Mackinder, like many a scientist of the time, was heavily influenced by nationalistic and racial ideology of the period. Reflecting the prevalence of Social Darwinist thought that likened social process to natural processes, Mackinder looked for geographical facts to account for British supremacy. For example, in order to justify British rule over Ireland he argued that the Irish Sea was an inlet: 'The seas which divide Ireland from Great Britain are truly inland waters' (cited in Mayhew 2000: 138). Reflecting Britain's imperial struggle against its European counterparts, Mackinder argued that geography in schools should teach students who, by visualizing the world, could 'think imperially' and would come to see the world as a 'theatre for British activity' (cited in Mayhew 2000: 134). In parallel with today's calls for global citizenship, Mackinder sought to blur the lines between national and international causes, arguing that Britons were 'citizens of an empire which had to hold its place according to the universal law of survival through efficiency and effort' (*ibid*. 2000: 134).

The utilization of education for political means at the end of the nineteenth century was, like today, driven by a political crisis in Britain, albeit one of a very different kind. Mayhew notes how geography's new moral mission was a reaction to the decline of Britain's global dominance and was supported by rival political parties: 'the new geography was a response to the crisis of rival national states, being firmly allied with these groups of both a liberal and conservative disposition who looked to the empire as Britain's salvation' (Mayhew 2000: 235). Nevertheless, the contribution of geographical education to statecraft would facilitate its establishment as an independent curricular subject for both schools and universities at the end of the nineteenth century. Not surprisingly, given the significance of empire in Britain at this time, geography became more firmly entrenched in its schools and higher education institutions than was the case in the US.

With the historically large influx of immigrants into the US at the end of the nineteenth and the beginning of the twentieth centuries there was growing preoccupation with the need to integrate new immigrants into American ways. In New York, Frances Kellor was actively campaigning for immigrants to reject their homelands and embrace Americanization. Her Committee for Immigrants in America championed the slogan 'Many peoples, one nation'. Support for nationalism in schools grew with the onset of the Great War. For example, the Fourth of July 1915 was celebrated as 'Americanization Day' in 107 cities nationwide. Kellor's organization was changed into the National Americanization Committee and developing patriotism became an integral aim of social studies education.

In the 1920s US schools routinely took the Pledge of Allegiance and Makler remarks that the social studies curriculum emphasized American values and taught about the republic as the 'form of government most favoured by God' (Makler 2004: 27). During this decade civics education embraced the mantle of national assimilation, teaching loyalty to America through pledges, oaths, patriotic songs, marches, salutes and English lessons. The objective was to espouse American values and the Anglo-Saxon Protestant vision of citizenship (Woyshner et al. 2004). American geography textbooks subsequently became more focused on teaching about the nation and in particular its commercial geography, while other countries were considered in terms of how they related to the US. For instance, world geography textbooks in the 1950s still retained a strong sense of national values (see Standish 2006).

Although moral education in the form of religious and nationalistic education continued in some form during the twentieth century, a growing understanding of the process of education and general movement towards intellectual rigour led many educators to recoil from the inclusion of political or moral agendas in schools.

Mid-to-late-twentieth century (1940s–early 1990s)

Of important note to mid-to-late-twentieth century geography are increased efforts to improve the scientific credentials of the subject, increasing specialization research, the decline of the nationalistic/ imperialist agenda, especially in schools, and in the 1980s moves in both the US and England and Wales towards a common national curriculum for geography (although not necessarily consensus).

Richard Hartshorne's (1939) *The Nature of Geography* was one of the most comprehensive attempts to clarify the nature and purpose of geography during this period. It is worth quoting Hartshorne at length, as his overview of the subject is exceptional. A good place to start is Hartshorne's broad description of geography:

> Geography seeks to acquire a complete knowledge of the areal differentiation of the world, and therefore discriminates among the phenomena that vary in different parts of the world only in terms of their geographic significance – *i.e.*, their relation to the total differentiation of areas. Phenomena significant to areal differentiation have areal expression – not necessarily in terms of physical extent over the ground, but as a characteristic of an area of more or less definite extent. Consequently, in studying the interrelation of these phenomena, geography depends first and fundamentally on the comparison of maps depicting the areal expression of individual phenomena, or of interrelated phenomena.
>
> (Hartshorne 1939)

Of course there are other ways to present spatial data than maps. But historically maps have been the primary tool of geographers. Like Kant and Humboldt before him, Hartshorne depicts geography as a synthesizing discipline in that it draws upon the phenomena studied by what he terms the systematic sciences. Geography's role then is to discern the spatial relations of these phenomena:

> The heterogeneous phenomena which these other sciences study by classes are not merely mixed together in terms of physical juxtaposition in the earth surface, but are causally interrelated in complex areal combinations. Geography must integrate the materials that other subjects study separately.
>
> (*ibid.*)

Hartshorne makes a distinction between the systematic sciences such as biology or mathematics with their own discrete phenomena or study and history and geography, which he terms chorographic subjects, meaning analysis of regions. However, he cautions that this does not demean them as disciplines in their own right and emphasizes the need for each to develop its own generic concepts and systems of classification. Geography's intellectual role is thus described by Hartshorne as:

> [T]o establish generic concepts of common characteristics of phenomena, or phenomenon-complexes that shall describe with certainty

the common characteristics that these features actually possess. On the basis of such generic concepts, geography seeks to establish principles of relationships between the phenomena that are areally related in the same or different areas, in order that it may correctly interpret the interrelations of such phenomena in any particular area.

(ibid.)

And finally:

[G]eography seeks to organize its knowledge of the world into interconnected systems, in order that any particular fragment of knowledge may be related to all others that bear upon it.

(ibid.)

Hartshorne also distinguished between systematic and regional geography. The clarity of Hartshorne's comprehension of the disciplinary role of geography stands in stark contrast to discussion today about the purpose of geographical education.

World War II was a turning point in Western thought as the experience of Nazism and the Holocaust led to the discrediting of racism, but also awareness of the role of nationalism in generating inter-imperialist rivalry resulted in more cautious and less overt national sentiment. Again, lessening geography's ties to external political agendas allowed for greater clarity in its intrinsic value. Hence many geography textbooks produced in the decades after World War II consciously sought to avoid political disputes and toned down nationalistic overtures. Nevertheless, the centrality of the nation state remained key to these textbooks and presentation of conflicts involving Western nations were far from neutral. This was especially the case as the Cold War began to dominate domestic and international political affairs in the 1960s.

Academic geography in the 1950s and 1960s made a significant break from the previous era. Regionalism, behaviouralism and environmental determinism were challenged by new approaches to geography which focused on quantification, modelling and a search for spatial laws. Positivism became a preferred approach of many geographers in the 1950s and 1960s as the subject sought greater scientific rigour. Of particular note was the work of Richard Chorley and Peter Haggett (1967). In the early 1960s they began to hold conferences and summer courses to explore new ideas in geography. Central to their geographical theories was the notion of space as a defining concept. Their courses and work attracted much interest in the field, including internationally, and helped to send the discipline in a new direction. In the 1960s and 1970s a number of curriculum development projects were launched in both the US and England/Wales. Spatial modelling was an important component in several of these.

Textbooks and school courses began to incorporate complex models and diagrams in order to mimic and predict spatial interactions. This included Christaller's central place theory, J. H. von Thunen's model of land use, Kansky's transportation networks model, urban land use models by Ernest Burgess and Homer Hoyt. Frequently these theories were not new. Von Thunen's model was developed in 1826 as the size and influence of towns began to swell. It was translated into English in 1966, soon to appear in textbooks in the US and UK. Burgess developed his model on 1920s Chicago to demonstrate its concentric growth from the central business district. In 1939 Hoyt proposed a modification of Burgess to include urban growth in sectors. Again, these became popular in geography textbooks later in the century.

In the early 1960s William Pattison (1961) sought to give some coherence to US geography at a time when the subject was struggling to retain its place in the curricula of American schools and universities. Pattison identified four traditions for geography: spatial, area studies, man–land interactions and earth science. The spatial tradition was evident in the great *Geographia* of Claudius Ptolemy in the second century AD and also foremost in the minds of the founders of the American Association of Geographers. Quite simply, the spatial tradition equates with the 'determination and display of spatial aspects of reality through mapping' (Pattison 1961: 212). The area studies tradition also dates back to antiquity, being represented in the work of Strabo, who sought to clarify 'the nature of places, their character and their differentiation' (*ibid*. 1961: 212). Pattison suggests that Hartshorne's depiction of geography as chorography fits best into this category. The history of geography also reveals a preoccupation with the relationship between people and their natural environments and how this varies spatially. Pattison cites Hippocrates, the Greek physician of the fifth century BC, as typifying the early work in this tradition in his *On Air, Waters and Places*.

The above three traditions can be placed under the umbrella of human geography or at least its interactions with natural phenomena. The final tradition identified by Pattison, the earth science tradition, approximates to physical geography. Geographers in this tradition have concerned themselves with explaining the spatial dimensions of natural processes and occurrences. In conclusion, Pattison highlights the unique contribution to geography of each tradition: 'The spatial tradition abstracts certain aspects of reality; area studies is distinguished by its point of view; the man–land tradition dwells upon relationships; but earth science is identified through concrete objects' (*ibid*. 1961: 215).

The 1960s and 1970s were also a period of significant curricular experimentation in both the US and England/Wales. Progressive thought became more popular in an era that continuously questioned tradition, the status quo and ruling establishments. In the US social studies was described as 'in crisis' from several quarters in the 1970s. Progressivism downplayed the role of content instead focusing on the process of education, viewing students as individuals with minds to be nurtured rather than vessels to be filled. This shift towards a focus on process is discussed in the next chapter.

There was a further development of Pattison's four themes in the 1980s as American professional geography associations began work on national geography standards. At this time the paucity of geographical knowledge among American school students, and the public at large, became a national concern and plans were initiated to improve the position of geography in the curriculum. A survey of high-school seniors by the National Association for Progress in Education (NAEP) found them lacking in knowledge of locations, geographical skills and tools, and understanding of cultural and physical geography (Allen *et al.* 1990). In 1984 the National Council for Geographic Education and the Association of American Geographers published *Guidelines for Geographic Education* detailing the geographical content that schools should be covering in geography. Five themes were identified: location, place, movement, human–environment relationships and region. Location best corresponds to Pattison's spatial tradition, man–land now reads human–environment, area studies has been split into the themes of place and region, movement has been added and earth science is no longer a separate theme. Subsequently, the Geography Education National Implementation Project (GENIP) assisted state alliances of teachers, geographers and academics to set about improving the profile and status of geography education.

In 1994 *Geography for Life: National Geography Standards* was published, the culmination of over a decade's work to identify a common American geography curriculum. *Geography for Life* identifies eighteen separate standards under the following headings: the world in spatial terms, places and regions, physical systems, human systems, environment and society, the uses of geography. The five themes are not explicit in the structure of the standards, but clearly remain key organizing concepts.

The American experience of constructing a national curriculum stands in stark contrast to that of England and Wales. Probably because of geography's weak position in US schools, this process was very much led by academic geographers with minimal political interference. This is not to say the American curriculum has been uncontested. Chapter 4 will show how the American culture wars directly influenced subjects such as geography, and the social studies standards produced by the National Council for Social Studies very much reflect this political process. Neither was *Geography for Life* immune from the cultural wars, but because geography was not a core subject in most schools it was subject to less political scrutiny.

In contrast, the generation of the geography national curriculum in England and Wales took place under very different circumstances, largely because of a stronger tradition of geographical education in schools. When discussion began about which subjects would feature on the national curriculum, it was by no means certain that geography would be included. With progressive ideals very much on the defensive during the 1980s, Eleanor Rawling (2001) suggested that geography organizations such as the Geographical Association to some extent went along with the 'utilitarian' approach to the subject, popularized under Margaret Thatcher's 1980s Conservative government, in order to ensure its inclusion as a foundation subject. The Geographical Association's submissions for the national curriculum emphasized the body of factual knowledge about the world that geography could supply and specific geographical skills that could be developed through map work and fieldwork. The outcome was that geography won acceptance as a foundation subject in the Education Reform Act of 1988.

The Geography Working Group, who wrote the geography curriculum document, comprised of ministers, Department of Education and Science officials, inspectors, industry representatives, academics, project leaders, a head teacher and a secondary school head of geography, all appointed by Kenneth Baker, the then Secretary of State. Rawling, who featured as a project leader of the group, described how the discussion and outcomes of the group were very much controlled by the chair, Sir Leslie Fielding (former diplomat, later Vice-Chancellor of Sussex University), the vice-chair David Thomas (Professor of Geography at the University of Birmingham) and DES and HMI representatives: 'There was never any doubt that this was a political exercise steered from central government' (Rawling 2001: 50). The clash between the government and progressive educationalists was likewise observed by Walford: 'If the government supported content, then the educationalists had to support process' (Walford 2001).

Debate continued during the production of later drafts and the content of the curriculum was reorganized to be more to teachers' liking. By the time the Final Order was revealed in March 1991 the then Secretary of State, Kenneth Clark, had intervened to strike out any 'references to enquiry skills and to attitudes and values' (Rawling 2001: 49). During a parliamentary debate in April 1991 he explained that the role of the Geography Order was 'To make sure our young people learn some geography, not just some vague concepts and attitudes which relate to various subjects, and to emphasise learning about places and where they are' (Hansard, 29 April 1991; cited in Rawling 2001: 64).

This first national curriculum document for geography was greeted with hostility from some teachers and educationalists. It included a heavy emphasis on content, maps and location knowledge both at home and abroad, including which regions to study, organized under the following headings: Geographical skills, Knowledge and understanding of places, Physical geography, Human geography and Environmental geography. However, the influence of progressive thought was also evident in the document: for instance 'enquiry should form an important part of pupils' work' and that study should 'take account of pupils' interests, experiences and capabilities' (Department for Education and Science 1991: 35). Investigations, group work and problem solving also featured, suggesting a student-centred approach to learning. Given the politically charged nature of the process, it was no surprise that the outcome was a poorly organized document lacking coherence and clarity.

Nevertheless, besides the political wrangling the *topics* covered in the national curriculum document were not so far from those being studied in schools, as reflected in textbooks, during the post-World War II period. These included: landscapes and geomorphology, weather and climate, natural hazards, population, settlements, migration, economic activity, transportation, land use, agriculture, natural resources and their management, and human–nature interactions. The document also suggested that students study contrasting locations, learn about different places around the globe, read and use maps and develop an understanding of key concepts such as scale, region and development. In the debate over the national curriculum teachers, as professionals, were correctly defending their right to determine the curriculum content and the way in which they teach it. In schools at this time there was a clear idea of the nature and purpose of geography and, despite the political nature of the construction of the geography curriculum, much of the content of geographical education made its way into the national curriculum document, albeit in an unstructured and incoherent form that was to be improved upon in subsequent drafts.

Concluding comments

This chapter has traced the origins of geography from the Ancient Greeks and Romans, European explorers and Enlightenment geographers, through to its founding as an independent school subject in the nineteenth century and subsequent evolution in the twentieth century. Only with the onset of modern science in the nineteenth century did subjects such as geography begin to develop as disciplines with inherent qualities, rather than as something attached to a moral agenda. Halford Mackinder was instrumental in seeking to establish a more scientific and more organized basis from which to study geography, yet he also viewed geography as linked with the promotion of national sentiment and empire. Others such as Hartshorne were to draw out the scientific and intellectual role of the subject. With nationalism in decline after World War II, geographers needed a stronger rationale for their subject. Over the course of the twentieth century geography established itself in both the US and England/Wales as a science for the study of spatially related phenomena. Geography's place in the curriculum was increasingly justified by its intrinsic educational benefits for students: it taught them about location, place, regions, natural systems, human–environment interactions, movement, and how phenomena are spatially interrelated. No doubt different teachers approached the subject in different ways, emphasizing different topics or utilizing different methodologies, yet all shared a common belief that, through the acquisition of geographical knowledge and skills, students would learn to make sense of the spatial distribution of physical and human phenomena. However, the next chapter will show that its intrinsic qualities were thrown into doubt by geography's ethical turn.

Suggested further reading

Chorley, R. and Haggett, P. (1967) *Models in Geography*, London: Methuen.

Hartshorne, R. (1939) *The Nature of Geography*, Lancaster, PA: Association of American Geographers.

Livingstone, D. (1992) *The Geographical Tradition: Episodes in the History of a Contested Enterprise*, Oxford: Blackwell.

Mackinder, H. (1887) 'On the Scope and Methods of Geography', paper given at the *Proceedings of the Royal Geographical Society and Monthly Record of Geography*, 31 January, London.

Marsden, W. (2001) *The School Textbook: Geography, History and Social Studies*, London: Woburn Press.

Mayhew, R. (2000) *Enlightenment Geography: The Political Languages of British Geography, 1650–1850*, New York: St Martin's Press.

National Council for Geographic Education (1994) *Geography National Standards: Geography for Life*, Washington, DC: National Geographic Society Committee for Research and Exploration.

Pattison, W.D. (1961) 'The Four Traditions of Geography', *Journal of Geography*, 63 (5): 211–16.

Walford, R. (2001) *Geography in British Schools, 1850–2000: Making a World of Difference*, London: Woburn Press.

Chapter 2

Geography's ethical turn

KEY QUESTIONS

1 Should geography seek to explain how the world *is* or how it *ought* to be?
2 What role if any do ethics have in the teaching of geography? Should ethical judgements be left to the individual student or taught?
3 Are ethics, and knowledge, specific to individuals and cultures or universal in nature?
4 What is the difference between subjective and objective knowledge?

Central to understanding geography's new citizenship role and advocacy for global perspectives is a shift that occurred within parts of the discipline, and social theory more widely, from the late 1960s. This change of direction was itself a response to a period of social and political upheaval in the US and UK, the so-called counter-cultural movement of the late 1960s and 1970s. This movement led to widespread questioning of social norms and practices, including capitalism, tradition, academic values, the role of academics and even the very basis of knowledge itself. With the intellectual basis of the academy thrown into question academics, and schoolteachers, began to interpret their roles differently, becoming more directly engaged with political causes. Detached, objective study was frowned upon as elitist and supportive of the status quo. Ethical rationale became increasingly important to justify research and education. This is what is meant by geography's ethical turn, which gave rise to the field of radical and/or Marxist geography. This has sometimes been described as the humanizing of geography, given its rejection of detached study. However, the proposition of this chapter is that while geography's search for a more ethical role has led to a better understanding of the context in which knowledge is produced, it has simultaneously eroded its intellectual foundations, ultimately serving to undermine its humanizing potential.

Geography's ethical turn differs from previous instrumental agendas for the subject that sought to use the subject as a vehicle to which their objectives could be attached. These moral and political agendas sometimes interfered with the intellectual freedom to pursue the subject, but otherwise the discipline remained intact. In contrast, the ethical turn has led to a question of the very intellectual and humanistic foundations upon which geography was built. In other words, it has had the opposite outcome to that of its stated intention: making geography less ethical and less humanizing.

The culture wars and the New Social Studies

Geography's radicalism and ethical turn was linked with the broader counter-cultural movement of the 1960s and 1970s. This movement shook the foundations of society, and consequently the curriculum, on both sides of the Atlantic, but especially in the US, where the movement was strongest. The outcome was nothing short of a wholesale revision of social norms and values, of the workings of liberal democracy and the nature and role of education.

The counter-cultural movement expressed itself in various forms: anti-establishment, anti-Western, anti-capitalism, anti-science, anti-authority, anti-war (especially the war in Vietnam) but for peace, the natural environment, alternative lifestyles and nonconformism. In the US this was the time of anti-Vietnam War, civil rights and pro-environment demonstrations. For the first time in its history, the values that America stood for, the notion of the good life and the American Dream were all thrown into question.

As adults became less sure of their perspective on the world and the values they should uphold, so its capacity to pass knowledge and values on to the next generation was diminished. Most moral education was decried as intellectually inhibiting, and imposing discipline came to be viewed as stifling of creativity. Given its focus on preparation for participation in liberal democracy, social studies in particular entered a period of uncertainty (see Shaver 1977). In response to this crisis, the National Council for Social Studies (NCSS) published a document of curriculum guidelines in 1971. Mullen notes that this publication reflected the ambiguity towards the subject of the previous decade, containing a number of contradictory statements. Nevertheless, there was a clear emphasis upon 'social problems/self-realization' (Mullen 2004).

The absence of a social consensus on the norms, values and knowledge that teachers should pass on to their charges led to a focus on the *process* of education. Education was viewed in scientific terms, with moral authority being imported from psychology. The ideas of Piaget and Kohlberg grew in popularity, resulting in a more student-centred approach. Two texts by Jerome Bruner epitomized this trend: *The Process of Education* (1960) and *The Culture of Education* (1966).

Increasingly, values inculcation was replaced by values clarification, whereby the individual students were expected to determine their own values through an exploration of social issues. The concept of value-free teaching gained credence at this time, reflecting the shift from socially to individually defined values. However, this relativist approach was not without criticism. Mullen cites a remark made by one teacher in an article appearing in *Social Education*. The teacher stated of the NCSS guidelines that they amounted to a 'non-curriculum', while others have referred to educational thought at this time as the 'de-schooling movement' (Bowen 1981).

In addition to confronting the values upon which society was based, the counter-cultural movement led academics to rethink conventional wisdom about the very nature of scientific enquiry and the basis of knowledge itself. This postmodern or cultural turn gave rise to social constructivist theories of knowledge in the humanities and social sciences, undermining geography's previous assumption of scientific objectivity. Social constructivists explore the social context in which knowledge is produced. They show how knowledge is coloured by the value systems of the individual or individuals who created it. However, some have taken social constructivism to an extreme, arguing that knowledge is entirely rooted to the social context in which it was produced, such that people with an alternative values system would never reach the same conclusions. This strong or deeply rooted version of social constructivism denies the possibility of individuals to abstract beyond their particular circumstances.

Social constructivism therefore gave credence to those challenging the status quo in the 1960s and 1970s. Non-Western stories were simply untold and unheard by mainstream accounts of history and society, and for some all versions of reality were viewed as equally valid. With the strong version of social constructivism, Western knowledge was presented as just one knowledge perspective of equal value and credibility to alternative perspectives or versions of knowledge. It is this line of thought that has given rise to Black or Jewish histories as different from those of the West. Similarly, Western civilization came to be seen by many as on a par with any other civilization (see Chapter 5).

The outcome of a deeply rooted social constructivist thought was to question the basis of objective truth: if knowledge could no longer be abstracted from the particular social context in which it arose, knowledge could not be separated from the values (or prejudices) of the individual who constructed it. Thus truth was denied its non-moral status. With social constructivism, all knowledge came to be viewed as political, and the act of acquiring knowledge itself was portrayed as political, since it was seen as inseparable from values held by the individuals who constructed it. Here, truth was to be replaced by truths and geography by geographies.

This challenge to Western knowledge and its value system had profound implications for society in general and its model of education in particular. The liberal democratic model of education was founded upon the basis that young people would inherit the knowledge of their elders and continue the pursuit of truth, changing society as they saw fit. Yet, if the pursuit of truth and acquisition of a body of knowledge were thrown into question, then so was the potential of people to change it. If one cannot know the world objectively, then how can one possibly see how to change it for the better? A new model of social change, and education, was sought. In this new model, social change was relocated to the individuals themselves.

The amalgamation of personal with political objectives has been noted elsewhere. For example, a study of race relations and education by historian Elizabeth Lasch-Quinn (2001) observed how the personal and the political became entwined in the US from the 1970s. While the civil rights movement raised awareness of the personal impact of socio-political conditions, Lasch-Quinn comments that people started to read the equation the other way: that socio-political conditions could be fixed through educating the individual. She observes, 'Concern with self-image, personal motivation, and therapy ultimately displaced concern with increased personal efficacy aimed at civic participation and social change' (Lasch-Quinn 2001: 104–5). Racial problems were rearticulated from the socio-political sphere to problems of the stereotypes and values held by individuals. The goal of social change was thus transformed into individual change.

The same conclusion was reached in a study of new directions in social studies education by Joe Kincheloe. The author described how, in the latter decades of the twentieth century, the cultural sphere had grown in significance for political expression, suggesting that 'social problems are rearticulated to the personal/individual level' (Kincheloe 2001: 57). Mullen (2004) observed how in the 1970s the social studies became more focused on contemporary social problems, including racism, urban decay, population explosion, pollution, natural resources and minority rights. For instance, the 1971 NCSS guidelines asserted the need for teachers to involve students in solutions to these problems as well as using them as a resource to shape the social studies curriculum. The idea of education as transformative of individuals and subsequently society has been expressed in educational theory as 'critical pedagogy', popularized by Brazilian Paulo Freire and bel hooks.

In geography this shift towards a student-centred rather than knowledge-centred curriculum led to curricular experimentation. In the US it took the form of High School Geography Projects. In the UK there were equivalent curricular initiatives. Both of these placed greater emphasis upon the role of the student in the learning process and are discussed in Chapters 3 and 4.

In America the 1980s saw a continuation of this trend towards a combined focus on social and psychological objectives for the social studies, but also there followed something of a backlash to the relativism of previous years. The idea that schools could be a solution to social, political and even economic problems became more widely held. In 1983 the government report *A Nation at Risk: America 2000* painted a damning picture of the state of US education. Describing a 'rising tide of mediocrity' in schools, the education system became a fall guy for the ailing state of the US economy and social fragmentation (cited in Gordon 2003). The report made reference to not only declining intellectual standards, but also the paucity of moral and spiritual strength of educational institutions. These accusations found sympathy among many Americans who felt the loss of moral certainties, traditions and social norms, and worried about the upbringing of their children. However, the response was not to reject values clarification as anti-intellectual, but instead critics sought to replace this approach with commonly agreed-upon values, retaining the focus on the psychological and social development of students. For instance, the Jefferson Center for Character Education identified six Pillars of Character for schools to nurture: trustworthiness, responsibility, caring, respect for others, fairness and citizenship (cited in De Roche and Williams 2001). A survey of educators by Phi Delta Kappa revealed that most thought young people should learn the importance of democracy, honesty, responsibility, freedom of speech, courtesy, tolerance, freedom of worship and integrating schools (Frymier *et al.* 1996). This has led many schools to regain a focus on the twin goals of academic and character (both personal and civic) education.

Hunter (2001) concluded that by the end of the 1980s a psychological regime had come to dominate American schools, with self-esteem and emotional intelligence becoming credible educational aims. For instance, in 1992 New Jersey passed legislation mandating that all schools boards should plan for the development of character and values in students: '"Character education" means programs intended to foster the development in each child of a commitment to our society's common core values' (New Jersey's 1992 Senate Resolution No. 13 and Assembly No. 298, cited in De Roche and Williams 2001). De Roche and Williams (2001) reported that by the end of the century over half of US states legislated for the teaching of values.

In England and Wales curricular experimentation in the 1970s and 1980s contributed to the growing popularity of student-centred teaching in mainstream schools. However, unlike the US, the curriculum remained focused on subject knowledge and skills until the early 1990s when psychological and social objectives rapidly began to transform several subjects, especially geography.

Radical geography

According to Richard Peet, 'Radical and Marxist geography responded to the political events of the 1960s and early 1970s in ways which transformed the discipline' (Peet 1998: 109). Two trends began to fundamentally alter the nature of geography: the search for a more 'humanized' understanding of the world and the postmodern reinterpretation of knowledge. What follows is a brief description and explanation of how these gave rise to a concern for ethics in geography. A more comprehensive description of this transition has been provided by David Smith (2000).

The 1970s gave rise to so-called 'radical geography', in part a response to the abstract and statistical world of the 1960s quantitative geography, but also to the political climate of the time, as described above. As geographers sought to bring greater scientific rigour to their subject, quantitative methods and statistical modelling had become their primary tools. However, by the 1970s people were beginning to question how much insight these abstract models provided in the real world, where individuals frequently did not behave as rationally as the models predicated. There is undoubtedly some truth in the accusation that geographers had been paying insufficient attention to the context in which events were unfolding. However, it would be wrong to then conclude that there is no place for abstract modelling and detached analysis, both of which are essential for identifying and comprehending spatial patterns. In radical geography there followed a quest to explore the human stories all too absent from quantitative analysis and abstract modelling. However, radical geography was more than this. In education it saw a role not only for describing and explaining the world, but also for challenging the status quo with a view to changing society.

The work of radical geographers keyed into this movement to challenge traditional capitalist society. Hence, studies at this time were at least in part motivated by ethical considerations. Popular topics for geographers included inequality, Third World development, social justice, racial discrimination, political domination, and environmental mismanagement. In particular, David Harvey (1973, 1982) began to explore the links between moral philosophy and geography.

Given the nature of the subject, geographers were especially drawn to study environmental problems as highlighted by the environmental movement of the late 1960s and 1970s. As noted in Chapter 1, modern geography has at times defined itself as a discipline which explores the interface between the human and physical sciences and hence was in prime position to analyse human impact on nature. While environmentalist thought in Western society has roots in the nineteenth century, the 1970s was the first time there was a widespread movement that questioned the possibility of future progress without running into environmental limits. This thinking was not simply a product of radical youth and academia but was expressed by national leaders and business executives.

Just how seriously the environmental agenda was taken by the political, business and academic world can be illustrated by the Club of Rome report *Limits to Growth* (Meadows *et al.* 1972). This group of thirty individuals came from ten countries – scientists, educators, economists, humanists, industrialists and civil servants – who gathered in the Academia dei Lincei in Rome. The report highlighted the perceived need for radical change: 'the major problems facing mankind are of such complexity and are so interrelated that traditional institutions and policies are no longer able to cope with them, nor even come to grips with their full content' (*ibid.*: 9). The urgency of the problem was succinctly expressed by U Thant, the Secretary General of the United Nations, in the following statement:

> The Members of the United Nations have perhaps ten years left in which to subordinate their ancient quarrels and launch a global partnership to curb the arms race, to improve the human environment, to defuse the population explosion, and to supply the required momentum to development efforts. If such a global partnership is not forged within the next decade, then I very much fear that the problems I have mentioned will have reached such proportions that they will be beyond our capacity to control.
>
> (*ibid.*: 17)

The Club of Rome believed that growth was limited by physical and social factors, including food production, raw materials, the ecological system, education, employment and technological progress. In certain respects their conclusions are reminiscent of those reached by Thomas Malthus in the late nineteenth century.

For geography, this gave rise to a heightened concern for environmental protection. Studies were conducted showing the environmental impact of society. Initially, environmental problems were viewed as something to be fixed via scientific and technical means or through greater state regulation. Later on this would change as people began to be viewed as part of the problem itself.

In the early 1970s American schools first celebrated Earth Day. Geography textbooks in the US began to include environmental values and multicultural sensitivity towards the end of the 1970s, but more prominently in the 1980s (see Standish 2006). In England and Wales this change would come later. In general, the strength of the counter-cultural movement was significantly larger in the US than in Europe, hence it had a more profound effect on American society at the time while in Europe its impact was gradual, with most change coming in the late 1980s and 1990s. Of course, on both sides of the Atlantic the 1980s were characterized by a reaction against the counter-cultural movement in the form of a neoconservative backlash. Both Reagan and Thatcher championed market principles, individualism and traditional values. The effect was only to temporarily offset geography's ethical turn.

Geographers in the 1970s and 1980s began to explore in more detail the links between their subject and ethics. Yi Fu Tuan in particular researched geography's contribution to moral issues, including their culturally specific character (Tuan 1977). David Smith notes that Tuan's work led other geographers to consider cultural differences in conceptions of the good life, trans-cultural moral experiences, the conflict between the particular and the abstract as sources of ethical understanding, and tensions between moral and aesthetic expressions of human culture (Smith 2000: 4).

By the early 1990s geographers' engagement with ethics was becoming more widespread within the profession. In 1991 the Social and Cultural Geography Study Group of the Institute of British Geographers called for geographers to engage with ethics, involving 'the articulation of the moral and the spatial' (Philo, cited in Smith 1997). A few years hence, a session at the 1994 Association of American Geographers conference entitled *Rethinking Metatheory: Ethics, Difference and Universals* furthered the rise of moral issues in geography. A new journal, *Ethics, Place and Environment*, was launched in which to collate work from an expanding field. The ethical concern towards those racially discriminated against or downtrodden by capitalism in the 1970s expanded to a more general concern for disadvantaged 'others'. This included cultural or ethnic minorities, women, the disabled, children, the politically oppressed and the economically disadvantaged.

Two important shifts took place at this time. First, the line between human society and the physical world was challenged. As David Smith observes: 'the very distinction between humankind and the physical environment is problematic, scientifically and also ethically: we are an integral and active part of nature, with consequent responsibilities' (Smith 2000: 2). Here, the modernist assumption that humans were distinct from nature because of their ability to consciously plan and construct societies was reversed. Environmental ethics was becoming more than just a concern for the environment and finding solutions to its mismanagement. Increasingly, it implied that humans, presented as an integral part of nature, were part of the problem. This shift was to dethrone humanity from its superior status, undermining our ability to know and, as far as possible, control the natural world. Instead, the new environmentalism demanded that we change ourselves to be conscious of our ecological impact.

Second, as noted above, social and political change was increasingly transposed to the level of the individual. If individuals could collectively change their attitudes then this would lead to societal change, was the logic employed. Here, geographers found a niche in the study of difference and identity, and how these varied spatially and culturally. In advocating geography's new ethical and political role, Claire Rasmussen and Michael Brown contend, 'Politics is not about defending the intrinsic interests of a political subject but about a struggle to construct subjects, making identity a primary ground for the operation of politics' (Rasmussen and Brown 2002: 182). This expanded the terrain of geography beyond the material world and into the realm of the psyche: how individuals perceive the world and their roles within it. This is explored further in the next chapter.

One dilemma that has challenged the exploration of moral geographies has been the conflict between the universal and particular as sources of moral authority. On the one hand, it would be out of keeping with contemporary geography to not respect the particular context in which moral values are shaped, but neither do some geographers want to subscribe to moral relativism. Different geographers have found different paths to tread the line between universal and particular morality or they have rejected the dualism out of hand. Seyla Benhabib argues that all people should be involved in a 'moral conversation' which can lead to debate and resolution of different perspectives. Smith himself notes that 'Principles must abstract from difference, but need not assume idealised accounts of human agents that deny their particularities' (Smith 2000: 17). Many other geographers take a similar line, arguing that morality has universal appeal, but can be applied differently in different contexts.

However, by its very nature ethics demands a consideration of others, as Smith contends. 'Ethical deliberation is often predicated on the principle of universalisation: that persons should be treated the same in the same circumstances' (Smith 2000: 18). What is the point of advocating an ethical position if one does not think it should apply to others? This principle was asserted by Immanuel Kant, who argued that the correct morality was one that could be willed for all human beings.

The confusion over particular versus universal morality for many geographers comes from the differential approach to ethics and knowledge assumed in geography's ethical turn. While social constructionists assert that knowledge is culturally situated, many simultaneously assert that all should conform to their ethical values of environmentalism, cultural tolerance, social justice and concern for an Other.

It is important to appreciate how geography's ethical turn has influenced the very nature of the subject itself. For one, it has led to a revival of moral objectives for the study of geography, an approach that was undermined earlier in the twentieth century for impeding independent thought. Further, it inhibits the scientific exploration and comprehension of spatial phenomena because it has conflated academic and ethical aims. Again, the words of David Smith are informative:

> At issue is not, then, whether geography is a positive or a normative endeavour, but how both perspectives are inseparably implicated in trying to make sense of the world, and perhaps to improve it.
>
> (Smith 2000: 2)

However, it is worth questioning whether it is the job of scientists and educators to decide how to improve the world. Commonly this is the prerogative of politics, while scientists are there to explain how things work. Yet this normative endeavour has become more central to geography, as well as other subjects, over recent years and mirrors the decline of its position as an objective science. With geography's ability to accurately map the world in question, ethics are frequently providing a new rationale for the subject. This has become especially clear in geographical education. Since knowledge acquisition is now seen as politicized and linked with identity formation, the school curriculum is designated a crucial role in shaping students' identities as embryonic citizens (Mitchell 2003: 387).

Teaching geography for a better world

Teaching Geography for a Better World was the title of a text brought out by John Fien and Rod Gerber (1988) that epitomizes the application of the new ethical approach to education. This book and subsequent publications by the authors have influenced geographical education across the English-speaking world, if not beyond. Geography's ethical turn, while making teachers more aware of the values systems they bring into the classroom, served to undermine the notion that teachers should take a neutral approach to their subject. Of course, in practice, it is not possible to teach without communicating at some level a sense of one's values. Teachers will always implicitly communicate some of their own and/or society's values. However, the question is, should they seek to minimize their personal viewpoint on matters that are political in nature, such as how to respond to global warming, or should they take an advocacy position? For much of the twentieth century teachers were expected to remain impartial or present alternative perspectives on political issues. Geography's ethical turn has reversed this position for some advocates for the subject. If knowledge is now viewed as inherently political then education is likewise seen as political in nature. With geography's ethical turn, the act of teaching has been recast as a political act. This has opened the floodgates for geography to become subservient to various social and political causes.

On opposing sides of the Atlantic Ocean, advocates variously want geography to adopt an 'active social science' approach, to be a new 'political geography' (Steinberg 1997: 118) or a 'transformative geography' which encourages students to 'practice the discipline of geography for the well-being of people and the environment' (Kirman 2003: 93), to involve teaching for 'social justice' (Merrett 2000), to encompass 'feminist pedagogy' where education is 'a fluid process whereby the student is empowered to act for social change' (Dowler 2002: 68) or even view geography as 'a means for social ends such as progress and problem solving' (Gerber and Williams 2002: 1). Others refer to promoting 'deep citizenship', linking 'public and private actions' with global concerns (Machon and Walkington 2000: 184). Thus the ethical turn in geography involves more emphasis in the classroom on personal transformation and participation, changing the personal values and attitudes of the student.

However, beneath the rhetoric of empowerment, social justice, citizenship education, and personal transformation lies a strong moral imperative with authoritarian consequences. The new ethical geography may superficially present itself as more enlightened and considerate of non-Western cultures than previous curricula with their Western-centrism, yet behind this veil of tolerance lies a new intolerance. The new ethical geography curriculum does not allow young people to develop their own moral compass; instead the issues and questions presented to students are designed to reinforce some strong contemporary moral messages. These are based around the ideas of environmentalism, cultural tolerance, human rights, social justice and equity, and caring for an 'Other'. Bill Marsden has noted the authoritarian impulse behind education *for* something, be it citizenship or the environment, in contrast to education *of* citizens: 'we can infer from the historical evidence that upholders of any "good cause" have found indoctrination more effective where schooling for some extrinsic end is envisaged' (Marsden 2001a: 21). Clearly this counters the spirit of free enquiry and rational discussion. It also means that education is being driven by something external to itself, as some academics have noted. Education *for* something:

> [I]mplies that education should aim for something external to itself and that educators are invited to prescribe a preferred end. It follows then that the slogan 'education for the environment' provides a linguistic invitation for co-option by those who feel they have the best answer.
>
> (Jickling and Spork 1998: 322)

While in the US the curriculum was being reoriented around values education in the 1980s, especially environmental values and cultural sensitivity, in the 1990s ethical issues have grown in significance in the curriculum and have cohered around the notion of global interconnectivity. In England and Wales the curriculum very rapidly embraced the themes of global citizenship in the mid to late 1990s. The new citizenship national curriculum was to embrace global citizenship and emphasized its links with other disciplines. Leading geographers and the Geographical Association began presenting the subject as capable of delivering the themes of global citizenship. In both the US and England/ Wales some geography curricula started to prominently include global issues, global connections and global responsibilities for students to consider.

Individual teachers may or may not hold back from encouraging students to take a given values perspective, but the new ethical curriculum is designed entirely for the purpose of engaging students in an examination of their personal responses to a given set of ethical problems. The simplistic manner in which this is done reinforces a contemporary moral imperative for young people to embrace. Global problems are not presented as issues to be interrogated for truth, knowledge and meaning, with a view to students developing ideas about the potential courses of social and political action. Instead, the solution is to be found in the personal realm and frequently is presented as a given: that people need to adhere to a new global values system that encourages them to consume less, have fewer children, take public transport rather than drive their cars, be less money-grabbing, support charities, and so forth. As one publication explains: 'The global dimension is concerned with exploring the interconnections between people and places. It asks us to observe the similarities and differences around our world today and relate these to our own lives' (Lambert *et al.* 2004: 2).

If the aims of geographical education are changing, then it is understandable that new teaching methods are proposed to deliver ethics education. Traditional 'chalk and talk' or lecturing is derided as too teacher-centred and criticized for its 'passive' approach to learning. Critics suggest that because students are given the answers they do not learn to think for themselves. Instead, several methods are proposed as leading to more 'meaningful' learning. Enquiry-based learning or problem solving are recommended because they encourage students to take some control for their own learning. Students help to define the problem, the questions that need to be answered and how they will go about their research. Here it is suggested that the role of the teacher is as a facilitator who guides students through their learning. Another approach is service learning whereby students undertake an activity beneficial to the local community, with a view to learning about the community and reflecting upon their role in it. Chapter 6 takes a more detailed look at the teaching methods used to explore global issues and ethics.

Evaluating geography's ethical turn in education

While geography's ethical turn has contributed valuable insight into the lives and stories of different people in their localities, the ethical approach to teaching geography is problematic. In particular, strong social constructivism has challenged the notion of geography as a body of knowledge, undermining the subject's ability to make sense of the world and communicate this meaning to young people. In place of theories, concepts and principles that can be utilized to gain insight across cultures and localities, geographical knowledge and theory become balkanized into small packages that have little relationship to each other and certainly are not pieces of a larger puzzle, arranged to provide students with a sequential and logical comprehension of spatial phenomena. This development alone reverses the scientific gains made by the subject since the beginning of the Enlightenment. As sociologist Frank Furedi has observed, 'without a relationship to Truth, knowledge has no intrinsic meaning' (Furedi 2004: 7). If all knowledge were relative, how could it possibly explain anything? While subjective stories from individuals in different localities are interesting and provide some insight into their individual lives, they do no more than this until a researcher undertakes an investigation into several people's stories using scientific methodology to conduct the interviews, analyse them and draw some conclusions. Using such an experimental method is a way of turning personal and values-laden observations and reasoning into knowledge that has a relationship to some reality, be it a social or natural reality. In the words of Yale Professor of Law Anthony Kronman:

> The experimental method is a technique for liberating our powers of reasoning from the limits to which the sense experience otherwise confines them, while at the same time providing a mechanism for testing the soundness of reason's abstractions against experience itself.
> (Kronman 2007: 213)

Through methodical data collection and analysis, individual stories can be transformed into a collection of stories from which insights can be drawn, patterns and trends identified. They are no longer subjective, because the observations have a grounding in evidence collected using a scientific methodology. Truly scientific investigations are conducted in such a way that anther person could replicate the methods and achieve the same result. This is why Enlightenment geographers such as Cook and Humboldt placed such a high value upon the accuracy of their work. A further check on whether the knowledge is accurate is through peer review. Before publication the work is scrutinized by other scientists in the field. Once approved for publication, this knowledge becomes accepted as a contribution to a wider body of subject knowledge. It has gained an objective existence beyond the individual who discovered it (not constructed out of thin air!) and can be used as a basis for future hypotheses or even theories. It gains a public existence, if you will.

Frequently, new knowledge supersedes old knowledge. Other scientists may develop different insights based upon new evidence, which prove the old knowledge partial, incomplete or even wrong. So long as the new research is accurate, genuine scientists will view the supersession of their findings positively because they will value the new knowledge and its insights above any personal attachment to their work. Again, the knowledge has an existence beyond the individuals who contributed to it. Objective knowledge is also something that we use every day. People use objective geographical knowledge of road names or numbers when they decide which road to drive on; they use knowledge of the compass when deciding which direction they need to be heading in; people use knowledge of locations, time zones, climate, culture and landscape when deciding where to travel and how to get there; pilots and sailors use very detailed and accurate maps when taking passengers to their destination. All this knowledge has both a basis in reality and an existence beyond the individuals who discovered it.

It is also important to recognize that our knowledge is not static, but frequently changing. Our understanding of the world is incomplete and sometimes errors have been made in measurements and observations. Moreover, the things that we hold to be 'true' about it sometimes change as new knowledge is discovered. This does not detract from truth as the ultimate objective of science and its pursuit by scientists.

This view of geography as a science for communicating an objective body of knowledge informed geographical education for much of the twentieth century, as illustrated in Chapter 1. The curriculum focused on knowledge that was public in nature and defined by the geography community. Teachers, by and large, concentrated on teaching knowledge, and as students gained knowledge of the world they would develop their own informed private opinions. This meant training students in a breadth of physical and human geographical knowledge, developing spatial skills and awareness. Through an engagement with abstract geographical ideas, theories and concepts, many of which were far removed from their everyday experiences, students developed intellectual skills of hypothesis testing, analysis, deduction, evaluation, and so forth.

Second, with the decline of truth and objective knowledge as the rationale for teaching geography, the ethical turn has led to the resurrection of extrinsic moral aims for the subject. Despite advocates' claims to respect difference and context, ethical geography does nothing to replace the Western-centrism of twentieth-century geography curricula. It simply replaces an emphasis upon nationalism, state-centrism and Western superiority with a curriculum built around a new set of ethics that are also Western in origin and character (environmentalism, cultural tolerance, etc.). These values have become prominent in some geography curricula, undermining the principle that young people should be free to determine their own ideas about social and political issues. However, there is a glaring contradiction in the differential approach taken in global citizenship education towards morality and knowledge which undermines the ethical claims of its advocates. Morality is given a universal quality while simultaneously denying the possibility that knowledge can be transferred from one context to the next. Yet how can those promoting an advocacy approach to education be confident in their ethical claims if they cannot be confident in knowledge? Wayne Veck realized this flaw in a paper exploring 'emancipatory research': 'In committing to social justice I was logically bound to the pursuit of truth. If the outcome of my research was to uncover injustice, to pronounce what was wrong, then what I had to say had to reflect the reality of that social injustice with the utmost accuracy' (Veck 2002).

Concluding comments

This chapter has traced geography's ethical turn both historically and logically, in order to ascertain its contribution to recent curricular reform in geography. This ethical turn has provided much valuable subjective knowledge about different people and localities, improved our understanding of the socially constructed nature of knowledge and exposed the Western-centrism of much modern geography. However, it has also popularized the notion that knowledge is *rooted* in the social context in which it was produced, denying the possibility for abstraction and shared cultural understanding. This view has undermined the view of geography as a body of knowledge and skills that all young people should have access to, regardless of their cultural background. The idea that all knowledge is equally values-laden has led some social theorists to deny the distinction between those accounts of the world that are grounded in reality and those that are not. This has opened geography's door to various extrinsic aims, politicizing or moralizing the content of the curriculum. The next two chapters trace this remoralization of the curriculum, first in the US (Chapter 3), and then in England and Wales (Chapter 4).

Suggested further reading

Gerber, R. and Williams, M. (eds) (2002) *Geography, Culture and Education*, London: Kluwer Academic Publications.
Kincheloe, J. (2001) *Getting beyond the Facts: Teaching Social Studies/Social Sciences in the Twenty-First Century*, New York: Peter Lang.

Machon, P. and Walkington, H. (2000) 'Citizenship: The Role of Geography?' in A. Kent (ed.) *Reflective Practice in Geography Teaching*, London: Paul Chapman, 179–91.

Peet, R. (1998) *Modern Geographical Thought*, Malden, MA: Blackwell.

Smith, D. (2000) *Moral Geographies: Ethics in a World of Difference*, Edinburgh: Edinburgh University Press.

Tuan, Y.F. (1977) *Space and Place: The Perspective of Experience*, Minneapolis, MN: University of Minnesota Press.

Chapter 3

From counter-cultural movement to global values

The US geography curriculum

KEY QUESTIONS

1 What are the significant influences in the transition from a national to multiple perspectives in the US geography curriculum?
2 How does the focus on values education relate to geography's new global orientation?
3 How does values education change the nature of geographical education?

It is helpful to make a distinction between societal values as reflected in textbooks and other teaching materials and using the curriculum to consciously attempt to change the values system of young people. Again, sometimes both of these things are going on simultaneously, as was the case with the national bias found in many twentieth-century textbooks. This chapter will show how, as a result of the ethical turn, the US geography curriculum has progressively embraced objectives that can be categorized as the latter, resulting in the growing inclusion of non-academic aims for the subject. This transition fits into a broader pattern in which all subjects have had to demonstrate their contribution to citizenship education. The teaching of geography in both the US and England/Wales, albeit with different timing, has become increasingly informed by social and political concerns rather than the demands of the discipline itself, as discussed in the previous chapter.

Over a similar time frame, US curricula have changed from delivering a homogeneous national perspective to offering multiple or global perspectives. This transition began with a reaction to the culture wars of the 1960s and 1970s as minorities gained a stronger position in American society and the multicultural make-up of the country became respected, over time.

Drawing on progressive educational thought, there was a conscious attempt to include schools in redressing past social injustice towards minorities. However, rather than a new unifying and representative discourse emerging from the collapse of the previously dominant Anglo-American perspective, the country, including schools, embraced diverse perspectives and celebrated different cultural identities. Here, nurturing students' identities to facilitate social integration became a central aspect of pedagogical theory.

In the 1980s and 1990s growing interest in global processes and inter-connections mirrored declining attachment to the nation state. Geography began to be seen as a subject with the potential for teaching young people about global interconnectivity and their global responsibilities. In particular, the 1990s saw school geography textbooks refocused around delivering a 'global perspective' and the teaching of 'global values', which continued an educational focus on students' interpersonal skills and attitudes.

While the post-World War II geography curriculum can be criticized for its preoccupation with the nation state and the international interests of the US, most textbooks were at least based on the assumption that students would develop into citizens with a public role through education and social experience, and some authors specifically sought to keep politics and national conflict out of their texts. Rather than seeking to influence the public role of young people as they mature into citizens, for some global values are promoted as the central core of the geography curriculum. They start from the assumption that young people lack the capacity to develop their own moral compass and hence they need to be directed towards a given values system. Geography's ethical turn has moved the core of the subject away from the key geographical knowledge and skills that students need to acquire to become competent in the subject and replaced it with focus on the moral and psychological constitution of individuals themselves. Where once geographers sought to offer students the subject's best insights into how the world looks and why, educators were being encouraged to offer different truths and geographies. Instead of delivering a world view, geography textbooks began exploring issues and different perspectives on the world. Therefore, it is important to emphasize that, in the transition from national to global orientation, a more fundamental shift has taken place in the nature of education itself: from learning subjects, national values and about social issues in preparation for participation in a liberal democracy to nurturing the psycho-social development of individuals.

Multicultural and environmental values in the US geography curriculum

Since the 1970s research using school textbooks has become an important methodology, providing reliable insight into the state of mind of any discipline at a point in time, and hence has demonstrated the potential to reveal curricular change over time. The central role of textbooks in the education of young people has been well documented (Woodward, Elliot and Nagel 1988; Johnsen 1993; Marsden 2001b). Woodward *et al.* (1988) concluded from a survey of US schools that 75–90 per cent of classroom time was structured by the school textbook, although with the Internet this figure has most likely decreased since this study was undertaken. The drawback of using textbooks is that they tend to be slow to adapt to disciplinary shifts; the time lag may be as much as ten years or even longer in extreme cases (Jackson 1976). The more successful textbooks are produced in several editions that are modified and updated with each subsequent edition. New ideas and concepts may well be added, but the overall approach to the subject is unlikely to alter significantly, at least until a completely new textbook is released. In the case of the US the school geography curriculum has been subjected to social and political pressures over recent decades and hence geography textbooks clearly reflect these broader pressures.

Multicultural education is not new in the US. With its history of diverse immigration, American schools have been looked to as a vehicle for cultural assimilation since the early twentieth century. Integration into a social democracy was very much the objective of progressives such as Dewey and Harold Rugg. Rachel DuBois pioneered the notion of inter-cultural education while teaching at a New Jersey high school in the 1920s. In the mid-1930s she became the leader of the Service Bureau for Intercultural Education. DuBois sought to challenge student attitudes by including stories of individuals from minority groups into the curricu-lum, teaching about how the law prevented equal social and political participation, and bringing aspects of students' lives into lessons (Pak 2004). Her ideas had resonance at a time of race riots in Harlem and Detroit and as people learnt of the experience of Jews in Europe during World War II. On the Pacific coast of the US, the Seattle public school boards were similarly promoting education with goals of 'respect for humanity, social justice, social understanding, critical judgment, tolerance, world citizenship and devotion to democracy' (Pak 2004: 64). Further, the National Council for Social Studies published a bulletin on intercultural understanding, written by Hilda Taba and William van Til, which became a bestseller in the 1940s. Nevertheless, Yoon Pak (2004) notes that the 'mainly white' teaching force 'delivered a version of intercultural education aimed at assimilation into the larger mainstream society' (Pak 2004: 58). Hence, intercultural education at this time was very different from that which evolved from the 1970s. It was also premised on the expectation that students would grow up to become citizens taking an active political role in society.

In high-school geography textbooks the transition from a homogeneous national culture to multiculturalism can be clearly traced over a span of a few decades following the counter-cultural movement of the 1960s. World geography textbooks in the 1950s sought to educate students primarily about the geography of the US, before considering its relations with the rest of the world, and this was approached in terms of its economic and political national self-interests. A good example is *World Geography: Economic, Political and Regional* (Pounds and Cooper 1957).

In the 1960s the international role of America was growing in importance and so geography textbooks focused more on the problems and needs of developing nations in Africa and Asia. The authors of one text noted that for most Americans interest in foreign policy was a new development: 'Now that the United States has become the leader of the Free World, we need to find out as much about our friends and allies as we possibly can' (Jones and Murphy 1962: 91). Cultural geography was a significantly more prominent theme and approach at this time. For instance, *The Wider World* (James and Davis 1967) examined the spread of Western ideals to other parts of the world, but they did so under the assumption that this was a positive process and that all nations would be better off if they too shared in these ideals.

The transition to multiculturalism in US geography textbooks began in the 1970s but was more evident in the 1980s. For instance, in *World Geography: The Earth and Its People*, regions were now called 'Cultural Regions' and were presented as less centred on the Western model, with every effort to value the contribution of different cultures. No longer was the culture of the US depicted as homogeneous: 'The Population of the United States is Diverse' and all immigrants contributed to this culture: 'With the exception of Native Americans, all the people of the United States are immigrants or descendants of immigrants who settled in North America after 1500' (Bacon 1989: 209). In other words, the previously dominant Anglo-American culture was no different from any other diaspora contributing to American culture. The consequence was a more diverse presentation of American culture. Thus, Bacon described the US as a melting-pot or a 'perfect example of cultural pluralism – a way of life in which people share a common culture while retaining parts of their traditional cultures' (Bacon 1989: 217).

Nevertheless, textbooks at this time still retained a strong sense of nationalism, even if the make-up of 'national culture' was changing. This was frequently evident in books discussing the international scale. Flemming (1981) conducted a study of six world geography textbooks published between 1975 and 1979. He found them to vary significantly in their approach to other nations, with some emphasizing political differences while others avoided such issues. Most of the textbooks portrayed the US and the West in a positive light through descriptions such as 'democracy' and 'free world' while communism was sometimes associated with 'totalitarianism' and 'propaganda' (Flemming 1981: 379).

In the 1980s geography was becoming more closely associated with learning about other cultures. In the teacher's edition of *World Geography* the author outlined the goals of the text for student learning: 'To help students appreciate the unique peoples and cultures of world regions. To help students develop a perspective on their own culture in relation to other cultures around the world' (Goss 1985: TG5). Similarly, in *Heath World Geography* the author proposed that 'Every culture is unique' and that 'People of different cultures also have different points of view. Even when they act in a similar way, people may have different reasons for their actions' (Gritzner 1987: 125). As an example Gritzner cited the different cultural reasons for tending cattle: in Hinduism they are sacred, on the Serengeti Plain they are a status-sign. Textbooks in the 1980s identified how cultural norms and values originated in different social settings and were becoming less judgemental of these differences.

A second significant change occurring in textbooks of the 1970s and 1980s was the growing importance of environmental values to the content and presentation of geography. Environmental values reflect a shift in emphasis away from a previous anthropocentric approach to society and the management of natural resources towards an approach that is sceptical of the righteousness and capacity of humans to intervene in or manage ecosystems. Instead, intrinsic value or authority over human endeavour is given to natural systems. The introduction of environmental education and its promotion of environmental values was a consequence of changing societal norms brought about by the environmental movement of the 1960s and 1970s, as noted in Chapter 2. A formal definition of environmental education was given by Dr William Stapp, University of Michigan, in 1969:

> Environmental education is aimed at producing citizenry that is knowledgeable concerning the biophysical environment and its associated problems, aware of how to help solve these problems, and motivated to work towards their solution.
>
> (cited by North American Association for
> Environmental Education 2003)

Shortly afterwards environmental education was enshrined in law with the passing of the 1970 Environmental Education Act.

Environmental education was introduced to schools in the form of several projects. In the 1970s Project Learning Tree taught students to value and care for forests, while Project Wild emphasized wildlife and ecosystems. Project Learning Tree (PLT) grew out of an education programme for elementary and secondary students developed by the

American Forest Institute (now the American Forest Foundation) and Western Regional Environmental Education Council (now the Council of Environmental Education). The Western Regional Environmental Council was set up as a three-year project with a $150,000 grant from the US Office of Education (Project Wild 2003). Two further programmes were introduced in the 1980s: Project WET (Water Education for Teachers) and GREEN (Global Rivers Environmental Education Network).

The growing number of environmental activists collectively formed the National Association for Environmental Education in 1971, which later became the North American Association for Environmental Education, reflecting its influence beyond US borders. Disinger reports that the organization drew more interest than it had anticipated, since it had initially not been intended to reach beyond community college level. He notes that conferences drew environmental activists who 'felt that an organization focused on "education" could and should afford them open opportunity to disseminate their pro-environmental messages to the full range of educational audiences' and that 'Those messages were sometimes (but not always) more propaganda than education' (Disinger 2001: 5).

Clearly, through such projects environmental education reached many students and teachers in virtually all US states. However, as McKeown and Hopkins observe, it advanced 'only because individual teachers have created thematic units and integrated them into the classroom curriculum' (McKeown and Hopkins 2003: 121). This approach stands in contrast to the state and national initiatives promoted by government from the late 1980s.

While geography itself was not a part of the environmental education projects, it evidently began to internalize the new approach to human–nature relationships through the inclusion of environmental values and teaching *for* not just *about* the environment. Geography is also a logical place to address interactions between people and the natural environment, given that this interface has historically been central to understanding spatial variation. However, previously these interactions were explored from an anthropocentric perspective: that the earth was there for people to utilize as best they could. This does not preclude conservation and sensible environmental management, but usually in terms of how this best suits people. In contrast, environmental values emphasize the value of the natural environment for reasons other than instrumental or aesthetic purpose.

In geography textbooks this has changed the way the human–natural systems are presented to students. Textbooks in the 1950s and 1960s mostly portrayed people's interaction with the natural environment in positive terms, focusing on utilization of natural resources to maximize output and wealth creation or taming of natural systems such as rivers, although pollution and other mismanagement were also cited. In textbooks written in the 1970s and 1980s natural resources were now described as 'Earth's resources' (not people's) and as 'fragile', 'under threat' and subject to 'abuse' from humans. For instance, in *World Geography: The Earth and its People* the global water supply was reported as 'A Fragile Resource' and that 'Pollution of surface waters is the most common abuse' (Bacon 1989: 113). The text continued, suggesting that 'Ground water in the United States is also threatened' (*ibid.*).

No longer were humans cast as a special case that could distance itself from nature. The new emphasis was on ecosystems as an interconnected whole, humans included. This approach was exemplified in *Heath World Geography*: 'An ecosystem represents a balance worked out in nature' and 'human activity also alters the balance within and among ecosystems' (Gritzner 1987: 96). The text further asserted that even small human actions such as dumping rubbish in a river or removing wood from a forest significantly disrupted ecosystems: 'Even a small change, multiplied thousands of times, can damage an entire ecosystem' (*ibid.*). Whereas previous textbooks emphasized the productive capacities of people to transform natural resources into commodities, in the 1980s resources were presented as limited in supply and likely to be used up by an expanding population. In *World Geography* Goss informed students: 'The days of cheap and abundant fossil fuels are over' (Goss 1985: 247), adding, 'How can we protect ourselves from the crisis that will certainly come if the earth's fossil fuels dry up before new sources are ready?' (*ibid.*: 256). This shifted geography's economic focus onto consumption rather than production, a pattern that is even more evident today.

Yet, at the same time, US geography textbooks produced in the 1980s still contained a strong geographical narrative. Environmental values and cultural sensitivity may have changed the way some topics were approached, but these textbooks still sought to describe and explain the world to students. In fact, in comparison with textbooks produced in the 1960s and 1970s they had more pages and chapters covering geographic themes and theory, including climate, landscape, resources, culture and population (see Figure 3.1)

Textbook publishing and the cultural wars

One of the main reasons for the increasing emphasis upon non-academic values of US textbooks was because they became a battleground for the cultural wars. After the civil rights demonstrations of the 1960s and 1970s there were moves to make textbooks more representative of non-Western contributions to history and the culturally diverse character of American society. In 1976 California enacted its 'social content standards'. These required textbook review committees to only approve books that:

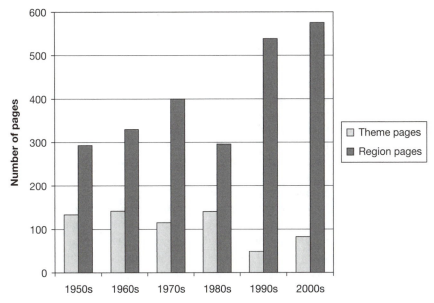

Figure 3.1 Thematic and regional content of US world high-school geography textbooks, 1950s–2005

[A]ccurately portray the cultural and racial diversity of our society, including the contributions of both men and women in all types of roles ... [and the] contributions of American Indians, American Negroes, Mexican Americans, Asian Americans, European Americans and members of other ethnic and cultural groups.

(cited by Finn and Ravitch 2004: 8)

However, what started as a laudable initiative took its remit to extreme measures. The social content standards continued to state that no textbook could contain 'any matter reflecting adversely upon any person because of their race, color, creed, national origin, ancestry, [or] sex' (*ibid.*). The consequence of this requirement was that textbooks sought to avoid negative portrayals of any group of people, even if this were a fair reflection of reality, such as the second-class status of women in most Muslim countries. There were other stipulations such as 'the junk food rule' whereby textbooks could not show food with low nutritional value, and textbooks were instructed to show positive images of people taking care of the environment.

Not only were California's social content standards a response to challenges to the dominance of the Anglo-American tradition in textbooks, but they also opened up the door to further legal challenges to the content of textbooks. In California this was mostly from groups on the political Left who had wholeheartedly embraced identity politics and hence sought equal representation of minorities and genders. By the 1990s there had already been a reaction from the political Right to the rising multi-cultural content of textbooks. In particular, this took place in Texas. Mel and Norma Gabler devoted vast resources to documenting textbook material they deemed objectionable to a Christian, American way of life (see Johnsen 1993). Similarly, the Texas Society of the Daughters of the American Revolution published a list of 170 'subversive' textbooks. As battles over books became highly charged and received national publicity, textbook content became highly politicized (see Keith 1991; Zimmerman 2002).

Publishing companies soon became wise to these protests, as well as California's social content standards. They took action to ensure that as many ethnic minorities as possible were represented and in equal amounts, genders were equally represented, that no group of people was depicted in a negative light, and that any *potentially* offensive material to any *conceivable* group or identity was removed from their textbooks. Not only were publishers reacting to particular objections that had been raised by groups, but they began a process of self-censorship in an effort to avoid future controversy over their publications. McGraw-Hill first produced its own bias and sensitivity guidelines in 1968. By 1993 its publication *Reflecting Diversity: Multicultural Guidelines for Educational Professionals* was prepared by twenty-eight staff with sixty-three consultants, underlining the seriousness with which the task was taken. Among its many require-ments, authors must use positive role models and avoid stereotypes for men, women, and people of different culture. For instance, African Americans should not be shown wearing loud colours, straw hats and white suits; they should not be depicted in crowded tenements or on chaotic streets. Traditional stereotypes, such as male construction workers, were to be avoided by authors and editors. Instead, they were encouraged to challenge stereotypes by showing people in unusual roles: the male nurse, the female engineer, and so forth. This also applied to minorities and the aged. Older people were no longer portrayed as inactive and frail, but must be shown to be active and in good health.

Likewise bias and sensitivity guidelines published by Harcourt instructed authors to 'beware of geographical chauvinism in the use of terms like America and Americans' (cited by Ravitch 2003). For example, they caution that there is no place called 'America' and terms such as the Orient or Orientalism and the Middle East (South West Asia) were banned. The guidelines argued that such terms have colonial connotations. Ravitch (2003) comments that at times this means telling lies about the cultural and historical roles of people. Evidently, publishers have been failing to make a distinction between racial bias in textbooks and removal of content that describes and explains cultural patterns, even if it portrays them in a negative manner.

There are several consequences of the self-censorship undertaken by publishers. One is that much of the imagination and life of textbook writing has been removed. Scott Foresman-Addison Wesley's 1996 guidelines detail 161 pages of restrictions defining political and social correctness for their authors. As Ravitch has pointed out, such a high level of control over one's writing, 'destroys the possibility of freedom of thought and expression' (*ibid.*: 49). This goes a long way to explaining the lifeless textbooks Tyson-Bernstein found as far back as the 1980s.

Another consequence is that the goal of textbook writing has become confused. While in the past most authors were principally trying to enlighten and interest students about their subject (and perhaps also instil patriotism), today the growing importance of social and political aims in curricula cloud this task. For instance, the Scott Foresman-Addison Wesley guidelines assert that the 'ultimate goal of the academic curriculum is to advance multiculturalism' (cited in *ibid.*: 40). While many textbooks in the past could be criticized for their nationalistic bias, today new ethical objectives have grown in significance for textbook production.

This development reflects the transition to identity politics and a belief that representations were damaging to the individual or group identity, but also that positive moral values and attitudes could be cultivated through education. As noted in the previous chapter, social change has been reduced to changing individuals and consequently schooling has grown in significance as a vehicle for social, political and even economic change (see Lasch-Quinn 2001). Subjects were now being asked to demonstrate how they contributed to the social and psychological well-being of young people, rather than how they develop their intellectual capabilities.

In addition to social and political goals the 1980s saw education become subservient to and presented as responsible for the economic destiny of the country. The 1983 report *A Nation at Risk* alerted the country to falling educational standards and established in people's minds the link between schools and the needs of employers. In subjects such as geography this led to a focus on pre-vocational skills of reading, writing, data analysis, communication, problem solving and so forth. These were introduced to textbooks in the 1980s and became significant highlighted features of those published in the 1990s and 2000s.

Environmentalism as personal responsibility

Besides respect for cultural diversity, environmental issues and values have become a dominant theme in geography textbooks. As the world has become more preoccupied with environmental problems geography has been one of the subjects best placed to address these concerns, given its focus on the relationship between people and natural world. So while national environmental concerns were addressed though environmental education in the 1970s and 1980s, an important shift took place at the end of the 1980s and the beginning of the 1990s. That a new direction was being sought was clear from some environmentalists who felt that environmental efforts to date had been unsuccessful. This included van Matre, a long-time advocate of environmental education and later director of the Institute for Earth Education. In his book *Earth Education* van Matre argued that 'we blew it' because the education projects failed to make a difference to how people live their lives (van Matre 1990: 4). Students who received environmental education did not internalize environmental values and develop a different world view. Van Matre suggests several reasons for this 'failure': that the projects externalized the problem as out there and not within us as individuals; that science was not necessarily the right place to teach environmental education since it suggests that the solution comes from the application of scientific method instead of a change of lifestyles; and that the content of the projects was sprinkled around rather than taught as a coherent programme and consequently basic ecological concepts such as the flow of energy did not get across to students (*ibid.*). A similar summation of environmental education at institutions of higher education was made by David Orr (1992). Part of the disappointment of environmentalists was that their radical ecological agenda from the 1960s had become incorporated into the modernist mainstream thought. Environmental problems were recognized, but people thought they could be fixed through the application of science and technology. A redistribution of resources was required, but otherwise capitalism marched onwards.

Nevertheless, change was afoot. A new approach to environmentalism was being advocated that would lead to a wholesale questioning of the modernist foundations upon which contemporary society had been built. Articulated through the concept of sustainable development, the new approach was precisely the one that van Matre was seeking: instead of seeing environmental problems as something external to ourselves it was humans that needed to change themselves. In other words, society needed to rethink its relationship to nature. Humanity could no longer be viewed as separate from and master of the natural world, but would need to consider itself a part of nature. Sustainable development was endorsed as an outcome of the World Commission on Environment and Development in 1987. It is described by Gro Brundtland, the author of the commission's report, as 'development that meet the needs of the present without compromising the ability of future generations to meet their own needs' (World Commission on Environment and Development 1987: 43).

This sustainability argument was eloquently presented by Daniel Sitarz (1998) in *Sustainable America: America's Environment, Economy and Society in the Twenty-First Century*. He suggests that since the end of the Cold War the emergence of the global economy, population growth and technological advance have changed the world in fundamental ways, such that humans are placing increasing stress on the natural world. Current levels of consumption and spending are not sustainable. To survive in this 'new world' requires a fresh approach to economic, environmental and social challenges. A sustainable approach means caring for the earth, developing a sense of stewardship, which is more of a perspective than a science, suggests Sitarz. For Sitarz, sustainable America means sustaining economic prosperity, a clean environment, population levels, nature, stable communities and education. Similarly, Al Gore (1990) was arguing for environmentalism to become the new organizing principle of society in place of the ideological 'glue' provided by Cold War ideology.

There are many interpretations of sustainable development and sustainability, which at time makes the topic confusing. However, they all share assumptions about the connectivity of social, economic and environmental phenomena or systems, and that humanity needs to modify its horizons to take account of its environmental and cultural impact. Hence, Wheeler writes that education about sustainability 'is about learning to make and understand the connections and interactions between these three complex systems' (Wheeler 2000: 2). Wheeler argues that sustainability education is about a way of thinking, that it necessitates thinking about the future, understanding communities, stewardship of natural resources, a broader interpretation of economics that includes intellectual, social, natural and spiritual capital as well as economic capital; and an understanding of the links between local and global issues. Similarly, Orr (1992) concludes that sustainability, citizenship and democracy are closely linked and that therefore sustainability can be achieved only through democratic participation and an informed citizenry.

With its focus on the relationship between places as well as the human and natural world, sustainability emphasizes the transnational character of environmental problems and views these as global problems necessitating global solutions, and something to which we should all contribute. Hence, environmental problems were now presented as the responsibility of all individuals. Thus environmentalism has become much more clearly a moral issue, not just a scientific one. This change is reflected in the concept of education for sustainable development, but its assumptions have subsequently been incorporated into US environmental education programmes and some geography curricula.

The Earth Summit held in Rio de Janeiro in 1992 and its report, *Agenda 21*, built international momentum, spurring many governments into action on environmental issues and the need for environment-related education to facilitate change. Sitarz reports that *Agenda 21* 'provides a comprehensive blueprint for humanity to use to forge its way into the next century by proceeding more gently upon the Earth' and that 'Deep and dramatic changes in human society are proposed by this monumental agreement' (Sitarz 1993: 1). The report argues that education will be indispensable for changing people's attitudes and hence urges governments to integrate environment and development into their education systems within three years, relates Sitarz. To ensure that this happens *Agenda 21* recommends several strategies for governments, including:

> A thorough review of curricula . . . to ensure that there is a multi-disciplinary approach which encompasses environment and development issues; . . . set up national advisory environmental education coordinating bodies; . . . set up pre-service and in-service training programs for all teachers and administrators which address the nature and methods of environment and development; . . . every school should be assisted in designing environmental activity work plans, with the participation of students and staff; . . . all countries should support university activities and networks for environmental and development education.
>
> (Sitarz 1993: 294–5)

The language in the report clearly endorses the notion of connectivity between social, economic and environmental issues through the linking of development and environment.

While in the 1970s and 1980s there was limited US government support for environmental education, it was only in the 1990s that environmental and sustainability projects received the kind of backing that would enable them to make a significant impact on mainstream education. This process began in 1990 with a second Environmental Education Act. The Act authorized an Office of Environmental Education in the US Environmental Protection Agency (EPA), an environmental education and training programme (later known as EETAP), environmental education grants, student fellowships related to environmental education, the President's Environmental Youth Awards, the Federal Task Force and National Advisory Council and the National Environmental Education and Training Foundation (NEETF) (North American Association for Environmental Education 2003). Many of these new organizations and initiatives had remits beyond formal education, but they have all worked towards mainstreaming environmentalism in some form. In 2001 the authors of a survey of state standards reported that environmental education in some form was 'gaining a foothold in both the formal and non-formal education infrastructure in many states' and that 'the US EPA has identified funding EE (environmental education) capacity building as the primary focus' (Ruskey *et al.* 2001: 13).

With environmental education preceding education for sustainability, the term 'sustainability' itself has only very recently begun to appear in US geography textbooks and frequently just in passing. The term is also becoming more prominent in state curriculum standards. Nevertheless, in the 1990s textbooks described environmental problems in global terms and were clearly influenced by the concept of sustainability. Thus, in *World Geography: Building a Global Perspective*, the authors reported that 'Officials are hoping that by rationing the use of resources now, long-term conservation will have a better chance of succeeding in the future' (Baerwald and Fraser 1995: 544). In practice, the authors said this meant limited access to the rainforest for hunting, fishing, farming and other activities for indigenous people. In this generation of textbooks there was a broader sense of environmental crisis brought about because humans had irreversibly disrupted natural systems. For example, in *Geography: People and Places in a Changing World* the author described the consequences of the unprecedented power of science and technology combined with a rise in population: 'As a result, people are rapidly changing Earth's land, air, and water to the extent that these basic elements of life have become issues of global concern' (English 1995: 70). The author surmised that 'The environmental problems that have resulted from human activity are among the primary problems we face today and in the future' (English 1995: 75).

Environmental education in the US has by no means been without criticism (see Holt 1991). Several studies have taken issue with the way it is approached in schools, while noting the importance of learning about the environment. For instance, one investigation noted how environmental education can bring 'life to scientific principles and information that underlie ecology' but found that in many schools lessons 'skip the basics, pushing students to complex and controversial topics such as endangered species without establishing a scientific basis of knowledge' (Sanera and Shaw 1999: 1). In these instances, the authors conclude that 'Education can play second fiddle to emotionalism and political activism' (*ibid.*). Because of this type of criticism an Independent Commission on Environmental Education was commissioned to undertake a thorough review of environmental teaching materials used in classrooms. The final report found that while some materials offered an informative balanced approach, in other cases 'factual errors are common', 'many environmental science textbooks have serious flaws' and 'others mix science with advocacy' (Independent Commission on Environmental Education 1997).

Global issues in the US geography curriculum

The late 1980s and the early 1990s were a significant moment of transition in social studies education. Increasing internationalized economies and the end of the Cold War gave rise to a new era of globalization and challenges to traditional national citizenship. The ethical values embraced in the social studies curriculum of the 1970s and 1980s became codified as part of a shift towards global or international education. Here, the new emphasis on citizenship education with a global orientation more closely resembles moral education than preparation for participation in a liberal democracy.

In 1990 Joseph Stoltman observed the need for geography to make links to citizenship in order to maintain a foothold in the social studies curriculum: 'While citizenship has not been a major goal of geography education, the research and writing on citizenship suggest that the discipline should play a prominent role' (Stoltman 1990: 37). Here, Stoltman was alluding to the fact that society was changing, with schools being looked to as institutions capable of infusing young people with a sense of values, where traditional social institutions (such as the church, family and marriage) were seen as failing. The link between a growing emphasis upon citizenship and ethics in the social sciences and a wider moral crisis in society has been made elsewhere (Smith 2000; Proctor and Smith 1999).

The 1990s was a decade when many scholars of civic education questioned the condition of American democracy (Ravitch and Viteritti 2001). In schools, the unpopularity of traditional citizenship classes and students' poor grasp of its themes are well documented (Cotton 1996; Braungart and Braungart 1998). A 1999 United States Department of Education survey revealed that only 20 per cent of youths have a proficient understanding of the US constitution and the principles underlying government (Ravitch and Viteritti 2001), while a declining interest in traditional history classes was noted among American students, who questioned its relevance for today's world (Jarolimek 1990). The decline of national culture and political life was partly an outcome of the transition to multiculturalism and multiple perspectives described above. Diane Ravitch comments that publishers' bias and sensitivity guidelines 'Actively prohibit the transmission of our national culture' (Ravitch 2003: 49). Her point is that it is not possible to uphold a common national culture and simultaneously celebrate the importance of other non-American cultures. The latter weakens the former. While politics at the national level has narrowed and become less relevant to people's lives, political initiatives and organizations on the international scene appear, by comparison, vibrant and dynamic, if not always successful. In this globalized era political, economic, social and environmental problems have become increasingly viewed in international terms. This has given rise to the promotion of human rights over national rights and humanitarian intervention over national sovereignty.

Social studies as a whole has embraced global issues as a more 'relevant' topic for students and has challenged the national model of citizenship with citizenship defined at multiple levels. The National Council for the Social Studies standards now include Global Connections as one of ten themes to study, with the following introduction:

> The realities of global interdependence require understanding the increasingly important and diverse global connections among world societies and the frequent tension between national interests and global priorities. Students will need to be able to address such international issues as health care, the environment, human rights, economic competition and interdependence, age-old ethnic enmities, and political and military alliances.
>
> (National Council for Social Studies 2003)

Learning about the US government has been reduced to one section of the theme Power, Authority and Governance and the role of the citizen is discussed at different levels: the community, the nation and the world. Another significant change was the addition of a new standard by the National Council for the Accreditation of Teacher Education to its Standards for Professional Development. The new standard was for the development of a 'multicultural and global perspective' (NCATE Standard 4) (Hayl and McCarty 2003).

The education system, as a vehicle for cultural transmission, has engaged in a concerted attempt to shape a new generation versed in global values (Strouse 2001; Stromquist 2002). Global change education is a burgeoning field not confined to international organizations (Mortensen 2000). Global citizenship education is not simply supported by NGOs with a global education remit such as the American Forum for Global Education and Global Education Associates in New York, or Global Citizens for Change, but is supported by professional associations such as the National Council for Social Studies, the National Education Association, various influential educational organizations such as the Asia Society and the Longview Foundation with financial backing from Goldman Sachs and the Bill and Melinda Gates Foundation (Burack 2003). This has given rise to state initiatives to develop international education in at least twenty-seven US states over recent years (Asia Society 2008).

While some geographers and geography textbooks have been advocating the virtues of internationalism and world peace for some time, for instance *Geography and World Affairs* (Jones and Murphy 1962), it is only in the post-Cold War era of globalization that the notion of global citizenship has grown in popularity, contributing to geography's renaissance in the US, evidenced by its growing inclusion in schools' curricula and the rapidly rising number of students taking Advanced Placement Human Geography in preparation for college (Association of American Geographers 2006). In February and March of 2007 the Teaching Geography is Fundamental Act was reintroduced to the 110th Congress. If passed this amendment to the Higher Education Act of 1965 will provide $15 million annually to improve geographic literacy for grades K-12. This would be the first time the subject has been federally funded.

Some American geographers began linking their subject with global citizenship back in the 1980s as the US was becoming more internationally focused. 'Geography instruction today must prepare students for citizenship in an increasingly global society' (Anderson 1983: 80) was a growing viewpoint. In 1992 the *International Charter on Geographical Education* proposed that through geography students should develop attitudes and values conducive to a 'concern for the quality of the environment, respect for rights of all people to equality, and dedication to seeking solutions to human problems' (International Geographic Union, cited in Edwards 2002: 31). Leading policy advisers began to look at geography's role in overcoming problems of 'connectivity' (Wilbanks 1994). Indicatively the previously neglected US geography curriculum was included as one of five core subjects in the 1994 Goals 2000: Educate America Act. Promoting geography's role in citizenship education has at times been linked with global citizenship. In this vein, Sarah Bednarz asserts that 'the definition of citizenship may in fact be broadening from national to international in scope' (Bednarz 2003: 74).

Geography textbooks such as Pearson's *World Geography: Building a Global Perspective* were quick to latch on to this sea change. However, textbooks mostly refrain from using the term 'global citizenship', presumably so as not to offend the significant patriotic lobby, and hence continue to emphasize nation symbols and flags. Yet, inside the covers, a very different approach to geography has emerged which discusses 'global issues', 'global connections' and the 'global community'. For instance, the Pearson textbook includes boxes under the heading 'Case study on global issues: a local perspective' whose goal is to learn about issues that are important for all of humanity and focus on 'the global implications of issues such as world population, conflict and its resolution, and human rights' (cited in Baerwald and Fraser 1995: T20). Other textbooks similarly advocate the importance of a global understanding. While some textbooks still refer to nation states to describe regions, they frequently discuss their problems as global concerns, whose management is the prerogative of the international community. Other textbooks examine the people or cultures of regions, rather than the political boundaries of nation states (see Standish 2006).

Some of the 'global issues' discussed in world geography textbooks include: cultures under threat from modernization/development/ Westernization, cultural and political conflict and the role of the United Nations in moderation/peacekeeping, deforestation, pollution (of air, water, soil), desertification, global warming, human rights, social justice for minorities, rising populations in developing countries, trade, consumption patterns, improving the social position of women in developing countries, development, poverty, disease and health, urbanization, land use conflict, the drugs trade, immigration, refugees and more recently terrorism. Discussion of issues such as these is not new to geography textbooks. However, it is possible to observe an increase in textbook content attributed to discussion of geographic issues from 11 per cent in the 1950s to 15.3 per cent in the 2000s (Figure 3.2). As the graph demonstrates, international issues are by no means new to geography textbooks. In the decades after World War II textbooks discussed problems of colonialism, decolonization, international peace, Third World development and Cold War ideology. While the data show that much of the rise of recent decades can be attributable to issues that appear at the national scale, this does not tell the whole story. What has changed is the way in which these issues are presented in textbooks. Today, national issues are frequently presented as part of larger global problems.

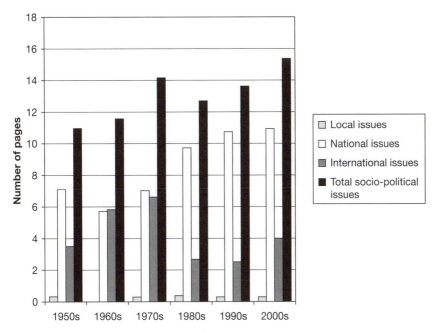

Figure 3.2 Socio-political issues per decade in US world geography textbooks, 1950s–2005

Until the 1990s authors usually discussed issues as the prerogative of nation states to resolve, although on occasion making reference to international bodies to deliver aid or to negotiate peace between two nations. From the 1990s the lines of responsibility are less clear. Certainly the role of international bodies, especially the United Nations, is more frequently cited, as are others such as the World Health Organization or non-governmental organizations like Oxfam and Save the Children. At other times broader global issues like global warming, consumption and cultural understanding are depicted as the responsibility of all, including the students reading the text. The motto 'Think global, act local' is often used in textbooks and by educators. It is also quoted in Standard 18 of the online national geography standards How to Apply Geography to Interpret the Present and Plan for the Future (National Council for Geographic Education 2003). Examples of global issues and their method of presentation will be illustrated in Chapter 7.

In the new global approach to geography, multicultural and environmental values have grown in significance, sometimes being cited as a primary purpose of the discipline. That geography was becoming more focused on learning about other cultures was made evident in an introduction by Riggs-Salter to the teacher's edition of World Geography: Building a Global Perspective: 'The study of geography is itself a way of focusing on different cultures' (cited in Baerwald and Fraser 1995: T9). The use of the phrase 'Building a Global Perspective' is indicative of a focus on the attitudes and values of students rather than the knowledge they will gain. Unfortunately, the text does not provide a definition of this term. However, the National Council for Accreditation of Teacher Education describes a global perspective as:

> An understanding of the interdependency of nations and peoples and the political, economic, ecological, and social concepts and values that affect lives within and across national boundaries. It allows for the exploration of multiple perspectives on events and issues.
>
> (National Council for Accreditation of Teacher
> Education 2006: 54)

The aim of this approach is to encourage students to see the world and people as interrelated and hence move away from viewing their nation as exceptional and pursuing self-interest. The meaning and consequences of teaching 'global perspectives' or 'multiple perspectives' are examined in Chapter 5. Here it is important to note that ethical considerations are being used to justify the teaching of geography.

During the 1990s the standards movement at both national and state level has simultaneously enhanced the breadth of geography covered in textbooks as well as the themes of global connections. Hence, most geography standards and textbooks today still retain much of the academic traditions identified in Chapter 1 that have come to provide the subject with scientific and intellectual credibility. This is largely an outcome of the standards movement that began work on a geography national curriculum in the 1980s, publishing *Geography for Life* in 1994. Some state standards are closely aligned to the national standards while others contain some strands but not others (see Kaufhold 2004). Also fortunate for geography in the US was that Texas chose to base its standards very closely upon *Geography for Life*. As one of the largest textbook markets (along with California and Florida) this very much influenced the content of subsequent textbooks by the four leading publishers (Prentice Hall/ Pearson, McDougle-Littell, Glencoe/McGraw-Hill and Holt, Reinhart & Winston). By tailoring textbooks to the extensive Texas market these publishers were forced to incorporate the national geography standards (Bednarz 2004). As Bednarz explains, 'Because the Texas curricula are aligned to *Geography for Life*, and Texas, in part, drives the creation of textbooks, one can surmise that this will influence the content of the books' (Bednarz 2004: 21). Bednarz found that in the 2003 editions of the Big Four high-school world geography textbooks the national standards had by and large been incorporated.

The theme of global connections is likewise found in many state social studies/geography standards. For instance, citizenship is identified at multiple levels in Wisconsin's geography standards: by the end of grade 4 students are expected to be able to 'Identify connections between the local community and other places in Wisconsin, the United States, and the world' (Standard A4.7, Wisconsin Department of Instruction 2006), while in the middle grades they are taught about global issues and how to respond to them: 'Give examples of the causes and consequences of current global issues, such as the expansion of global markets, the urbanization of the developing world, the consumption of natural resources, and the extinction of species, and suggest possible responses by various individuals, groups, and nations' (Standard A 8.11, Wisconsin Department of Instruction 2006).

The New Jersey geography standards present the subject at different scales. In the middle grades the notion of global interdependence is again present: 'Explain and identify examples of global interdependence' (Statement D7, New Jersey Department for Education 2006), while at high school students are required to learn about the virtues of sustainable development: 'Analyze the human need for respect for and informed management of all resources (sustainability), including humanpopulations, energy, air, land, and water to insure that the earth will support future generations' (Statement E6, New Jersey Department for Education 2006).

Nevertheless, at the same time as the national standards have become prominent in geography textbooks so have global values and some of the themes of global citizenship. As textbooks were sucked into the cultural wars their content has become increasingly politicized through the inclusion of fashionable social, economic, environmental and political causes. The outcome has been that they frequently seek to be all things to all people, as well as devoid of any potentially controversial material whatsoever. Further, it is important to remember that textbooks are not synonymous with the curriculum, as studied by students in the class-room. While in the case of the US geography textbooks are probably more widely used than in England or Wales given that many social studies teachers lack a grounding in geographical education from their own education and training, the way in which textbooks are used by teachers will vary. The Internet has also made readily available voluminous alternative geographical resources, upon which many teachers draw. Hence, prominent websites offering geographical education resources such as National Geographic also need to be considered, especially as they are able to respond more rapidly to new trends and ideas.

The National Geographic campaign My Wonderful World, supported by numerous geographical and educational organizations, has adopted many themes of global citizenship. The campaign lists ten ways to 'give students the world' that include 'Finding global connections close to home . . . Connect students with people from other countries and cultures. . . . Help students envision their futures' (National Geographic Society 2006). Again, the campaign is promoting the subject of geography and clearly aims to teach students about the geography of other parts of the world. But there is also a moral undercurrent. In a section encouraging teachers to make their schools 'geography-ready' the campaign suggests that each school's mission should include 'fostering cultural understanding . . . Appreciating differences and/or finding strength in diversity . . . Developing global citizens and preparing students to live in a global, multicultural society' (ibid.). Suggested ways to achieve this include displaying artefacts from different cultures, writing signs, banners and labels in languages other than English and sending teachers for diversity and cultural sensitivity training. The campaign has a number of useful resources for teachers, including maps, technology guides and lesson plans.

What has changed is not necessarily that people are seeking to use textbooks for instrumental ends. Chapter 1 illustrated how this has been the case in the past. However, geography's ethical turn has thrown into question the intellectual and humanistic foundations of the subject and thus for many the moral claims of global values offer a more solid basis for their teaching. As discussed above, the relativist approach has precipi-tated a crisis of disciplinary knowledge in which subject specialists feel less able to defend a body of knowledge as something independent of the subjective viewpoints of those who created it. This has opened the floodgates for political interference in the curriculum and increasingly subjects are justifying their place in the curriculum through ethical, psychological or vocation goals rather than intellectual ones.

If the aims of the subject are changing then no doubt the nature and content of geography are also in transition. Today, the study of other cultures seems less focused on understanding their spatial distribution and changing dynamics and more about representing the practices and achievements of other cultures in order to encourage students to have respect for them. This change is important because now promoting specific moral values, in this case respect for other cultures, is increasingly informing the content and presentation of the curriculum, rather than the principles of the subject. How this alters the content of cultural geography is the topic of Chapter 5.

Concluding comments

The purpose of the chapter has been to examine changes to the direction and content of the US geography curriculum. The emphasis has been upon highlighting these changes. However, it is essential to recognize that the changes identified above by no means apply to all geography teachers and classes. There remain many geographers committed to the foundations of their discipline who are busy teaching geography rather than global issues and values. In particular, the formal geography curriculum, in the form of national and state standards, retains geography's intellectual traditions and where taught offers students a strong foundation in the subject. Most state standards reflect much of the content of the national standards (Kaufhold 2004) and the National Council for Geographic Education (NCGE) similarly promotes a traditional role for the subject in its curricular documentation. For example, NCGE promotes a book by Phil Gersmehl (*Teaching Geography*), who likewise grounds his approach in geography's academic traditions. In the introduction Gersmehl entices the reader with 'Welcome to the world of geography, the art/science that deals with where things are located, why they are located there, and what difference their location makes' (Gersmehl 2005: 3).

Teachers and textbook authors have made it clear that the geography community is divided on its educational role, with some emphasizing its links with global citizenship and moral education, others taking a more traditional approach and some seeking a combination of the two. Similarly, the most recent editions of the Big Four world geography high-school textbooks include most of the content of the national standards (Bednarz 2004) but at the same time promote geography as a discipline for exploring global issues with a view to informing the ethical values students hold. In seeking to be all things to all people, textbooks have become extremely large and also confused about the purpose of geography. While introductory pages usually describe the origins of geography, its different traditions and highlight its inclusion of the national standards, much of the text seems to be a factual tour of the world infused with boxes exploring 'global issues' and 'multicultural perspectives'. The inclusion of ethical objectives leads to confusion about the central purpose of the text, inhibiting the analysis of geographical trends. The absence of direction and the manner in which textbooks are written today result in a superficial text lacking a coherent narrative.

Suggested further reading

Bednarz, S. (2004) 'US World Geography Textbooks: Their Role in Education Reform', *International Research in Geographical and Environmental Education*, 13 (3): 16–31.

Finn, C. and Ravitch, D. (2004) *The Mad, Mad World of Textbook Adoption*, Washington, DC: Thomas Fordham Institute.

Independent Commission on Environmental Education (1997) *Are We Building Environmental Literacy?* Washington DC: George C. Marshall Institute.

Mortensen, L. (2000) 'Global Change Education: Education Resources for Sustainability', in K. Wheeler and A. Bijur (eds) *Education for a Sustainable Future: A Paradigm of Hope for the Twenty-First Century*, New York: Kluwer Academic/ Plenum Publishers.

Sitarz, D. (1993) *Agenda 21: The Earth Summit Strategy to Save our Planet*, Boulder, CO: Earthpress.

Woyshner, C., Watras, J. and Crocco, M. S. (eds) (2004) *Social Education in the Twentieth Century*, New York: Peter Lang.

Chapter 4

Global citizenship and the geography curriculum in England and Wales

KEY QUESTIONS

1 What have been the main drivers of change in the English/Welsh geography curriculum?
2 How is this new geography curriculum similar to and different from that which has emerged in the US?

In the UK geography has traditionally had a stronger place in the school curriculum, not unrelated to its colonial past. Here, the focus will be on the combined curriculum for England and Wales, as Scotland and Northern Ireland have their own independent school systems. Unlike the US, the curriculum in England and Wales had been relatively free from political debate until the 1980s. Launched in 1991, the first geography national curriculum included geographical knowledge and skills drawn from its past traditions: landforms, rivers, climate, population, settlements, urbanization, development, and required study of both the UK and different world regions. The focus on knowledge content, as well as process, was to the dismay of progressive educationalists, who had been developing enquiry-based teaching materials for geography since the 1960s. This child-centred approach laid down the foundations for geography to embrace global citizenship education in the late 1990s. This did not happen until after a decade of New Right Thatcherism, which included the implementation of the geography national curriculum, and the end of the Cold War, leading to a period of global advocacy.

In England and Wales the curriculum based on geographical knowledge and skills rapidly began to unravel from the mid-1990s, as a result of three dynamics that led to the subject's new focus on global citizenship: a shift in government education policy from a defence of subjects to psycho-social objectives exemplified by the new citizenship national curriculum, the growing influence of non-governmental organizations (NGOs) in the production of national curricular documentation and general teaching materials, and geography's self-reinvention as global citizenship education by some prominent geographers. This transition was facilitated by New Labour's rise to power in 1997. Tony Blair's Third Way approach to politics and education led to scepticism towards traditional subjects and calls for a complete reinvention of education with psycho-social objectives, similar to those already in place in the US education system. This chapter will commence with curricular developments in the 1970s.

Curriculum experimentation in the 1970s

The 1970s have been described as 'the decade of curriculum development for geography' (Rawling 2001: 27). Impetus and money came from the Schools Council. Established in 1964, the Schools Council was responsible for curriculum reform and development in schools in England and Wales. It launched several influential geography projects in schools to research and to promote curriculum development. It was also a time when the comprehensive reorganization of schools was taking place, prompting a broader questioning of schooling. The curriculum, untouched by government intervention, was an arena for experimentation by teachers.

Based at Avery Hill College of Education, Geography for the Young School Leaver (GYSL) was one project established in 1970 that aimed to examine the contribution that geography can make to the education of average and below-average students between the ages of fourteen and sixteen. In part this was a response to the raising of the school-leaving age from fourteen to sixteen in 1967. The idea was to produce a curriculum that was more 'relevant' to these 'less academic types' who were not aiming for higher education and hence less likely to succeed in examinations. The project sought to produce high-quality resource materials and adopted a theme-based approach to learning.

In the same year the Geography 14–18 (Bristol) Project examined the curriculum and assessment of fourteen- to sixteen-year-olds to find out why many students were failing at this level. It blamed the narrow focus of essay-style assessment and an examination syllabus that was factual and descriptive. Orrell (1990) notes that 'From the beginning the Bristol Project held the view that more able students should have the opportunity to undertake a geographical enquiry of their own' (Orrell 1990: 39). A new O level was developed such that 'more able' students could have 'the same stimulation and enjoyment from geography as their "less able" colleagues' (Walford 2001: 178). Hence, decision making, problem solving and course work became an important part of this innovative curriculum for students, involving teachers in both the planning of curriculum and the assessment of course work. This model became the norm for General Certificate of Secondary Education (GCSE) course work from its introduction in 1986.

Subsequently, the Geography 16–19 Project was launched in 1976 at the Institute of Education, London. It established a distinctive people–environment approach to geography and an enquiry-based approach to learning. Hall (1991) described an example of an enquiry-based question from an A-level decision-making paper. Students were asked to review the major problems of an area of east Manchester and produce a statement of priorities for its redevelopment. To complete the task it was necessary for:

> Candidates to handle a wide range of enclosures from photographs, statements from residents, maps, graphs and statistics: considerable skills of data handling, including spatial distributions, patterns and quantities were required as well as linguistic skills of communication in preparing a 'report' for the planning committee.
>
> (*ibid.*: 23)

To complete such a task would require knowledge of the social and economic needs of an urban area in addition to taxing all the skills mentioned. Hall also noted that the above example highlighted the 'growth of the importance of values analysis'. A wide range of course and syllabuses derived from this framework, including the University of London A-level syllabus. Further, Rawling observed that the Schools Council projects of the 1970s were exemplary in their involvement of teachers in the complete process of curriculum change. Common sense suggests that this 'is the most effective way to ensure continuing and effective development work' (Rawling 1990: 37).

These curriculum developments were in part the consequence of the growing popularity of student-centred educational theories. As noted in Chapter 1, the 'radical' geography of the 1970s focused on social issues was in part a response to the counter-cultural movement, but also a reaction to the abstract, quantitative geographical theories of the 1950s and 1960s.

Progressive education in the UK became more widespread, initially in primary education and later in secondary education, after the influential Plowden Report (Department for Education and Science 1967). Student-centred education advocated a less teacher-centred approach to learning. Knowledge should be built on what the student already knows. Therefore the starting point for education was seen as 'what the student knows' rather than 'what the teacher knows'. The development of the child became the focus rather than the teaching of knowledge.

As distinguished geographer Bill Marsden noted, the outcome was that 'process increasingly took precedence over content' (Marsden 1997). With this approach geography becomes a medium through which the child is developed rather than a subject to be taught. Consequently, classroom activities became less structured and more activity-based.

Curricular experimentation and innovation are to be welcomed as they can lead to fresh ideas and methods for teaching students about the world, and certainly some interesting materials and teaching methods were developed through the Schools Council projects. In particular, the new spatial modelling approach promoted by Chorley and Haggett was incorporated into some of the project materials (see Chapter 1). Also, the enquiry approach offered teachers an alternative method to approach the subject. Project work can be intellectually demanding and very meaningful when grounded in real-life situations. When taught effectively, students will learn how to pose questions in a meaningful way, decide which questions should be investigated, the method of addressing them, where to collect information and data, how to organize, present and interpret the data and the conclusions to be reached. To complete these tasks means learning to become competent in a number of research skills, which is why projects of this nature are more likely to be used successfully with higher levels of education.

However, for many teachers the enquiry approach advocated in child-centred education means more than simply teaching students how to undertake project work. It seeks to adopt this approach to education in a wholesale manner in which the student is very much involved in the process of learning and the teacher's role is diminished. One problem with this approach is that the student lacks the intellectual overview and experience of the teacher. Students do not know which are the most important questions to ask, which are the concepts they needs to learn and in what order, and they do not have the equivalent knowledge of methodology and research resources to the teacher. That is why students undertaking project work through an enquiry approach need much guidance from the teacher and also why it cannot replace subjects as a foundation of knowledge. Rex Walford comments that the enquiry approach came to dominate the curriculum at the expense of fundamental knowledge and concepts: 'in the hands of less skilled practitioners the system also allowed curriculum mayhem, with some essential components of knowledge and skills rarely visited, and with some children quite at sea in an apparent jumble of projects' (Walford 2001: 141).

The affirmation of the student in progressive educational theory reflects a further problem with this approach: implicit scepticism towards subject content. Again Marsden observed, 'educational theorists strongly favoured integration, dismissing subject-based syllabuses as mere social constructions and/or historical accidents' (Marsden 1997: 249). By 'integration' Marsden was referring to the thematic approach often championed in progressive educational theory. Marsden added that the moves away from a distinctive subject focus were also driven by 'the forces of structuralism, radicalism and postmodernism' (*ibid.*: 249). The influence of postmodern thought on notions of citizenship and geographical education is considered in Chapters 2 and 8.

Upon closer inspection it is evident that very different educational objectives were being pursued through enquiry-based projects. For some the significance of the projects was their focus on the values and attitudes the students hold towards social and political events, rather than the knowledge and skills they need to acquire to become competent geographers. Rawling explained that the projects

> Encourage pupils to clarify their own values and attitudinal stance when faced with issues and conflicts about the environment and quality of life. In this sense, geography has become an important medium for political literacy and citizenship in the broadest sense.
>
> (Rawling 1990: 36)

Again, Marsden cautions that teaching about social issues will necessarily distract from the foundations of the discipline: 'issues dominance must mean some withdrawal from a distinctive geography' (Marsden 1997: 249). A further problem identified by Marsden was the declining input of academic geographers into school geography from the 1970s, again fed by disillusion with the positivist basis of geographical theories.

The linking of geography with citizenship and moral education which began in the 1970s would become the dominant approach of the Geographical Association and the government in the late 1990s. The interim period was dominated by a New Right reaction against the progressive 1960s and 1970s. The outcome was a confusing geography national curriculum that mixed the enquiry approach with subject content knowledge.

Rising utilitarian and progressive aims for geography

After Callaghan's 1976 Ruskin speech the curriculum would no longer be a place of freedom for teachers. The notion of the 'skills gap' between Britain and the rest of Europe became popular during Margaret Thatcher's reign and education was under scrutiny to deliver. Three further Schools Council projects exemplify this trend in geography. The Geography, Schools and Industry Project, started in 1984, sought to develop geography's contribution to economic understanding and links between school and industry. Second, the GYSL/TRIST Project of 87/1988 encouraged pre-vocational courses in schools. Third, Humanities and Information Technology in 1988 examined how IT skills could be taught through history and geography. All three led to a greater focus on skills, both those specific to geography, such as map drawing and interpretation, and those with broader applicability, such as reading and writing, oral communication, use of information technology, decision making and problem solving (Rawling 1990). Skills teaching and pre-vocationalism were fundamental to the formation of GCSEs. The significance of geography's utilitarian agenda to its foundational status in the national curriculum was noted in Chapter 1.

Progressive educational ideas did not disappear during this period. Instead, they were placed on the defensive by the New Right. For instance, the World Studies 8–13 Project (1980–89) continued to emphasize geography's connections with personal, planetary and political issues. Hall described how at a personal level 'geography needs to make an appeal both to the psychological and to the social elements of personality: to the concept of individuation/self identity and self-respect' (Hall 1991: 24). The World Studies 8–13 Project also illustrated the growing affiliations between geography and development education, environmental education, peace studies as well as non-governmental organizations such as Oxfam and the World Wide Fund for Nature. In the 1980s environmental issues were beginning to capture wider public attention in the UK and were also being pursued by geographers. Rawling (1990) noted that the 'radically oriented' *Bulletin of Environmental Education* became popular with geographers and informed curricular materials created for the World Studies project. And for Hall 'the greening of an ecologically affine geography linked with a humanistic viewpoint of the subject is emerging as a major strength of the subject at this moment in time' (Hall 1991: 24). Although, by 'humanistic', Hall was referring to students' 'understanding of self and other in terms of values, attitudes, hopes and fears' (*ibid.*) rather than the knowledge of the world generated by humanity and embodied in subject disciplines.

While environmental education had been implemented in the US in the early 1970s, environmental issues began to draw more attention at the international level and subsequently within European nations themselves. An important document in this regard was the Belgrade Charter (1975), ratified as the Tbilisi Declaration, that was part of the Final Report of the Intergovernmental Conference on Environmental Education held in Tbilisi, USSR, in 1977. The Belgrade Charter sought to develop international environmental education programmes:

> To develop a world population that is aware of, and concerned about, the environment and its associated problems, and which has the knowledge, skills, attitudes, motivations and commitment to work

individually and collectively towards solutions of current problems and the prevention of new ones.

(UNESCO–UNEP 1978)

A decade later, at the request of the General Assembly of the United Nations, the World Commission on Environment and Development report *Our Common Future* called on national leaders

To re-examine the critical environmental and development issues and to formulate realistic proposals for dealing with them; to propose new forms of international cooperation on these issues that will influence policies and events in the direction of needed changes; and to raise levels of understanding and commitment to action of individuals, voluntary organizations, businesses, institutions and governments.

(World Commission on Environment and
Development 1987: 3)

Shortly after this report, the European Community at a meeting of its council in 1988 noted:

The need to take concrete steps for the promotion of environmental education, so that this can be intensified in a comprehensive way throughout the community.

(Palmer and Neal 1994: 15)

A resolution on environmental education was later adopted to 'lay the foundations for a fully informed and active participation of the individual in the protection of the environment and the prudent and rational use of natural resources' (*ibid.*: 16). In the 1990s environmental values were subsequently introduced into the English and Welsh curriculum in the form of sustainable development education. Hence, as government education policy began to switch from subject knowledge to social issues, not surprisingly, it would find common ground with progressive educationalists in the shape of values and citizenship education.

By the mid-1990s the subject content of the geography national curriculum was already being cut. Many geography teachers found the initial national curriculum orders overloaded and unworkable (Walford 1995). In particular, there was confusion between Programmes of Study and Statements of Attainment. After problems with testing in English and mathematics, many teachers decided to boycott national curriculum testing. The new Secretary of State, John Patten, called on Sir Ron Dearing in April 1993 to review the whole curriculum. The review process led to a reduction and simplification of content in the 1995 geography national curriculum document. The number of attainment targets was decreased and its structure allowed clearer presentation of what was required at each key stage. However, at this time the government also determined that geography and history would no longer be compulsory subjects at Key Stage 4 (fourteen to sixteen years), a massive blow to the curricular standing of both these subjects.

During this period there was also less political contestation of the curriculum. There was almost a pragmatic acceptance that this was the form that the geography national curriculum would take, while many teachers felt there was sufficient flexibility to teach the subject as they saw fit. The Geographical Association reported positively about the working relationship they held with the Schools Curriculum Assessment Authority (SCAA) and the newly formed Qualifications and Curriculum Council (QCA), a later amalgamation of the National Council for Vocational Qualifications and SCAA. Various publications reflected this co-operative approach, such as the Geographical Association's *Curriculum Guidance* series. The change that was afoot was triggered by the demise of the New Right and its arguments for traditional subjects. John Major's government was a mere grey shadow of Thatcherism. His tenancy in Downing Street is perhaps best understood as a transition from Conservatism to New Labour. The evolution of the citizenship national curriculum during the 1990s illustrates the continuity between these two governments as well as change.

The making of a (global) citizenship national curriculum

During the 1990s several government initiatives sought to make citizenship an explicit goal of schooling. The question of citizenship was investigated by the House of Commons Speaker's Commission on Education (1990), the National Curriculum Council (1990), the Commission on Social Justice (1994) and the Citizenship Foundation (1995). Following the 1997 White Paper *Excellence in Schools*, the Advisory Group on Citizenship was formed to make recommendations for the introduction of a citizenship curriculum for schools. Bernard Crick, leader of the advisory group, described its rationale for mandating citizenship education:

> It can no longer sensibly be left as unco-ordinated local initiatives which vary greatly in number, content and method. This is an inade-quate basis for animating the idea of a common citizenship with democratic values.
>
> (Advisory Group on Citizenship 1998: 7)

The goal of the Advisory Group on Citizenship was nothing less than to change the 'political culture' of the country and to enact a 'shift of emphasis between, on the one hand, state welfare provision and responsibility and, on the other, community and individual responsibility' (Advisory Group on Citizenship 1998: 10). Although, in actuality, this shift in responsibility is about the state taking a more direct role in ensuring that young people have 'socially responsible' attitudes and behaviours through their adoption as curricular aims. Arguably, this leaves young people with less responsibility for making their own decisions about such matters.

The aims and content of the emergent citizenship national curriculum were somewhat confused. However, what was being proposed was clearly not in line with traditional models of citizenship. Documentation discussed the need for most subjects to contribute to citizenship education, including geography, English and Personal, Social and Health Education (PSHE), and while it did emphasize British citizenship and learning about national politics it also promoted the idea of citizenship at multiple scales. The centrality of global citizenship to the emergent citizenship national curriculum was indicated by the joint government/ non-governmental organization (NGO) publication *Developing a Global Dimension in the School Curriculum* released in 2000. The booklet stated that it was aimed at head teachers, governors and those teachers responsible for planning and implementing the curriculum because 'the importance of education in helping young people recognise their role and responsibilities as members of this global community is becoming increasingly apparent' (Department for Education and Skills/Department for International Development 2000). The report explained how curricula should develop a global dimension:

> [T]he content of what is taught is informed by international and global matters, so preparing pupils to live their lives in a global society . . . addressing issues such as sustainable development, interdependence and social justice at both the local and global levels . . . It builds knowledge and understanding, as well as developing key skills and attitudes.
>
> (Department for Education and Skills/Department for International Development 2000: 2)

This document borrowed heavily from Oxfam's *A Curriculum for Global Citizenship* (1997) and highlighted the direct input of NGOs in the creation of the citizenship national curriculum. Oxfam's curriculum has been used and cited by educators far and wide, including in the US. Its vision of a global citizen is someone who

> Is aware of the wider world and has a sense of their own role as a world citizen; respects and values diversity; has an understanding of how the world works economically, politically, socially, culturally,

technologically, and environmentally; is outraged by social injustice; participates in and contributes to the community at a range of levels from the local to the global; is willing to act to make the world a more sustainable place; takes responsibility for their actions.

(Oxfam 1997)

Two other important documents that contributed to the rise of global citizenship education in the UK were *A Framework for the International Dimension for Schools in England*, produced by the Central Bureau and the Development Education Association, and *Citizenship Education: The Global Dimension*, also published by the Development Association (2001). The former claimed that 'the international dimension provides a wider and more relevant context for initiatives such as citizenship education' (Central Bureau/Development Education Association 2000: 7). The latter was a more substantial document that detailed the global dimension for each of the three citizenship national curriculum programmes of study – political literacy, social and moral responsibility, and community involvement – and how each can be addressed through other national curriculum subject areas.

Oxfam has not been the only NGO to contribute to the new citizenship curriculum. Other influential NGOs which have been busily promoting global education/citizenship include the Central Bureau for International Education and Training, the Commonwealth Institute, the Council for Environmental Education, the Council for Education in World Citizenship, the Development Education Association, the Nuffield Foundation, ActionAid, CAFOD, Comic Relief, Voluntary Service Overseas, UNICEF, Worldaware and organizations involved with the On the Line project. While global education, in different guises, has been promoted by an array of NGOs for over thirty years (see Hicks 2003) it was only as nations struggled to retain a sense of coherence and national purpose after the end of the Cold War that some coherence within the movement for global education began to emerge and common ground was established in the growing acceptance of global citizenship education. Educational theorist Harriet Marshall identified seven key changes within the field of global education which have contributed to its curricular prominence:

The coordination of global education NGOs and consolidation of global education traditions; the continued significance of a few key individuals; the increased emphasis on working with teachers . . . and teacher educators; the increased interest of official or government educational institutions and individuals in global education; the broadening media coverage of the global agenda; the growing interest and concern about globalisation and its meanings and effects upon society (and education); and the new world threats provoking new calls for global education and understanding.

(Marshall 2005: 78)

Probably the most significant of the changes identified by Marshall is the official government endorsement of global citizenship as exemplified in the above documentation. Also significant is the agreement found among the non-governmental organizations. Proponents of human rights education, environmental education, sustainable development education, anti-racist education, world studies, development education and global education found common ground in the growing acceptance of global citizenship education. Many NGOs produce detailed teaching resources on global citizenship themes, which have become more acceptable teaching instruments in schools. For example, Amnesty has several resources for teaching about human rights such as *Learning about Human Rights through Citizenship* and a scheme called TeachRights. UNICEF in the UK has published teaching resources on global issues and children's rights, including *For Every Child* and *Discussing Global Issues: What is Participation?* And the Cumbria Development Education Centre has produced a *Survival Pack for Future Citizens: Global Issues and Sustainable Development for Key Stage 2* (ages seven to eleven) and *Exploring Values for Key Stages 3 and 4* (eleven to sixteen). Nevertheless, as Marshall noted, perhaps the most important shift has been the new-found advocacy of global citizenship by government education bodies.

In September 2000 citizenship education became part of the national curriculum for English and Welsh primary schools. In September 2002 citizenship education was mandated as a separate discipline for secondary schools, implementing many of the Crick Report's recommendations providing official government endorsement to global citizenship. So, while knowledge about government, politics and British history was included, so were personal values and community involvement, practising democracy and global citizenship. These latter elements and the emphasis on personal, social and health education (PSHE), geography and English, not traditionally subjects associated with citizenship education, were indicative of a new approach to citizenship education and one that is no longer tied to the nation state.

Hence, teachers are required to teach students about how the United Kingdom is governed and how they should contribute to the national democratic process. However, the nation is presented as just one scale at which politics is conducted along a continuum from local to global. For instance, at Key Stage 2 (ages seven to eleven) students are encouraged to 'develop their sense of social justice and moral responsibility and begin to understand that their own choices and behaviour can affect local, national or global issues and political and social institutions' (Qualifications and Curriculum Authority 2002a). Once the nation becomes one of several levels at which politics gets conducted it loses its uniqueness. Hence, it has been argued that individuals today demonstrate identities existing at different levels rather than an overriding commitment to the nation state (Isin and Turner 2002). Other parts of the citizenship national curriculum explicitly emphasize the global scale. At Key Stage 3 (ages eleven to fourteen), teachers are instructed to teach pupils about 'The world as a global community, and the political, economic, environmental and social implications of this, and the role of the European Union, the Commonwealth and the United Nations' (Qualifications and Curriculum Authority 2001). Similarly, at Key Stage 4 (ages fourteen to sixteen), students should be taught about 'the wider issues and challenges of global interdependence and responsibility, including sustainable development and Local Agenda 21' (Qualifications and Curriculum Authority 2002b).

A prominent theme of the citizenship national curriculum has been its promotion through other subject areas. With its emphasis on interdependence of people, places and the natural environment geography has logically been looked to for delivery of significant aspects of its 'content'. For instance, the schemes of work at Key Stage 3 describe how geography contributes to citizenship by enabling students to:

> Understand the diversity of cultures and identities in the UK and the wider world; understand the issues and challenges of global interdependence; reflect on the consequences of their own actions in situations concerning places and environments; understand their rights and responsibilities to other people and the environment.
>
> (Qualifications and Curriculum Authority 2001)

Many in the geography community have willingly gone along with the idea that geography should contribute towards citizenship education, especially at a time when the subject's curricular standing was under pressure. But, more than this, geography's reinvention in England and Wales as global citizenship education suits those with progressive ideals, who are more interested in extraneous political and psychological agendas than teaching them about the geography of the world.

Geography reinvented as global citizenship education

During the mid-1990s concern began to develop about geography's status as a national curriculum subject. Warning signs were appearing from several directions, including its new optional status at Key Stage 4 in the post-Dearing curriculum.

Ofsted reports began to detect weakness in geography teaching. Rawling notes that 'After 1996, the Ofsted inspections began to reveal that geography was not holding its position relative to other subjects with respect to quality of teaching and progress made by pupils' (Rawling 2001: 74). Lack of specialist teaching staff at Key Stage 3 (ages eleven to fourteen years) and poor short-term planning were two of the reasons given by Ofsted. There was also concern about a downturn in the number of pupils taking A levels and GCSEs in geography. A-level entries decreased by 8.5 per cent in the years 1994–96 and at GCSE level geography went from being the fourth most popular subject in 1990 to the seventh in 1998 (Walford 2001: 230–3). Geography was also under pressure from new government initiatives to promote vocational qualifications in schools. General National Vocational Qualifications were piloted in 1985 and to be launched in 1991. They included Leisure and Tourism, which geography perceived as a threat. Likewise, in 1996 new GCSE courses were announced which included humanities. Geography's place as a national curriculum subject was now being questioned by the SCAA: 'The key issue in a review of geography is its place in the curriculum rather than any demand for major review of its subject orders' (Schools Curriculum Assessment Authority 1997: 74).

With the subject under heavy pressure to justify its place in the curriculum at this time, leading geographers were perhaps more easily attracted to the trendy new themes of global citizenship education than they might otherwise have been. In January 1998 the recently formed Qualifications and Curriculum Authority (QCA) held a conference to examine the character, place and future of geography and history in the fourteen-to-nineteen curriculum. The conference discussed 'the need for students to develop personal and social skills, including tolerance of other people and other cultures ... and the ability to handle moral dilemmas in a responsible way' (Geographical Association 1998: 125). A common ground was now clearly evident between the government and the geography community in the form of global citizenship with its focus on the personal values and the social development of children. This new-found co-operation was especially facilitated by the election of New Labour, who sought to use education for a host of social, economic and political initiatives. When Tony Blair famously outlined his top three priorities as 'education, education and education', Furedi makes the point that for schools this should be equated with 'politics, politics and politics' (Furedi 2007). In contrast to the New Right, Tony Blair's government embraced student-centred education, but continued moves towards education in pre-vocational skills and target setting. The various initiatives and approaches to emerge under New Labour should be seen less as stemming from a coherent ideological standpoint and more as reactionary attempts to be seen as doing something to address political problems, which were now being conducted through schools rather than the world of politics.

At the end of the 1990s the government and leading geographers had found a common alliance in seeking to reform society by changing individuals. These geographers and the geographical associations began promoting the subject as one that could deliver global citizenship, embracing global issues of environmentalism, sustainability, human rights, equality, democracy and social justice (see Grimwade *et al.* 2000; Lambert and Machon 2001). There followed an explosion of articles and documents pertaining to geography's new mission. In April 1999 the Geographical Association released a new position statement that set out a new citizenship role for geography. One of the new aims for geography was to 'develop an informed concern for the world around us and an ability and willingness to take positive action, both locally and globally' (Geographical Association 1999: 57). Launched in September 2000, the revised geography national curriculum highlighted four important elements for the subject: sustainable development, global citizenship, values and attitudes in addition to location knowledge (Department for Education and Employment/ Qualifications and Curriculum Authority 1999).

Also in 2000, the Geographical Association brought out *Geography and the New Agenda: Citizenship, PSHE and Sustainable Development,* with different versions for primary and secondary education. This publication by several leading geographers more clearly defined geography's new direction. The meaning of this New Agenda can be drawn out by illustrating quotes from articles and documentation.

Geographers were of course drawn to the 1990s discussion of globalization. Geographers have been keen to investigate globalization because it is a time/space concept that attempts to describe how the world is changing. However, frequently people mean much more than this when they talk about global interdependence. Often describing material change is accompanied by a discussion of our responsibility to other people and nature. As Sinclair explains, 'Globalization is about our personal links to other people and their environment' (Sinclair 1997: 162). Effectively it has become a framework for interpreting problems with moral strings attached. Global issues are not just there to be understood, but for everybody to take responsibility for them and 'do their part'. Globalization provides the spatial framework while citizenship, PSHE and SDE draw out the moral imperative behind the New Agenda.

In an editorial to an edition of *Teaching Geography* devoted to New Agenda issues, Robinson presented the case:

> So how can we enable students to become adults who feel responsible for the impact of their own 'global footprints'? How can we

provide them with the will to be more active in developing their own future society and environment? Perhaps the answer should be: in geography.

(Robinson 2001: 56)

Robinson considered geography to be a natural vehicle for such a task, as students already investigate interrelationships and issues from the local to the global level. She makes the point, however, that to encourage active citizenship it is necessary not to apportion blame, but to teach students to see issues as their own responsibility:

> In geography the question of who is responsible is often followed up with a consideration of what other people, known as 'they', should be doing about it. It is crucial that we encourage students to appreciate that everyone is involved in an issue and that everyone should become actively engaged in it.

(*ibid.*)

Robinson set the tone for how teachers should change their approach to teaching citizenship through geography. Machon described the concepts that lie behind citizenship, in particular individuals' rights and responsibilities:

> Citizenship is not an elusive concept but one that is usually formulated in terms of individuals' duties and rights in a social context; that is to say that citizenship is the foundation of civic order. The ethical imperative here is the obligation on effective citizens that they work towards the improvement and the maintenance of the health of that civic order.

(Machon 1998: 115)

Machon further suggested that the balance between rights and responsibilities has been too heavily weighted in favour of rights and that geography teachers should begin to redress this imbalance by 'helping the learner to identify the collective consequences of their individual actions' (*ibid.*). Contributing to the greenhouse effect by driving your car would suffice as one such example.

Hicks explained that to achieve effective citizenship 'requires that a person (a) has some knowledge and understanding of public affairs; (b) is concerned about the welfare of the wider community; and (c) has the skills needed to participate in the political arena' (Hicks 2001: 57). Hicks suggested that geographers can contribute at all three of the levels identified. In teaching students to become informed citizens, geography can teach them about 'human rights, responsibilities, issues of justice and fairness'; in relation to enquiry and communication skills 'thinking about political, moral, social and cultural issues'; and in relation to skills of participation and responsible action 'taking part in school and community activities' (Hicks 2001: 57).

Other publications documenting the potential of geography's contribution to citizenship vary from the QCA's (1998) *Areas of Cross-Curricular Concern within Citizenship Education* to the *Oxfam Curriculum for Global Citizenship* review by Douglas (2001) in *Teaching Geography*. The QCA lists the issues to be covered, including development education, multicultural education and peace education. The QCA also suggests that values and disposition should be taught, including belief in human dignity and equality, practice of tolerance and concern to resolve conflicts with others. Douglas also suggests that 'teachers who embrace global citizenship themselves will thereby encourage the young people in their charge to develop into active and responsible global citizens' (Douglas 2001: 89).

The second national curriculum review in 1998–99, this time conducted by the QCA, placed a heavy emphasis on personal, social and health education (PSHE) (Grimwade *et al.* 2000). A non-statutory framework across all key stages was produced based upon a report of the National Advisory Group on Personal, Social and Health Education called *Preparing Young People for Adult Life* (Department for Education and Employment 1999). The role of PSHE suggested by the QCA was in helping 'to give pupils knowledge, skills, and understanding they need to lead confident, healthy and independent lives, and to become informed, active and responsible citizens' (Department for Education and Employment/ Qualifications and Curriculum Authority 1999). The non-statutory guidelines at Key Stages 3 and 4 (ages eleven to sixteen years) divide PSHE into two sections: 'knowledge, skills and understanding' and 'breadth of opportunities'. Under 'Knowledge, skills and understanding' it is suggested that students should focus on:

1   Developing confidence and responsibility and making the most of their abilities.
2   Developing a healthy, safer lifestyle.
3   Developing good relationships and respecting the differences between people.

(*ibid.*)

Grimwade *et al.* (2000) illustrated some of the geographical opportunities available to address some of these aims. Learning about different people and cultures around the world will help students to respect differences between people. Fieldwork teaches students the importance of teamwork and developing relationships. Recognizing and following health and safety requirements can also be a feature of fieldwork. Furthermore, students can learn about the health risks associated with food choices and sun-bathing.

The 'breadth of opportunities' section was described by a series of state-ments. 'Feeling positive about themselves' could be achieved at Key Stage 4 (ages fourteen to sixteen years) by 'communicating the results of a shopping survey to the manager of a local supermarket'. 'Making real choices and decisions' could be achieved at Key Stage 3 (ages eleven to fourteen years) if a student were 'to be involved with a decision on how to improve the environment of the house or area'. Likewise, at Key Stage 3 'participating' can be accomplished if students 'help clean up part of the school grounds' (*ibid.*: 39).

There is some overlap between PSHE and citizenship, not just in its content, but also its general message. Both are geared towards educating the individual to act in a 'socially/ethically responsible' way. The last aspect of the New Agenda, sustainable development, continues this theme.

In the late 1990s, Sustainable Development Education (SDE) became more widely embraced by both geographers and New Labour. As a con-cept it is entwined with environmental education, but some would argue that SDE is more than just learning about the environment because it demands that pupils develop certain attitudes and behaviours towards the environment and people. Reid noted how the new geography curriculum 2000 emphasized sustainable development and citizenship rather than environmental change. He reported that, for pupils, geography

> should develop their awareness and understanding of, and respect for, the environments in which they live, and secure their commitment to sustainable development at the personal, local, national and global levels. It should also equip pupils as consumers to make informed judgements and independent decisions and to understand their responsibilities and rights.

> (Reid 2001: 72)

Reid also noted the distinction between sustainable development and environmental education in the new curriculum:

> Education for sustainable development enables pupils to develop their knowledge, skills and understanding and values to participate in decisions about the way we do things individually and collectively, both locally and globally, that will improve the quality of life now without damaging the planet for the future.

> (*ibid.*)

There are two related aspects to SDE. First, it presents a picture about how the world should or should not develop. Second, it teaches people to act in the 'socially and ethically responsible' way illustrated above.

Reid described some typical SDE that might take place under geography. He stated that teaching often focuses on the interactions between:

- Natural systems that provide the resources (e.g. air, water, soil, food) that support all life – human and non-human.
- Social and cultural systems that provide family, community and wider support for people to live together in ways that are culturally appropriate.
- Economic systems that provide for a means of livelihood (jobs and income) for people.
- Political systems through which social power is exercised to make policies and decisions about the way social and economic systems use their resources in the natural environment.

(*ibid*.: 58)

This gives an indication of the broad range of topics that can be taught as part of SDE. Effectively, it is a new way of approaching geography teaching.

John Huckle, who was previously a critic of values education, is today a strong advocate of environmental values in the curriculum in the form of SDE. He believes that teachers should base their teaching and the ethos of the school on values relating to the environment, including maintenance of a sustainable environment, preservation of diversity and beauty in nature and accepting responsibility for other species. Huckle (2002) suggests that capitalism has furnished us with 'limited ecological responsibility' and has separated us from nature. The challenge of sustainable development then is to 'rethink and restructure production and consumption in the light of ecological constraints'. The consequences of education, argues Huckle, are that:

Pupils should discuss the extent to which they and others feel alienated from nature and should engage in activities and projects that can put them back in touch with their bodies, the land, the relevance of their school work to viable futures.

(*ibid*.: 67)

And:

Teachers should acknowledge that abstract and specialist knowledge intensifies alienation and should interpret geography generously so that it integrates a wide range of knowledge from the natural and social sciences and the humanities, and builds on the lay and tacit knowledge of the community.

(ibid.)

This is an example of postmodernist thinking that has come to influence the curriculum. Huckle wants to dispense with the traditional curriculum based on subjects and replace it with a more student-centred or holistic curriculum.

The Nuffield Foundation, a UK charitable trust, also makes a point of the links between geography and the new citizenship:

> Knowledge and understanding of human behaviour, its consequences for other humans and the world they inhabit are indisputably important to all students in a healthy democracy. The same can be said about the development of the political, social and ethical values which guide their behaviour.

(Nuffield Foundation 2006)

What the foundation fails to address, however, is that there is no world system of democracy and hence there are no formal mechanisms for citizens to shape politics beyond the confines of their nation state.

Geography textbooks and examination boards in England and Wales have also appropriated the concepts of global citizenship, sustainable development and issues-based approaches to geography. A study of the changing nature of the geography curriculum in England and Wales found a growing focus on the values and attitudes of students themselves (Standish 2002). The study included a small survey of geographers teaching in schools in the south of England. The survey revealed that most teachers thought there had been increasing emphasis upon values and attitudes education, including environmental values and cultural sensitivity. For instance, 80 per cent of interviewees thought that 'geography should teach pupils to respect and reconnect with nature' (Standish 2002: 38). Most teachers in the survey were in support of this new role and saw geography as having links with citizenship education. However, 68 per cent also identified a decline in the geographical knowledge that students were expected to learn and were concerned about this trend. Similarly, a study of geography textbooks in the UK by Zhang and Foskett found that 'the teaching emphasis in the subject has switched from reciting cause–effect relations to investigation into geographical issues through attitude-related and activity-involved learning' (Zhang and Foskett 2003: 327).

Of particular relevance to this study, Zhang and Foskett comment of international understanding: 'the issue of interrelation and cooperation between different parts of the world . . . has been noticed by some textbook writers for a long time, but only recently has this issue been explicitly and positively expressed in texts' (*ibid.*: 328). The authors concluded that there has been a shift in the nature of the subject: 'it was formerly a mixture of place knowledge, physical science and social studies, but now it has switched its focus on to the development of children's sense of place, the sense of the globe, the sense of environment, and the skills of geographical enquiry' (*ibid.*: 329).

A few examples will illustrate this trend. Students are expected to consider their own responsibility for global issues in the A-level geography textbook *Global Challenge* by McNaught and Witherick (2001), including the 'overconsumption' of resources, high fertility rates and growing numbers of refugees. In earlier geography textbooks social, economic and political processes were portrayed as something that was addressed though the nation state and its political framework. Yet, today, the elevation of governance at multiple scales over national government has prompted some geographers to call for geography textbooks to move beyond state-centrism (Agnew 2003). Nevertheless, as noted in the previous chapter, change for textbooks is frequently slow. Hence, fortunately, many textbooks continue to include significant geographical content and skills, inherited from the discipline's academic traditions.

In contrast to textbooks, examination boards are frequently more responsive to new thinking in a discipline. London's main examination board, Edexcel, has dedicated large sections of its geography GCSE syllabus to 'managing the environment' (Edexcel 2000). Early in the new millennium, Edexcel's specifications for GCSE geography made a virtue of the reduced knowledge content, suggesting that it 'contains the same core geography but in less depth' (Edexcel 2000: 1). This, it argued, has created room for teachers to focus on other areas like teaching about the environment and citizenship. Likewise, the Assessment and Qualification Alliance examination board makes reference to 'an appreciation of the environment' and 'an understanding of global citizenship' in its aims for GCSE geography (Assessment and Qualifications Alliance 2002: 13). Exam questions might ask students, for example, to detail a sustainable approach to tourism. Yet there has been little discussion of the educational consequences of reducing the quantity and range of concepts that students are expected to learn at this age. At Advanced level examination boards drew heavily from the QCA's *Subject Criteria for Geography*. One of the document's aims was for students to 'clarify and develop their own values and attitudes in relation to geographical issues and questions' (section 2.1, Qualifications and Curriculum Authority 2002c).

In 2002 the Geovisions Working Group of the Geographical Association began work on a new 'hybrid' GCSE geography course. One of its aims was described as being to:

[P]romote global citizenship by leading towards awareness and understanding of global systems, global patterns, the processes and impacts of globalization and the opportunities and responsibilities of the individual.

(Westaway and Rawling 2003: 61)

This new GSCE is presented as more 'relevant' to pupils and is now being used in a number of schools (Wood 2005). Its emphasis upon the personal ethics of students is apparent in its specification content document:

Candidates should be encouraged to examine their own values as they analyse the values of others and to become aware of the power relations implicit in any situation and the conflicts and inequalities which may arise.

(Oxford, Cambridge and RSA Examinations 2004: 1)

In 2004 the Development Education Association published *Geography: The Global Dimension*, illustrating the organization's commitment to teaching about global citizenship. The document highlights the same key concepts as the Department for Education and Skills/NGO publication above as the 'core of learning' about global issues: citizenship, sustainable development, social justice, values and perceptions, diversity, interdependence, conflict resolution, and human rights. These 'concepts' are also very reminiscent of Oxfam's 1997 curriculum for global citizenship.

In February 2007 the much awaited revised programmes of study for Key Stage 3 (ages eleven to fourteen) were released in draft form by the QCA. As far as geography is concerned, the above trend towards making the subject synonymous with the themes of global citizenship education was reinforced. An introductory section on the importance of geography specifies that: 'Geography inspires pupils to become global citizens by exploring their place in the world, their values and responsibilities to other people, to the environment and to the sustainability of the planet' (Qualifications and Curriculum Authority 2007: 1). Again, the key concepts include interdependence, sustainable development, cultural understanding and diversity.

Concluding comments

While geography's transition from a subject founded on geographical knowledge, concepts and skills to one that seeks to shape the social values and psychological identities of students began in the 1970s with progressive educational theories, the period from the late 1990s to the current day has witnessed a most dramatic destruction of the subject's foundations. Partly because geography is a field of knowledge rather than a discrete discipline with clear boundaries (see Hirst 1974), such as physics for example, it has always tended to be a more malleable subject reflecting the prevailing cultural and political climate of the times, as discussed in Chapter 1. It is also a spatial subject that seeks to make links between different scales and between the human and the natural world; hence its suitability to the themes of global citizenship. Today, the themes of globalization, interdependence, environmentalism and human rights have substantially altered the very meaning of the discipline, at least for many subject leaders. However, as previously discussed, this does not mean that all geography lessons are like this. There are still many geography teachers in English and Welsh schools who know how to educate young people to become students of geography and teach them about how the world is changing. What is concerning is the impact that policy makers and subject leaders are having on school geography through their promotion of the New Agenda. As Marsden has cautioned, not only has this focus on social causes been 'taking the *geography* out of geographical education' (my italics) but also has led to the politicization of the geography curriculum. The result of importing political and moral causes into the curriculum has been to 'generate inculcation and indoctrination rather than genuine education' (Marsden 1997: 245).

Suggested further reading

Department for Education and Skills/Department for International Development (2000, updated 2005) *Developing a Global Dimension in the School Curriculum*, London: Department for Education and Employment/Department for International Development/Qualifications and Curriculum Authority *et al.*

Grimwade, K., Reid, A. and Thompson, L. (2000) *Geography and the New Agenda*, Sheffield: Geographical Association.

Lambert, D. and Machon, P. (2001) *Citizenship through Secondary Geography*, London: RoutledgeFalmer.

Marsden, W. (1997) 'On Taking the Geography out of Geographical Education: Some Historical Pointers in Geography', *Geography*, 82 (3): 241–52.

Oxfam (1997) *Curriculum for Global Citizenship, Oxfam Development Educational Programme*, Oxford: Oxfam.

Rawlings, E. M. (2001) *Changing the Subject: The Impact of National Policy on School Geography, 1980–2000*, Sheffield: Geographical Association.

Walford, R. (2001) *Geography in British Schools, 1850–2000: Making a World of Difference*, London: Woburn Press.

Westaway, J. and Rawling, E. (2003) 'A New Look for GCSE Geography?' *Teaching Geography*, 28 (1): 60–2.

Chapter 5

The geography of culture or respecting cultural diversity?

KEY QUESTIONS

1 What do school students need to learn about culture in geography?
2 Is the primary purpose of studying the geography of culture to learn about different cultural practices and traits or to change students' ideas and attitudes towards people from a different cultural region?

As noted in the Introduction, developing a global or a multiple perspective has become a central theme of many American, English and Welsh geography curricula today. In essence, this entails 'the cultivation of cross-cultural understanding, which includes development of the skill of perspective-taking – that is, being able to see life from someone else's point of view' (Tye and Tye 1992). This objective fits into a broader educational pattern whereby multiculturalism and the celebration of cultural diversity have become central to the functioning of school life. Diverse cultural experiences are today promoted as an essential part of a young person's education in an increasingly globalized world, leading to empathy and understanding between people of different cultures. Geography is frequently looked to as a subject that can help to offer diverse cultural experiences through its exploration of the variety of human life on the planet.

The purpose of this chapter is to illustrate how multiculturalism and cultural diversity, as pedagogical aims, have changed both the nature of cultural geography and our understanding of culture itself. While geography curricula have long sought to describe differences in culture found at different geographical locations, today this descriptive approach is being supplemented by teaching multiculturalism as the way the world *should be*. This chapter illustrates that the objectives of multicultural education, to encourage students to become respectful of other cultures and to learn to see issues from another point of view, are in some instances also becoming an aim of teaching cultural geography. In effect, cultural geography is becoming less concerned with learning about the lives and cultural practices of people in distant places and more focused on students learning about themselves, how they interact with people from other cultural backgrounds and their attitudes towards them. Genuine tolerance of people from different cultural backgrounds can only arise out of knowledge of differences but also recognition of our common humanity. The problem with multiculturalism, as it is currently being promoted in many schools, is that it presents an acultural view of humanity in which our ideas and perspectives are seen as deeply rooted to our past experiences, and hence difficult to transcend. This leads to a static and fragmented view of culture in which many cultures have replaced culture as a potentially unifying force for humanity. It encourages students to look for and respect cultural differences, rather than seeking to overcome them, the consequence of which is to place greater, not less, distance between people with different cultural backgrounds.

Cultural geography

It is perhaps best to try to understand the meaning of cultural geography through historically specific examples, since the meaning of culture itself has changed significantly over time. In the nineteenth century Friedrich Ratzel (1844–1904) studied the ecological relations between the earth's surface and human cultures, while Franz Boas (1858–1942) took a more ethnographic approach to examine localized human communities. In this historical period, scientists had yet to mark a clear distinction between natural and social science. Darwin's theories of evolution were applied to civilizations, emphasizing the influence of natural systems upon people, otherwise known as environmental determinism.

At the end of the nineteenth century there were some early signs of change, in the work of Mackinder and vidal de la Blache, as they explored how humans interacted with their environment. At times, Mackinder discussed the role of human consciousness, while de la Blache went further in describing how people directly shape the natural world. Although de la Blache's regional division of rural France emphasized the interrelationship of people and the natural landscape, he also viewed the landscape as 'a medal struck in the likeness of a people' (cited in Knox and Marston 2004). This newly anointed role for humanity challenged previous environmental determinism, opening the door for cultural geography, even though it would be some time before deterministic ideas and theories were surpassed in the geography curriculum.

In the US, the most influential cultural geographer of the twentieth century was Carl Sauer (1889–1975). Sauer received his Ph.D. from the University of Chicago in 1915 and moved to Berkeley in 1923. In 1925 he wrote *The Morphology of Landscape*, which clearly outlined his view of culture as a departure from environmental determinist thought. Unlike his predecessors, Sauer viewed humans as having a more active role in shaping the landscapes they inhabited, rather than being a product of them. The Berkeley school subsequently became a prominent home of cultural geography for Sauer and his colleagues until the 1980s. A broad definition was provided by two of its scholars identifying cultural geography as 'the application of the idea of culture to geographic problems' (Wagner and Mikesell 1962). More useful perhaps is to identify the three principal themes for cultural geography that were to emerge from this school: the diffusion of cultural traits, the identification of cultural regions and cultural ecology (focused on how the perception and use of the environment are culturally specific) (Johnston *et al.* 2000: 46).

The cultural approach to geography became popular in the 1950s and 1960s with the discrediting of racist and deterministic thought. For instance, *Land and People: A World Geography* had a chapter looking at 'What makes humans special' and another about how 'People change the landscape' (Danzer and Larson 1982). The cultural approach led authors to describe the spatial dispersion of Western civilization to other lands, using the concepts of industrial and democratic revolutions, of course from a Western perspective. With both revolutions emanating from Europe, the text presented eleven cultural regions shaped according to the reaction of the people to the spread of these ideas: 'In some places the new ideas were eagerly adopted; in others they were resisted' (James and Davis 1967: 10). Similarly, in *World Geography*, all countries were discussed in terms of their progress on a path towards development that all will take, albeit at different rates. For instance, 'India has taken several steps towards modernizing the lives of its people' (Israel *et al.* 1976: 293), which included universal voting rights. Likewise, in Africa, former colonies still look to France as 'a source of culture and trade' (*ibid.*: 85). This approach towards culture was to change drastically in the late 1960s and 1970s with the shift in focus to cultural identities rather than culture as a dynamic human process.

Multicultural geography

The transition from viewing culture in universal terms to something that is rooted in a particular social context came about as a result of the postmodern or cultural turn in the 1960s and 1970s. Drawing on constructivist theory, culture, like knowledge, was now presented as a social construct with meaning only for the people who created it. Of course, culture is created by people in a given social context. What is at stake is whether cultural traits and ideas can be extrapolated beyond a given social and geographical context. With multiculturalism, cultural traits and ideas lose meaning outside of the context in which they were created. The effect of this shift in outlook has been to replace culture with cultures, and also to present culture as something deeply rooted and difficult to change. With culture now seen as a deeply rooted social construct, an identity, it has become more about *who we are*, our ethnicity, our heritage, or fixed personal attributes, rather than *what we do*. In multiculturalism our culture is dominated by our past rather than a vision of where we are heading. Over time, multiculturalism has become the main prism through which culture is viewed, but also a value to be communicated to students. As such it informs geographical education in both the US and England/Wales. This section will begin by tracing the rise of multiculturalism in American schools before turning attention to the other side of the Atlantic.

Since the 1970s multicultural education has become a central feature of the social studies curriculum in US schools, promoting the value of and respect for all cultures, not just Western culture, and presenting knowledge and truth as culturally specific. As a movement for change it has literally transformed the American education system. Two authors on the topic suggest that the aim of multicultural education is the 'promotion of an activist agenda', in which schools advocate 'the reconstruction of society by transforming power relationships and redressing past grievances through various compensatory measures' (Ellington and Eaton 2003: 74). This has meant turning a political objective into a 'pedagogical value', in the process transforming the meaning and purpose of subjects which pursue multicultural objectives (Kronman 2007: 141). Indeed, multicultural education has been a defining objective of the American education system for the past couple of decades. Hence, it should come as no surprise to find this as a goal of some geography textbooks. Multicultural education or teaching about diversity is also specified in the national and state social studies standards, NCATE standards and teacher resources. Of importance to note here is that today learning about other cultures is no longer viewed in purely descriptive and analytical terms, but is seen as a way to teach students to be respectful and tolerant of people from different cultural backgrounds. However, a problem arises in that the latter aim begins to interfere with the former.

In the 1970s the language used in high-school world geography texts changed to reflect a more inclusive approach to people of non-Western culture. More wholesale change in the approach and constitution of textbooks was evident in the 1980s. Here, there was significantly more coverage of world regions than in earlier textbooks, with many whole chapters dedicated to examining other nations and places (see Figure 5.1). Greater international coverage certainly is beneficial to geography students, but in

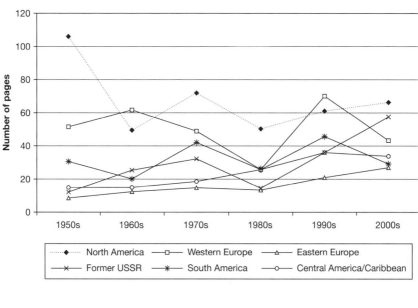

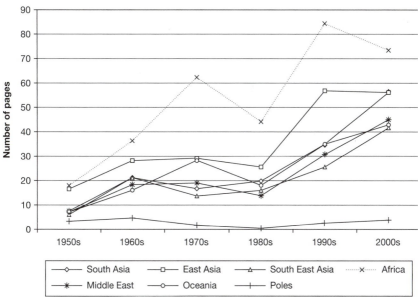

Figure 5.1 Regional coverage in US world geography high-school textbooks, 1950s–2005: (a) The Americas, Europe and the former Soviet Union; (b) Asia, Africa, Oceania and the Poles

some textbooks there is a tendency to *cover* different cultural regions rather than *analyse* them from a geographical perspective. With multicultural objectives in mind, publishers seek to ensure that different cultures are represented and portrayed in a positive image, rather than seeking to understand their practices and values.

Recent US world geography textbooks address multicultural objectives in several ways. These include focusing on a number of non-Western cultures (which are often presented as under threat from Westernization), by elevating ethnicity over political affiliation and by 'mentioning' the contributions and 'voices' of non-Western cultural groups. An example of how each of these appears in textbooks follows. Over time the centrality of these objectives to geography textbooks has shifted multiculturalism from an attempt to address cultural bias in the curriculum to a means of understanding ourselves and our society.

All of the leading high-school world geography textbooks have a significant focus on non-Western cultures. A simple page number comparison shows that Africa has become the world region covered in most detail since the 1980s, taking up on average 9–10 per cent of the books. The chapters on Africa include significant descriptions of a number of ethnic types. Aspects of their culture that are detailed include their settlements, dress, eating habits, and recreational activities. For example, a description of rainforest hunter-gatherers from *World Geography: People in Place and Time*:

> The Efe are nomadic and survive as hunters and gatherers. The men skillfully hunt small animals, using bows and arrows or spears and nets. Efe women search the forest to gather vegetables, roots, berries, fruits, and nuts.
>
> (Ainsley *et al.* 1992: 576)

This detailing of the lives of distant non-Western cultures in this manner was absent from geography textbooks produced earlier in the century. Further, the nomadic lifestyle of the Efe in this textbook is presented as under threat from modernization, in particular the tightening of national border controls that restricts their movement: 'the nomadic way of life is disappearing in the modern world' (*ibid.*: 540). East Africa is a focus in a number of textbooks, given its array of ethnic groups. Under the heading 'Maintaining traditional cultures' *McDougal Littell World Geography* informs students that 'East Africa's position as a major trading region has given it a diverse culture' (Arreola *et al.* 2005: 444). However, none of these textbooks enters into a discussion of why primitive cultures should be 'maintained'. There seems to be an underlying assumption that modernization and cultural change are undesirable. This pattern is repeated in chapters on other regions that also focus on indigenous cultures, including Native Americans, tribes of the Amazon, or Australian aborigines.

In post-World War II American geography textbooks there was an emphasis on nation building for people in the developing world who were freeing themselves from the shackles of colonialism. This was depicted as a positive process in that indigenous people were being given the opportunity to define their own destinies and political priorities. For instance, in *The World Today: Its Patterns and Cultures* the authors argued that 'Tribal states are fast disappearing. Most of the states that exist in the world today are national states' (Kohn and Drummond 1971: 130). The authors went on to express the benefits this brought to people: 'A sovereign state has the legal right to go to war, commission ships, exercise jurisdiction over territory, acquire citizens, negotiate treaties, exchange diplomats, levy tariffs, and do many other things' (*ibid*.: 135). Yet, in more recent textbooks, the opposite is the case: ethnicity or tribal affiliations are held above political ones: 'Many Africans have stronger loyalties to their ethnic group than they do to their country' (Gritzner 1987: 126), reported the author of *Heath World Geography*. Here, ethnicity has become the principal means for organizing central aspects of life: 'each group has its own customs, beliefs, and rules for behavior' (*ibid*.). In many recent textbooks, maps of Africa detail ethnic groupings and highlight their lack of correspondence to political boundaries, or define populations by ethnicity rather than by nation state. Yet there is a glaring contradiction between how these parts of the world and nation states in the developed world are approached. Multicultural nations are considered problematic in the developing world while celebrated in Western societies.

Since the 1980s textbook authors and publishers have presented culture as historically rooted and less transient than their predecessors. This might account for the emphasis placed on cultural diversity rather than cultural integration. Because of this there was less discussion about dispersion of cultural practices and traits that humanity has in common. In part, this simply reflects how people's ideas about the world have changed in recent years. It is undoubtedly true that many people place greater emphasis upon ethnicity in their lives today. Hence, a theory like Huntington's *Clash of Civilizations* has resonance for many. So at one level these textbooks are simply reflecting changing social trends, but their representation of culture as tied to ethnicity and past-orientated also fits the socio-political objective of promoting multiculturalism as a central pedagogical aim.

Some authors and publishers are also careful to emphasize the contribution of non-Western cultures to civilization, in contrast to earlier textbooks in which civilization was, by and large, disingenuously presented as synonymous with Western society. For instance, the Arabic development of learning and knowledge in the Middle Ages was noted by Ainsley *et al.* among others: 'The Arabs preserved that tradition of learning and took it with them as they spread their people and culture across North Africa' (Ainsley *et al.* 1992: 537). The same is true with respect to the contribution of other cultures to the American tradition. In one textbook, the unit objectives specified: 'Describe how the United States and Canada, nations of immigrants, have been enriched by cultural diversity' (English 1995: 237). Several recent textbooks now include 'multiculturalism' or 'respecting diversity' as American values.

While it is a positive development for textbooks to acknowledge where genuine contributions of other cultures to the development of knowledge, science, civilization or a shared meaning of culture have taken place, it is important to recognize that this is frequently not the objective of multicultural education. The contribution of Muslims to the advancement of civilization in the Middle Ages or how non-Western cultures have informed American society are two such examples. However, oftentimes textbooks do not give sufficient detail for students to understand how knowledge was advanced or where social norms have changed because of challenges to the dominant Euro-American traditions. Statements like the ones cited above are given without real explanation. This technique has come to be known as 'mentioning' in the textbook world and has replaced detailed analysis (Finn and Ravitch 2004). The message given to students is that respect for other cultures should be given regardless of the nature of their 'contribution' and students are discouraged from evaluating the intrinsic worth of the different cultural practices or viewing them as a contribution to a universal culture.

Again, there is a tendency for including the 'voices' of non-Western people in piecemeal fashion, seemingly to give a text the multicultural stamp of approval rather than for the purpose of truly interrogating different world views. For instance, *World Geography: Building a Global Perspective* sought to encourage students to have respect for other cultures through the inclusion of 'Multicultural notes' in each chapter that 'help students visualize other cultures through the voices of inhabitants of other countries' (cited in Baerwald and Fraser 1995: T13). The same emphasis was reiterated in *McDougal Littell World Geography* that included features on 'Growing up in . . .' and 'Comparing cultures'. The former focused on the lives of children in other countries: 'students learn about the common activities of young people in other countries, as well as key milestones in growing up' (Arreola *et al.* 2005: T7), while it is suggested that the 'Comparing cultures' sections 'help students relate the experiences of other people and places to their own lives' (*ibid.*). The emphasis here is upon gaining respect for and valuing the contributions and viewpoints of other cultures. In essence, empathy is being elevated above intellectual analysis or moral comparison of cultural practices and their spatial dimensions.

This development becomes even more apparent in the way in which geography textbooks approach Western society itself. While in the 1950s and 1960s North America was the main focus of US school geography, today its geography is frequently glossed over. While it would not be expected that a world geography textbook would necessarily focus on North America, most cover it in similar detail to other world regions, few schools themselves offer courses in the geography of North America and there are few textbooks published on this topic today. Instead, geography is usually offered at either middle or high school, or both, as a World Geography class. The geography of North America tends to be included or lost within a history course on the subject. And again, in world geography textbooks, Western culture is treated more as an object of study, with a focus on symbols, cultural traits or recreational activities, than as something actively shaped by its citizens. Even historical figures seem to take on a more symbolic role, with little appreciation of how society was changed as a result of their actions. However, this problem is not merely one of education and publishing. The degraded understanding of culture and the inability of textbooks to communicate a sense of Western culture reflect the modern social and political crisis in society itself (see Ravitch 2003).

Thus, while previous textbooks or curricula should be criticized for their Western-centrism and for promoting values of nationalism, their objective was to explain knowledge and provide truth, communicated to students by the author's narrative. However, rather than replace this Western narrative with a more balanced analysis of world cultures, textbooks offer multiple perspectives without analysis and evaluation of culture itself. This leaves students with a very weak sense of their own culture. When one of the main aims of society and textbooks has become to celebrate diversity, the obvious question to ask is what is left that people hold in common. This contradiction was highlighted in one textbook while detailing the history of immigration in the US and Canada: 'The process of protecting and promoting diversity while remaining unified presents a challenge to both countries' (Arreola *et al.* 2005: 101).

While many American geographers may still hold a strong sense of the intellectual merits of their discipline, some geography textbooks used in schools today confuse socio-political and geographical objectives, despite the inclusion of national standards. Perhaps because textbooks have been placed under the political microscope, they have embraced social, economic and political objectives which frequently undermine the teaching of geography. Critical to this process has been the shift from the author's responsibility for the text to the publisher's. Not only do publishers of recent geography textbooks in the US control much of the writing, but also they scrutinize every word for potentially offensive content (Ravitch 2003). Hence, a twenty-first-century high-school world geography textbook is quite a different species from those that came before. While it has grown in size, is more colourful, has improved maps, graphics, Web links, boxes, challenges, reviews and so forth, its aims are confused and its understanding of geography frequently weak. It has far more page coverage of world regions and cultures than textbooks of previous decades, but its expansiveness has come at the expense of depth, coherence and cultural analysis. Its approach to covering the world has become standardized, with fewer publications dominating the US market (Bednarz 2004; Standish 2006). These textbooks cover most world regions in a similar amount of detail, often taking a formulaic approach to describing each. Frequently, world regions and countries are examined under the same headings: history, people and culture, economic development, climates and vegetation, natural resources, landforms and rivers and urban development. These geography textbooks may well be factually loaded and attractive to the eye, but they lack clarity of purpose. What has been lost is the narrative that synthesizes the information, theories, models and concepts into a body of knowledge.

Many of the above trends have become apparent in recent changes to the English/Welsh geography curriculum. Politically, the UK was still clinging on to the notion of a homogeneous national world view until the end of the 1980s and the then Conservative government attempted to instil this perspective into the new national curriculum, with limited success. However, head teacher Chris McGovern reports that school history had already embraced teaching multiple perspectives over a common narrative in the 1980s, which led to an unworkable history national curriculum document for teachers released in 1991 (McGovern 2007). Calls to internationalize the curriculum and include global citizenship grew stronger with the globalization debate of the 1990s and coincided with the decline of a common national perspective. Hence, unlike the US, it was not until the 1990s that multiculturalism became a significant and officially endorsed educational objective. Sometimes the language used in England and Wales differs slightly from that in the US. For instance, the phrase 'respecting diversity' occurs more than 'multiculturalism', which partially reflects the more individualized approach to the topic that was to emerge in the 1990s. Respecting and valuing diversity were central to Oxfam's 1997 *Curriculum for Global Citizenship* and have subsequently become one of the Department for Education and Skills' eight key concepts of global education, and promoted as part of geography's global curriculum (Lambert *et al.* 2004).

As in the US, geography has been looked to for teaching about the virtues of multiculturalism. Again, the main terms of reference include cultural diversity and interdependence. For instance, a 1998 QCA conference emphasized geography's role in promoting 'tolerance of other people and other cultures' (Geographical Association 1998: 125). The following year the Geographical Association's position statement demonstrated their concurrence with the government's prognosis for geography. The statement highlighted the need for students to develop an informed concern for the world around them, including working with others and spiritual, moral, social and cultural development (Geographical Association 1999: 57).

The introduction of the citizenship national curriculum solidified geography's role in promoting cultural diversity. The scheme of work *Citizenship through Geography at Key Stage 3* (ages eleven to fourteen) suggests that geography enables students to 'understand the diversity of cultures and identities in the UK and the wider world' as well as 'understand the issues and challenges of global interdependence' (Qualifications and Curriculum Authority 2001). The document provides activities to meet these aims: for example, studying the religious or ethnic dimension of housing or employment patterns or investigating regional differences in development and their effects on the quality of life of different groups of people. The 2007 draft programme of study for geography also includes 'cultural understanding and diversity' as one of its key concepts (Qualifications and Curriculum Authority 2007).

Unlike the US, multiculturalism is a relatively new educational initiative in England and Wales. Hence, it is not surprising that most geography curricula and textbooks have yet to be restructured around its mission. This has not halted its many advocates and there are signs that change is on its way for the geography curriculum. In particular, the new pilot geography GCSE includes 'Introducing cultural geography' as one of nine options students can select. The syllabus states that this option 'places emphasis on the idea of a plurality of cultures' and aims to teach students about the 'challenges of living in a multicultural society' (Oxford, Cambridge and RSA Examinations 2004: 77, 78). The recommended content for achieving this goal is to study different images of Britain's communities and landscapes, through films, poems and literature.

The narrative to the study of culture has been lost in some geography curricula because the aims of multicultural values education interfere with analytical aims. Because students are taught to respect different cultures, regardless of their contribution, the purpose of study becomes simply an awareness of difference, rather than seeking to understand and compare different cultural practices and ideas.

What do students learn from lessons in cultural diversity?

It is important to consider in more detail what educators and policy makers think students will learn from studying other cultures today and whether this will have the desired outcome. As noted above, multicultural education began life in the US as an attempt to correct previous political and social injustices of the way in which minority groups were treated in the country. Textbooks and curricula were rightly altered to be more inclusive of the different peoples who had contributed to American history. However, what began life as a worthy objective became a socio-political curricular initiative as educators began to focus on the identity and social interaction of students rather than cultural comparisons.

Many textbooks and curricular documentation do not provide a rationale for why students need to learn about other cultures. It is almost as if cross-cultural contact has come to be seen as virtuous in and of itself and there is no need to account for its inclusion. Where explanation is provided, statements are frequently ambiguous and the intended outcomes not always tangible. The term 'global perspectives' is frequently rolled out as part of the rationale, although again the terms of reference are often less than concrete. For example, in the introduction to *World Geography: Building a Global Perspective* Riggs-Salter suggests that 'A global perspective is essential if students are to understand the connections among the world's people and places and indeed understand their own situations and their own futures' (cited in Baerwald and Fraser 1995: T5). For the author, learning about the diverse range of cultural types in the world is seen as necessary to valuing cultural diversity and obtaining a 'global perspective'. Hence, she defines multicultural education as 'a curriculum and way of teaching that acknowledges the cultural diversity of the United States and the world and sees this diversity as a positive fact of life' (cited in *ibid.*: T12), but does not see the need to account for why diversity should be viewed with esteem.

Nevertheless, there are at least three explanations that can be discerned from rationales provided in textbooks or curricular documentation (including those on international or global education): that it is necessary to learn social skills and cultural sensitivity to be able to work with people from other cultures, that knowledge of other people and places has potential practical use for employees of companies operating or trading overseas, and finally, that learning about how other people see the world helps one to reflect and to become less partisan. For each of these there may be a degree of truth, but the more important change has been to replace the intellectual and moral examination of cultures in geography with an approach that seeks to shape the values and attitudes of students. This development fits into the rise of psycho-social objectives in the curriculum identified above. According to one study of multicultural aims in social studies education:

> The theorists are not interested in students learning a body of knowledge about different ethnic groups. Instead their objective is to change student attitudes about themselves and others. They place a high priority on multicultural education as a tool to improve ethnic group relations, raise specific groups' self-esteem, and stimulate citizen action to transform America.
>
> (Ellington and Eaton 2003: 76)

The changing demands of the global market are a prominent theme in the US initiatives for reforming the curriculum around an international dimension, which helps to account for the prominence of business leaders on many committees for international curricular initiatives. It is argued that young people need more knowledge of other countries, other cultures, other languages and to develop cultural sensitivity in order to work with individuals from other countries. For example, one US international education initiative stipulates that students need to 'foster understanding and appreciation for diverse cultures' (New Jersey Department for Education 2006) while the Wisconsin Department of Public Instruction asserts the need for young people to develop flexibility and creativity to work across cultures. Similarly, the influential Asia Society describes social and cultural integration in its discussion of why international education matters. The society argues that this is a necessary focus of education today because of 'Increased diversity in our nation's classrooms, workplaces and communities' (Asia Society 2007). Again, geography education is viewed as having an important role to play here.

Of course it helps to know something about someone else's culture to be able to get along with them: for example, Muslims fasting in the month of Ramadan or Jews not celebrating Christmas. Being aware of cultural differences can prevent potentially embarrassing situations. However, it is worth questioning why this has needed to become an educational objective only in recent years. The make-up of the population in the UK has been growing more ethnically diverse since post-World War II immigration, while the US was built by immigrants from a multitude of nations. Hence, in both there has been a diverse mix of cultures in classrooms, workplaces and communities for decades. National and state policy based on racial differences certainly enhanced social division, but plenty of people learned to see past this ideology and, through their own personal experience, worked out how to get along with people of different cultural backgrounds. The discrediting of racist ideology has helped to make cities in both the US and the UK some of the most international locations in the world. Plenty of people from different cultural backgrounds have learnt how to get along without being 'educated' about their cultural differences. And if someone makes a cultural *faux pas* someone else can put them straight. If anything, multiculturalism encourages people to view each other through the prism of cultural identities rather than as people with a common humanity (this is explored more below). So this doesn't explain why knowledge of other people's culture has become a central part of the curriculum.

As economies have become more internationally integrated, it also appears logical that multinational employers would want to hire people who know something about the places and people in foreign parts they need to work or trade with, and maybe even speak the local language. Business leaders in the US have been particularly active in the development of international education programmes in numerous states, as was noted in Chapter 3. Spearheaded by the Asia Society, a coalition of national education institutions (including the National Council for Social Studies and the National Education Association), policy makers and business leaders was formed in the early 2000s. The coalition's strategy is to:

> [B]uild on the interests of governors, and international relations and corporate leaders, who realize the centrality of international know-ledge and skills to America's future, and to link them to education leaders in order to increase the policy priority given to education about other world regions, cultures and languages.
>
> (Asia Society 2007)

The Asia Society is a non-profit educational organization that presents itself as seeking to strengthen relations between Asian people and the US. In 2001 it released a report, *Asia in the Schools: Preparing Young Americans for Today's Interconnected World*, which highlighted the dearth of knowledge about Asia among American students at a time when Asia's economic relationship with the US had reached unprecedented levels. The society then co-ordinated a national coalition to promote Asian and international education in US schools and has evidently struck a chord with educators and policy makers. The National Coalition on Asia and International Education comprises over thirty organizations and companies and is co-chaired by John Engler, former governor of Michigan, and James B. Hunt, former governor of North Carolina. Its members include the president of the American Federation of Teachers, the president of the National Education Association, the president and CEO of the American Association of Colleges for Teacher Education, the executive director of the National Association for Secondary School Principals, and repre-sentatives from the National Council for Social Studies, the National School Boards Association and the National Geographic Society. Its stated goals are to raise awareness of the importance of international education, to build political momentum for change, and to encourage education institutions to embrace international education (Asia Society 2007).

In the UK, the business community also made a significant contribution to the global orientation of the curriculum. In particular, business leaders and associations contributed to the framing of the Department for Education and Skills documents on global education in the curriculum. And it would appear these are not just face-saving appearances on behalf of the business community. On its website Hewlett Packard declares that global citizenship is one of its seven company objectives (Hewlett Packard 2007). Similarly, Intel has stated its commitment to nurturing global citizenship.

However, again it is worth questioning education's new-found role in preparing a work force equipped for the global economy. Many studies of the relationship of education to work show that there is little schools do that directly prepares young people for work. Beyond literacy, numeracy and computer knowledge and skills most employees learn what they need to on the job. Many employers simply want to hire intelligent and well-educated individuals who are adaptable to the changing demands of business (Wellington 1993). While some general knowledge of the world is undoubtedly useful, it is unlikely that at school a student would learn about the localities where a company was investing in sufficient detail, nor would they be approaching the question in the same way. No doubt a company has specific objectives in mind when it comes to international business and its employees would be pursuant of these. Even the new-found 'commitment' to learning foreign languages in England and Wales is not likely to reverse their decline in schools. Researcher Shirley Lawes found an impoverished view of foreign language learning in schools, which reduces language study to 'a functional skill that teaches the sort of thing you find in a "get by" phrase book. It is selling young people short and unlikely to inspire anyone to see languages as anything other than mechanical and boring' (Lawes 2007: 92). Whether a similar outlook prevails in the US remains to be seen. And it is worth reminding ourselves that the international language of business, including in countries like India and China, is English. So a potential employee is unlikely to be passed over because they haven't learnt Mandarin or Hindu.

Upon closer inspection there is little content of intellectual substance to 'international knowledge and skills', as the next chapter will demonstrate (see Marshall 2005). Instead, they are more focused on the values, attitudes and social skills of students. Advocates of international education promote cultural contact as a means of learning to see the world through multiple perspectives. They encourage students to not think of their viewpoints as superior to others and to view all perspectives as equally valid. In order to achieve this goal, initiatives advocate first-hand contact with people of distant cultures. They seek to establish or improve links between education institutions in the US and those abroad. Partnerships or sister schools have already been or are in the process of being created for schools in New Jersey, Wisconsin, North Carolina and many other states. The objective of these partnerships is to increase cross-cultural contact for both students and teachers. This can take place through student and/or teacher exchange programmes or by utilizing the Internet for joint project work or simple e-mail communication. International education initiatives also seek to draw upon the cultural diversity of students and teachers already within the school. At one New Jersey-based conference on international education, teachers were informed that they should be seeking to internationalize their curricula and work towards global citizenship for themselves and their students (Standish 2006). Being a 'global citizen' meant being deeply engaged in other cultures, learning the language and joining in local traditions.

Undoubtedly, diverse cultural experiences provide valuable learning opportunities for students and teachers alike. The cultural diversity of many classrooms in America and England/Wales today provides a ready resource for learning about cultural differences. International exchange programmes have been run in many schools for many years with both linguistic and cultural educational objectives in mind. However, what differentiates multicultural education and some of the recent initiatives to internationalize students' cultural experiences is that the learning outcomes are focused on predetermined values young people should acquire. Rather than allowing young people from different cultural backgrounds to freely interact and learn about each other, students are told that the objective is to be tolerant and respectful of others. The values and attitudes of 'global citizens' have already been established as goals for students to aspire to *before* they commence their cultural experiences. This transforms a potentially enlightening experience to one which is governed by an externally imposed morality.

The final explanation is that learning about other cultures helps students to learn about themselves, and evidently this also informs the aforementioned push for a globally trained work force. Phrases such as 'fostering understanding and appreciation' are value statements. These educational objectives, albeit ambiguous ones, do not necessarily require students to walk away with new knowledge, but simply to acquire certain dispositions, values or attitudes of mind. For instance, the UK geography programme of study for Key Stage 3 (ages eleven to fourteen) explains that in developing cultural understanding and diversity students are 'Appreciating how people's values and attitudes differ and may influence social, environmental, economic, and political issues, and develop their own values and attitudes about such issues' (Qualifications and Curriculum Authority 2007: 3). While values education has been a growing objective in US education over the past two decades, its inclusion in UK curricula is a more recent phenomenon.

Interviews conducted with middle and high-school social studies teachers and textbook authors revealed that cultural tolerance and empathy were two values that some American educators view as central to learning about other cultures. For some, tolerance and empathy have replaced the modernist belief in cultural improvement. As one teacher explained:

> In many American minds we are still judged by how strong we are and we pride ourselves on that in many cases. I do think it is changing. I think that as education continues and borders expand through technology many Americans are realizing that that isn't necessarily the best approach and why do you have to be better. I prefer to think that we are one of many and can share and expand.
>
> (Standish 2006: 201)

This teacher, like others, was uncomfortable with the idea of nationalism, which she said encouraged chauvinism. 'I think it is very difficult to say God Bless America rather than God Bless All,' she proposed. Cultural tolerance and empathy encourage students not to pass judgement on which culture is better. They promote deference and philanthropy over pride and self-interest; co-operation and compromise over confrontation and competition; and inclusion over exclusion. The teacher explained, 'I think we need to stop judging the differences and looking at them as just that – differences – and still feel comfortable about going back to your own comfort zone' (*ibid.*: 202). Similarly, one geography textbook author commented that 'without empathy the knowledge is kind of sterile' (*ibid.*). In other words, don't learn something because it interests you or because you want to know something about the world, rather learning is becoming tied to specific socio-political values in the curriculum.

A similar mission is expressed by some leading geographers in the UK. The authors of *Geography: The Global Dimension* assert that 'In some ways learning about the global dimension in geography is about decreasing pupils' egocentricity' (Lambert *et al.* 2004: 23). This, the authors argue, can be achieved by students 'considering their own place and then transferring this understanding to other places' (*ibid.*).

The reorientation of education away from knowledge about the world towards the moral viewpoint of young people reflects both contemporary disenchantment with the value of subject knowledge and also the belief that social problems can be addressed by reforming individuals.

In the minds of some, this is fast becoming a new rationale for subjects such as geography. In the case of learning about other cultures, the new curriculum is trying to encourage cultural co-operation in a world where cultures are perceived to clash. Greater understanding of other cultures for individuals is viewed as central to alleviating cultural conflict and misunderstanding. This is why advocates for multicultural education or developing a global perspective see 'increasingly diverse workplaces and communities' when in truth they have been diverse for some time. It is less reality that has changed, but more some people's perceptions of it that have shifted.

How multiculturalism undermines the geographical study of culture

Multiculturalism is problematic for the study of geography because it both presents an acultural view of humanity and it replaces the analysis and comparison of cultural difference with values education as curricular ends. First, the perspective of strong constructivism which holds that people's knowledge and culture is contextually grounded leads to a deeply rooted view of culture, dominated by our past rather than a vision of our future and hence is much harder to change. Because culture is presented as a product of our identity (ethnicity, gender, class, nationality), *who we are*, there is a tendency to view people as prisoners of their past. While it is possible to change nationality and class, and even gender, our culture is presented as harder to change, given its rootedness. With multiculturalism there is a tendency to view culture as static or even an object to be preserved, as if a museum piece, rather than a dynamic entity produced by human ideas and creations. This helps to explain the tendency to present indigenous cultures as under threat from Westernization in some geography textbooks. The result is that some geography curricula focus on the more banal aspects of culture such as dress, food, music, recreation or symbols, instead of norms, values and institutions which shape society and in turn are also a product of the human imagination. The outcome is to portray culture in almost inhuman terms: not as a social process guided by people, but as something from the past that needs protecting from contemporary social processes. The celebration and preservation of traditional cultures has elsewhere been criticized for its functional approach and resistance to change (see Butcher 2007). 'The logic of functionalism,' suggests Butcher, is that 'culture makes man, rather than man makes culture' (*ibid.*: 120). This perspective runs counter to humanism, in which change and adaptability are the very essence of human existence.

A similar observation was noted by Ross Dunn, professor of history at San Diego University, in response to a new world history curriculum:

Many multiculturalist leaders have been so intent on demonstrating the respectability of Asian, African, and pre-1500 American civilizations and on giving them their rightful place in the school day that they have assumed the global curriculum to be mostly descriptive of 'other cultures' rather than a study of the social processes and historical changes in the world. Too frequently, they have accepted the notion that 'cultures' exist as internally stable, homogeneous mechanisms.

(Dunn 2002: 12)

The concern is that students are being taught about culture as something divorced from social processes and to view cultures determined by the past, rather than something they actively partake in. One student commented to me after a class on the cultural geography of America, 'I didn't think we had a culture.' Clearly, she had learnt to see culture as something existing only outside of the US and unrelated to her life.

This fragmentation of culture into a series of immutable artefacts leads to a further problematic outcome, one which undermines the central objective of multicultural education: to bring people of different cultures closer together through mutual understanding. Where cultural identity is portrayed as deeply rooted and socially grounded, this implies that individuals are different from each other as a consequence of their different social and cultural environments. Multicultural education teaches people to focus on these differences and respect them as differences. In essence, people are taught to see people of other cultures as different from themselves, rather than focusing on what people hold in common. They are taught to see individuals as representatives of a different culture rather than as fellow human beings with similar needs and desires. This insight has been articulated by Jim Butcher (2003) in a book about how travel is being transformed into lessons in morality. The book reports that tour companies are increasingly seeking to 'educate' tourists to be culturally sensitive to their 'hosts' and act in environmentally responsible ways. In parallel to developments in the geography curriculum, tour companies have written travel codes specifying acceptable values and behaviour, which are duly communicated to the travellers. Again, this creates predetermined rules of engagement and encourages tourists to look for cultural differences rather than what they have in common. The result is to present people from other cultural regions as different, which can have the effect of placing a barrier between people. Butcher makes the point that if tour operators encourage visitors to see culture instead of people, then that is what they see. Conversely, he suggests that it is when visitor and host sit down and freely communicate with each other that they begin to see each other as fellow human beings and not representatives of some alien culture. In effect, multicultural education attempts to formalize relations between individuals, with each playing a pre-allotted role that requires them both to tread carefully and respect the other's cultural identity. But again, formal relations are generally more distant and superficial than those that develop spontaneously and informally.

The claim of multiculturalism that all cultures are different but equal is also disingenuous (see Kronman 2007). While it is important to learn about the diversity of cultural practices around the world and how they do or do not interact this does not make them of equal worth, as any student can deduce for themselves. The dominance of Western civilization, at least until its recent cultural turn, was no accident. Much of what we take for granted today is a product of the advances made in Western societies in the modern era: science, medicine, law, high levels of production and consumption, efficient transport networks, information technology, communication systems and so forth, have all been rapidly advanced over the past two centuries. There are examples of non-Western contributions to some of these areas, but the overwhelming advance of knowledge, technology, political, social and environmental aims have been a product of Western societies. There is also a question of whether Eastern societies, such as Japan and South Korea, can be categorized as part of the 'West', but certainly they have subscribed to its economic and political model.

In presenting different cultures as of equal worth and failing to analyse their relative merits and shortcomings, some geography textbooks tend to offer multiple truths. Here, obtaining a global perspective equates with not believing in one version of the truth and refraining from making judgements about different accounts because truth is now seen as relative. This observation was made by the late Albert Shanker, a former president of the American Federation of Teachers:

> The claims of multiculturalists and other separatists reflect the attitude that no one group may make judgment on any other, since all 'depends on your point of view'. This extremely relativistic viewpoint conflicts with the need that all societies have of establishing some basic values, guidelines, and beliefs.
>
> (Shanker 1996)

In this respect, many geography curricula are failing to encourage students to do what comes naturally: to make judgements about life and find for themselves answers to significant cultural conflicts, such as the place of women in some Muslim countries or the banning of religious symbols by French schools. The purpose here is not necessarily to judge other cultures as misguided or wrong but simply 'to understand why, in specific historical circumstances, human beings behaved in the ways they did' (Dunn 2002: 12). Geography has the potential to offer students insight into the workings and values of different peoples across the world. This is an invaluable educational experience in that it helps young people to determine their own moral compass. The multicultural approach fails to offer students both an approach for analysing culture and the means for comprehending it as social practice.

It is in this regard that geography is sometimes seen as having a role to play as part of the humanities. In analysing different cultures in different settings geography may cross over from being a social science to an interpretive science. The question is one of approach: is the given culture being analysed empirically to learn about its spatial connections and distribution or is it being evaluated in terms of the values it holds and the practices undertaken? The former approach is that of a social science, the latter humanities. The humanities explicitly seek to examine the human condition, which involves making judgements about the worth of different human products: art, social institutions, values, norms, practices, literature and so forth. In geography, this means that teachers should try to convey a sense of what different societies and cultures stand for and allow students to evaluate them on their own terms.

But despite its claims to offer a more ethical approach to geography, the multicultural approach *inhibits* students' ability to evaluate their own and other cultures. Again, because it sees an individual's value system as rooted in a given social and cultural context, it presumes that one cannot abstract from this to gain a distanced perspective upon one's own life and the lives of others. Young people are frequently taught that Black history is different from White history, that a female's perspective is different from a male's, and so forth. Yet this jars with real-world experience because 'We are not prisoners of our upbringing' (Kronman 2007: 147). Through education, travel or social interaction young people learn to see the world through the eyes of others and begin to look critically at the partial viewpoints held in younger days. Of course, it is possible to abstract from a personal viewpoint, so long as one recognizes that identity is dynamic and a function of *what we do* rather than as something which dictates *who we are*.

The irony of the multicultural approach to geography is that for all its talk of tolerance its avoidance of interrogating cultural values promotes a new form of intolerance: that of passing judgement about different cultural practice and ideas. In multicultural geography textbooks, learning about cultures and developing a strong sense of the meaning of culture have been replaced by turning respect for diversity of culture into a value itself. Again, Shanker highlights the contradictory approach taken by multi-culturalists who reject making judgements about other cultures and then proceed to make tolerance into a value: 'And, it should be pointed out that those who reject this claim are ironically making an absolute value of tolerance, for in its name they are unwilling to make any other value judgment' (Shanker 1996).

Therefore, a main aim of multicultural education is for students to take on the value of respect for other cultures. In the end, global perspectives seek to avoid any perspective on human life at all: we can't make judgements about other cultures and other viewpoints, since all cultural practices and knowledge of the world are portrayed as equally valid. However, one study of global education ideology concluded that such an approach is more likely to lead students to indifference than to genuine tolerance of others:

> [T]he pressure not to apply moral standards is more likely to produce an ethic of 'indifference' than one of true tolerance – as young people learn not to pass judgment on all kinds of horrendous practices, especially when they are non-western. In trying to suppress what is probably a natural human tendency (to judge), these students are more likely to become morally numb, certain not 'sensitive' to the 'other'.
>
> (Burack 2003: 53)

This explanation helps to account for the paucity of cultural analysis and moral evaluation in some contemporary geography curricula. The effect of adopting a multicultural approach to geography therefore has the opposite outcome of that which it claims: instead of widening perspectives and challenging students' moral world, it seeks to impose a restrictive and inhuman moral outlook upon young people.

Concluding comments

The primary concern of this chapter has been the effect of teaching multiculturalism and/or global perspectives on geographical education. Again, this is not to argue that all geography lessons use this model. Nevertheless, there are many advocates in the subject who wish to see cultural geography as the teaching of multicultural values. What is clear is that where this approach informs the study of other cultures, the aims of geography education have changed. No longer are students being given an insight into the practices, dynamics and interrelationships of people of different cultures. Instead, they are taught to see culture as immutable and external to the creative capacity of human beings. The likely outcome of the multicultural approach is to place greater, rather than less, social distance between people from different cultural regions. In one sense the phrase 'learning about other cultures' is an inaccurate description of multicultural education. As its aims state, the objective is to change the students themselves, their attitudes towards other people, rather than to teach them about world cultures. Of course they might also learn something about other people and places in the process, but this has become a secondary consideration and the approach taken negates genuine cultural understanding.

Suggested further reading

Banks, J. (ed.) (2004) *Diversity and Citizenship Education: Global Perspectives*, San Francisco, CA: Jossey-Bass.

Burack, J. (2003) 'The Student, the World, and the Global Education Ideology', in J. Leming, L. Ellington and K. Porter-Magee (eds) *Where Did the Social Studies Go Wrong?* Washington, DC: Thomas B. Fordham Institute.

Ellington, L. and Eaton, J. (2003) 'Multiculturalism and the Social Studies', in J. Leming, L. Ellington and K. Porter-Magee, *Where Did the Social Studies Go Wrong?* Washington, DC: Thomas B. Fordham Foundation.

Finn, C. and Ravitch, D. (2004) *The Mad, Mad World of Textbook Adoption*, Washington, DC: Thomas Fordham Institute.

Johnston, R., Gregory, D., Pratt, G. and Watts, M. (2000) 'Cultural Geography', in *The Dictionary of Human Geography*, 4th edn, Oxford: Blackwell.

Ravitch, D. (2003) *The Language Police: How Pressure Groups Restrict What Students Learn*, New York: Knopf.

Chapter 6

Approaches to teaching global issues

<hr>

KEY QUESTIONS

1 Why study issues in geography? What do they contribute to a geographical understanding of the world?
2 Which issues should be in the curriculum and why?
3 What is different about global issues in today's curricula in comparison with the teaching of issues in the past?
4 What role do students have in learning about issues? Is it simply to understand them or should they also be taking some responsibility for issues themselves?

<hr>

This chapter will explore the growing popularity of global issues in the geography curriculum. As discussed in the previous chapters, seeing the world as interdependent and engaging with contemporary global issues are seen as essential parts of developing a global perspective. The implication is that if issues are truly global in nature then everybody has a responsibility towards solving them no matter where they occur. Some of the issues appearing in geography curricula include environmental problems, sustainable development projects, trade, social justice, protecting human rights or the rights of minorities, equality, fighting poverty and responding to natural disasters.

Yet in considering the educational merits of studying issues it is important to think about what students of geography gain from such a task. Is the objective to further geographical understanding or to encourage young people to think in a particular way about the topic of consideration? What does learning about the problems people face around the world contribute to an understanding of geography and how best should this be approached? The chapter will show how the study of issues and problems faced by societies at a given locality is an important part of developing a geographical understanding of the world. Nevertheless, in the transition from viewing issues as global rather than through the national political framework these problems are being removed from their geographical and political context and reinterpreted from a Western perspective. The objective of studying global issues has changed from seeking to understand the problems people face in their given locality to encouraging students to empathize and personally engage with the issue. Global issues are seen as our responsibility, including students', not just something that people face in their own country. This means that learning about these issues is very much a process of increasing self-awareness: what do students think about global warming or the preference for boys over girls in some Asian countries? What do they think should be done about malnutrition in parts of Africa or tropical deforestation? Thus some contemporary curricula include the expression 'doing geography' where students are expected to *make a connection* with people in a distant locality or contribute to the relief effort after a natural or humanitarian disaster. Here, students are not simply learning about issues; they are being asked to make an emotional and personal commitment to them.

This new approach can be criticized because it is not about teaching geography and neither does it contribute to the intellectual development of young people. Instead, global issues set emotional and values goals for students to obtain, which themselves serve to undermine knowledge and the moral capacity of people to advance their own well-being. The chapter will begin by discussing how global issues are approached differently from curricula which addressed issues from a national context before proceeding to illustrate the methods used to approach teaching about global issues.

What is different about global issues?

Learning about issues means studying problems of a social, political, environmental or economic nature faced at different localities. Learning about the problems that different people face contributes to our understanding of spatial difference and the unique human and physical qualities that contribute to a sense of place. Because of differences in culture and natural landscape it would be anticipated that the issues faced by people would vary across the globe. Learning about the problems encountered in different places is part of the human story that geography seeks to reveal.

Therefore, studying issues is not something new to geography. However, given that in modern times the nation state has been the vehicle for expressing human will legally through the notion of national citizenship, most geographers have naturally approached issues through this concept.

Ultimately citizens of nation states are the ones responsible for the issues that arise within the territorial bounds of the nation state and hence at liberty to decide on a course of action. Hence the principle of national sovereignty became an important principle to uphold. Of course this principle applied only to some citizens and some states for much of modernity. During the colonial period sovereignty was reserved for the powerful nations of Europe, America and Japan. Nevertheless, in the post-World War II period citizens of all nations gained formal equality and the sovereignty of nations underpinned international relations, if it was not always respected in practice. Hence, geography textbooks in the post-war decades, by and large, addressed issues as the responsibility of individual nation states, moving away from the perspective of colonial responsibility for occupied territory. However, in these decades the vast majority of issues discussed were viewed in national terms with the expectation that they would be addressed through the national political framework, although the West established new relations with many developing nations through development and aid policy.

What has changed in the twenty-first century is the way in which these issues are approached and their centrality to the discipline itself. Global issues are presented as problems that are larger in scale, crossing national boundaries and necessitating a transnational response because of the interconnected nature of societies in this globalized era. The post-Cold War period has witnessed the increasingly international nature of politics, evidenced by the expansion of intergovernmental organizations, the growing importance of non-governmental organizations, and the expansion in international law (Duffield 2001). The growing popularity of the phrase 'the international community' also signifies this trend towards transnational co-operation to address problems that are seen in humanitarian rather than political terms (Chandler 2002). One consequence of this shift is that nation states are seen to be impotent to solve these global problems alone and indeed acting alone in the 'international community' is frequently frowned upon.

Subsequently, the theme of interdependence has become central to many geography curricula in recent years. Again, this is not to say that geographers in the past did not look at the connections between distant localities, they did. But today interdependence captures the essence of this new approach to global issues. In American social studies and geography curricula the concept of interdependence has become popular. As noted in Chapter 3, the social studies national standards include 'Global connections' as one of their ten themes discussing the 'realities of global interdependence' (National Council for Social Studies Standards 2003) and several state standards also include interdependence in their geography standards. The 2005 edition of *World Geography: Building a Global Perspective* introduces students to geography, suggesting that it will help them 'understand the connections between global and local events' (Baerwald and Fraser 2005: 32).

In England and Wales, interdependence is one of the key concepts highlighted for students to learn in the 2007 draft geography national curriculum programme of study for Key Stage 3 (ages eleven to fourteen). Likewise in the new pilot geography GCSE, interdependence features as one of five fundamental concepts to be addressed. The examination syllabus describes the thinking behind the concept of interdependence:

> Candidates should understand and explain the multi-dimensional links between places and people, the different scales at which the causes and effects of these links operate and the impacts of these upon people and places.
>
> (Oxford, Cambridge and RSA Examinations 2004: 4)

Nevertheless, it is important to recognize that the change from viewing issues in national to global terms is not just a matter of scale. Beneath the surface of this discussion a more fundamental change has taken place in the way problems are being identified and addressed. Geographers by nature seek to comprehend and demonstrate how phenomena are spatially related, as pointed out in Chapter 1. For example, geographers look at how economies in different localities complement one another through trade and investment or how settlement patterns are related to the natural landscape and climate or how people of different cultural background have exchanged goods and ideas. Discovering interconnections is at the very heart of geography and essential for any geography student to explore.

Yet the language with which global interdependence is discussed today reveals that the concept has been taken to a new level of meaning. Not only are geography curricula exploring links between phenomena, they seek to examine how individuals themselves are connected to the social and natural world. For instance, this approach is made quite explicit in the elementary and middle-school social studies text *Self in the World* (McEachron 2001). The author's approach is different in that she advocates learning about the world, but only from the perspective of how it relates to the individual student. In the UK, some leading geographers similarly assert the importance of the global dimension to students' self-awareness. This they suggest helps students:

> To rediscover and further develop strategies of values education which not only help pupils see values as a variable that affects and explains human behaviour but helps them to understand their own feelings about places and the people who make them.
>
> (Lambert *et al.* 2004: 7)

The objective here is not just to make students aware of how their lives are connected with those of others and with nature, but also to explore the moral obligations these connections carry with them. The teacher support material for the Oxford, Cambridge and RSA pilot geography GCSE explains the moral dimension of exploring global connections: 'But interdependence is also about relationships – trust, dependency, support – and so there is a values dimension to the study of interdependence whether it is people, countries or companies which are being studied' (GeoVisions GCSE Working Party n. d.).

While it can be argued that there is always a values dimension to studying social, political and other issues, when geography textbooks presented issues in national terms it was up to the citizens of each nation to decide how to respond to the issue, even if students reading the text developed opinions themselves. However, when people across the world are portrayed as dependent on each other and also on nature, the implication is that we all have a moral obligation to each other and to nature. Here, political issues have been removed from their wider social and political context and reinterpreted as interpersonal relations. This development flows from the idea of politics as identity and parallels the discussion of cultural interaction in Chapter 5. Under a heading 'Geography and you', the authors of Holt's *World Geography Today* explain how geography is being recast as a personal act:

> Anyone can influence the geography of our world. For example, the actions of individuals affect local environments. Some individual actions might pollute the environment. Other actions might contribute efforts to keep the environment clean and healthy . . . Understanding geography helps us evaluate the consequences of our actions.
>
> (Helgren and Sager 2005: xxiii)

Hence, many geography curricula of the twenty-first century present issues as if they are of direct relevance to the daily lives of students themselves, that geography should inform their interaction with other people, the commodities they purchase, how they choose to travel and where and even how many children they decide to have.

'Relevance' is another buzzword of recent curricular reform that provides insight into the global approach to teaching about issues. Increasingly educators presume that what is taught must have some immediate or direct relevance, or utility, to the lives of students, otherwise why are they learning it? Chapter 4 showed how the notion of relevance informed some of the geography projects of the 1970s and 1980s. For instance, the Geography for the Young School Leaver (Avery Hill) project was an attempt to offer a more relevant geography curriculum for 'non-academic' students, the assumption being that learning the discipline of geography was not for everyone. This same scepticism towards the value of geographical content to young people informs the contemporary calls for relevance. The idea of a relevant curriculum can be applied to basic utility skills such as learning to read maps, knowledge about services in the local community and learning about global issues, such as global warming, in order that people can take an 'appropriate' course of action. The logical implication of this development is that students should learn in school only that which will be of use in their everyday lives. Learning about theories of landscape evolution, urban land-use models, glacial cycles, patterns of settlement, cultural hearths are all thrown into question, unless they can be shown to be of direct utility to students. This is why issues themselves have grown in significance to geography curricula in recent years. While abstract geographical knowledge and theories are viewed as less relevant, global issues are seen as something that everybody has a responsibility towards.

In this regard, geographical education has followed the wider discipline's ethical turn from the study of not only what the world *is* like but also to how the world *ought* to be (see Chapter 2). Again, the Holt high-school text informs students that 'The study of geography helps us make connections between what was, what is and what may be' (Helgren and Sager 2005: xxiii) and *Geography for Life: The National Standards* promotes the role of geography in helping people plan for the future. Standard 18, 'To apply geography to interpret the present and plan for the future', suggests that 'Geographic concepts also help us think clearly about alternative futures and make us wise decision-makers' and the Web site encourages teaching students to 'Think globally, act locally' (National Council for Geographic Education 2003).

The term 'futures' has also been highlighted as a key theme for the new geography. The pilot GCSE syllabus in England and Wales includes 'Futures' as another key concept. Again, students are told to consider their actions and plan for alternative future scenarios. This concept is concerned with providing opportunities to 'develop a futures perspective that takes account of historical change and encourages them to envisage alternative scenarios and interpretations, and also makes them aware of the possibilities for involvement in planning and creating for the future' (Oxford, Cambridge and RSA Examinations 2004: 12).

Of course thinking about the future and one's political role in shaping it can be a progressive activity, if approached in the right way. It is important that students learn about contemporary problems facing humanity and are given opportunities to think about how society could do things differently. However, global issues are frequently presented to students as if they are adult citizens themselves and so need to be taking responsibility for them in the here and how. The citizenship national curriculum scheme of work at Key Stage 3 (ages eleven to fourteen) asserts that geography contributes to citizenship by enabling students to:

> Understand the issues and challenges of global interdependence; reflect on the consequences of their own actions in situations concerning places and environments; understand their rights and responsibilities to other people and the environment.
>
> (Qualifications and Curriculum Authority 2001)

The idea is that through global issues students will learn about the rights and responsibilities of citizenship. As discussed in Chapter 4, the curriculum in England and Wales has clearly defined this as global citizenship, while in the US the term is rarely used in current geography curricula although issues are often presented in global terms.

However, most children lack the intellectual insight required to understand complex socio-political issues in depth and general experience of how the world works. This is why they are not fully developed citizens and are prevented from voting until they reach adulthood. A distinction needs to be made between having opportunities to consider socio-political issues in order that young people can begin to form their own opinions about the world and having political responsibility for dealing with them. Under national citizenship the latter is reserved for adults. In contrast global citizenship tends to blur the lines between adulthood and childhood, with the expectation that students should become political actors in the here and now: 'It is only when we have a vision for the future that we can act towards it' (Lambert *et al.* 2004: 8). The contrasting approaches to national and global citizenship are explored in greater depth in Chapter 8.

The moral imperative behind global issues implies that something must be done regardless of national political boundaries. Although it is not always clear what action is being implied and especially who should be carrying it out, there are generally two forms of action that global issues suggest: modification of personal behaviour by students themselves, such as consumption patterns or doing community work, and/or support for international, intergovernmental or non-governmental organizations (though usually Western-led). This recourse to action helps to explain the recent reinvention of the subject as a verb: *doing geography*. In this context, geography is seen as some sort of action that has social or environmental consequences rather than an academic discipline that requires abstract thought and understanding.

A similar trend has been identified in the English and Welsh science curriculum. Physics teacher David Perks has written about how the science curriculum has been changed to 'empower students as future citizens and consumers of science, rather than to train them as future scientists – the *producers* of science' (Perks 2006: 11). Perks notes the recent introduction of ideas and issues about science and how it works into the curriculum at the expense of teaching basic scientific principles.

By implication learning about theories for glacial cycles, landscape formation or urban patterns in geography must be irrelevant. The outcome of a relevance approach to learning is that education becomes training in life skills rather than learning to understand the world through subjects such as geography. Students need to develop an understanding of the world while at school so that they play an active part in shaping its future as adults. Teaching global issues circumvents educating young people about the complexity of problems, undermining their capacity to develop as moral citizens. Seeking to direct their values, attitudes and behaviour in the present denies students the opportunity to develop their own opinions and ideas about how the world ought to be.

Which methods are employed to teach global issues?

No doubt geography teachers in classrooms across the US, England and Wales are employing a variety of approaches to teach students about issues that arise in the course of teaching geography. Which methods are employed by the teachers will very much depend upon their educational aims. Here, educators need to consider the *process* of education in addition to the *content*. In some cases teachers will be seeking to teach students about the issues faced in different localities with a view to furthering their geographical comprehension, in others some extraneous objective to geography is being pursued such as learning how to research a topic for oneself. With global issues the aims of geography education are shifting towards self-reflection and analysis, as noted above, and so different methods are proposed to engage students in this pursuit. This section will review these different methodologies.

It is logical that a teacher might utilize an alternative method for teaching about issues to that which they employ for teaching concepts, theories or general geographical knowledge, as issues are political in nature. This means that different people or groups of people may well have different ways of looking at a problem and consequently have different opinions about the best course of action to follow. A simple example would be a proposal to build a new supermarket in a village or part of a town. Some people might welcome the convenience of a larger store near by, but others object to the potential increase in traffic and congestion associated with the supermarket. In this case it is simply a matter of personal preference. With other issues, such as poverty, the question is likely to be how best to alleviate people's plight. With aid and development a whole range of other questions arise such as their impact on local economies or what type of development will help and how this could be initiated.

Because of the political nature of issues, geography textbooks frequently, but not always, present the views of different groups of affected people. A skilled teacher will provide students with insight into the complexity of the issue in question, the range of possible strategies to solve it, the likely consequences of each and also how people affected by the issue might feel about it. Given the expansive and open-ended nature of learning about geographical issues some educators take an investigative or enquiry approach. For some teachers this means getting students to do some of their own research to explore the issue. The objective of such an approach is not only that students learn about the issue itself but they also begin to develop research skills. Margaret Roberts, the current editor of *Teaching Geography*, identifies five stages in the sequence of enquiry skills:

1   Planning the enquiry, identifying the issue, questions and/or hypotheses, and planning how to investigate
2   Collecting, recording and presenting data
3   Analysing and interpreting data
4   Reaching conclusions
5   Evaluating the enquiry.

(Roberts 2006: 93)

Learning to conduct research in a scientific manner as outlined by Roberts is no easy task. All of these skills are difficult to master, need to be developed through the practice of research itself, but also necessitate an overview of the subject material itself. This is why research skills are frequently honed during higher education. The researcher needs to have an overview of the subject in order to identify the best questions to ask, the appropriate methods and sources for gathering data, and to know how to analyse and interpret the results. In schools students can mimic this research process, so long as they are skilfully guided by the teacher. Given the intellectual demands of this approach, it naturally works best with more mature students. Lower down the school an investigative approach can be successfully employed if the teacher tightly controls the parameters and the research materials.

US high-school geography textbooks also suggest that students can investigate current issues themselves. In the teacher's edition of McDougal Littell's *World Geography* case studies are highlighted to provide insight into issues. The text advises teachers 'Every Case Study includes a Project that gives students the opportunity to work in groups, use primary sources, conduct in-depth research, and make a presentation. A Research Link helps students do research on the Web' (Arreola *et al.* 2005: T8). Prentice

Hall's *World Geography: Building a Global Perspective* advertises its New Tracker Web link that helps students to 'find information on global issues' (Baerwald and Fraser 2005: xxii).

However, as noted in Chapter 4, for many teachers an enquiry approach means more than investigating one issue or conducting a piece of project work. Roberts explains that enquiry can mean 'an approach to learning to be used for all themes and places studied' (Roberts 2006: 93). In other words all geography education should be approached in this way. The holistic enquiry approach is founded upon progressive educational ideals and was popularized through the American High School Geography projects of the 1960s and in England and Wales through the Schools Council geography projects of the 1970s and 1980s. Today this approach to learning features heavily in the latest geography national curriculum for England and Wales. The enquiry method claims to actively engage students in the learning process, encouraging them to enquire into questions and issues rather than receiving knowledge 'passively' and to mimic the research process employed by academic geographers themselves. According to Roberts, this approach to learning is superior to didactic teaching in that it

> [I]nvolves the students in making sense of new information for themselves . . . It acknowledges that geographical knowledge is not 'out there' as some absolute reality, but that it has been constructed by geographers . . . It has the potential to give students more control over their own learning.
>
> *(ibid.:* 95–96)

While some of the innovative teaching materials and approaches to teaching geography generated through enquiry learning are a valuable resource for teachers, its focus on the student rather than the knowledge they need to acquire illustrates how this is a fundamentally different approach to education. The *process* of learning has become divorced from the *content* that students need to learn. Adopting the postmodern scepticism towards a common geographical body of knowledge, this approach focuses on subjective knowledge (different people's accounts of geographical information) and the values and attitudes of the students rather than the key concepts and theories required for geographical analysis. This turn towards an ethical approach to teaching in geography, exemplified by global issues, reflects growing psychological and social objectives for the curricula in the twenty-first century, filling the void previously occupied by the inherent virtues of the subject itself.

Focusing geography lessons on ethical concerns rather than geography leads the attention of educators away from what students need to learn to master the subject. The dominance of issues- and enquiry-based learning at the expense of essential geographical knowledge and skills has been noted by Walford (2001) and Marsden (1997). The outcome is to undermine both the *content* and also the *process* by which they can best learn geography, since the curriculum becomes filled with aims extrinsic to the subject, such as the exploration of feelings and attitudes. Likewise, in a paper discussing the 'global gaze' in the UK citizenship curriculum, Harriet Marshall points to the weak nature of the 'knowledge base of global education':

> [G]lobal educators were sometimes more concerned with the 'how' of global education rather than the 'what', in other words there appeared to be more clarity about the affective and participatory domains of global education than the cognitive.
>
> (Marshall 2005: 82)

The implication is that participation in a dialogue about global issues is more important than the knowledge developed.

One example, *Geography: The Global Dimension*, illustrates the change from viewing issues as part of the geography of the world to the internal life of the student. The booklet lists six themes to aid students in pursuit of global citizenship: developing talk, developing maps, developing sustainable futures, developing empathy and understanding, developing interpretations and developing partnerships. In the theme 'developing maps' teachers are advised to teach their students not to construct and read maps that model the real world but instead to use *affective maps*. Creating affective maps involves 'Plotting on maps the feelings that particular places evoke. Feelings are shown by symbols, possibly supplemented by annotation' (Roberts 2003). *The Global Dimensions* booklet includes a guide for constructing an affective map:

1 Sketch an area you know well.
2 Think of about 10 feelings.
3 Create symbols for each feeling to make a key.
4 Annotate the map with symbols.

(Lambert *et al.* 2004: 21)

While this activity does involve some geographical mapping, the focus of the lesson has shifted away from the accuracy and readability of the map to the feelings students attach to places on the map.

The publication continues to explain that teaching about the global dimension is not about delivering a curriculum. Instead, it seeks to engage students in a 'conversation' about issues in which they get to explore what they think and feel about them. The authors suggest the following teaching and learning sequence results in 'education as conversation':

1   *Initial Stimulus:* Generates the motivation to find out more.
2   *Mediation of Geographical Understanding:* What do we need to find out about and to describe, analyse and explain this geographical phenomenon or narrative?
3   *Making Sense of the Matter:* Applying learning and developing learners' understanding through activities that develop their abilities to 'think geographically'.
4   *Refining Thinking:* Learners sort and re-present in some form their own geographical understanding to others.
5   *Reflection:* Learners reflect on their own geographical under-standing.

(ibid.: 14)

This model follows a similar pattern to the sequence of enquiry skills out-lined by Roberts above. However, in this sequence there is more emphasis on 'thinking' and 'reflecting' than on the actual research skills identified by Roberts. This shift points to a further twist evident in geography's new approach to global issues. Skills are being redefined as dispositions or attitudes of mind rather than tools for analysing or processing informa-tion and data. One might imagine that 'thinking geographically' would refer to spatial oversight, yet according to one project 'Thinking geo-graphically involves thinking about you, your place and how your place connects with other people's places' ('Valuing places', cited by Lambert *et al.* 2004: 7).

The same can be said of other 'skills' in geography and other curricular subjects today such as 'critical thinking'. One US geography textbook describes the importance of this skill and its relevance for citizenship education:

> The development of critical thinking skills is essential to effective citizenship. Such skills empower you to exercise your civic rights and responsibilities as well as learn more about the world around you. Helping you develop critical thinking skills is an important goal of *World Geography Today*.
>
> (Helgren and Sager 2005: S2)

The precise meaning of critical thinking is not always given and is often vague. One definition suggests that it means not accepting things at face value: 'Put simply, critical thinking involves recognising that "things are not always what they seem to be" or "there's more to this than meets the eye"' (Lambert *et al.* 2004: 7). Such an attitude towards learning about the world would be welcome if this was its intended outcome. However, in the context of an approach that is sceptical of a common body of geographical knowledge, the phrase rings hollow. Knowledge itself should be used to nurture in young people the ability to discern accurate information from prejudicial opinion. Yet, when this attitude of mind is increasingly replacing the content of education, this cannot possibly result in enlightened individuals. Its inclusion in the curricula may be worse still, in that students are encouraged to be sceptical of objective knowledge itself, instead viewing all knowledge as subjective and equally valid. Again, Perks has made the equivalent observation of the science curriculum in England and Wales (Perks 2006).

The topic of the pervious chapter, developing multiple or global perspectives, is another disposition disguised as a skill. Exploring global issues is not only a way for students to reflect on how they think and feel about the world, but is also a way to consider multiple perspectives. A given issue can be explored from the perspective of different people or groups affected, in turn potentially influencing the student's viewpoint. This process of considering alternative views of the same issues adds to the focus on subjective knowledge without seeking a resolution to the different perspectives considered. *The Global Dimensions* booklet explains this approach: 'Global geography lessons try to involve pupils in complexity and open-endedness, where clear-cut answers to enquiry questions do not always exist' (Lambert *et al.* 2004: 9). When the objective of considering alternative viewpoints is simply to respect them and empathize with rather than criticize and evaluate, students are left without a means for assessing the relative merits of different opinions. All opinions should be considered, but not all are equally grounded in the best real-world solution. The danger of the multiple perspectives approach is to leave students will lots of questions and no answers. Again, this illustrates that for some educators the social attitudes and dispositions of students are becoming more important than learning real skills that can be used for intellectual enquiry.

In learning about global issues it is often presumed that this will lead to some kind of action or participation in a project. Oftentimes the exploration of global issues leads to the question of what can be done to address the problem. As noted above, global issues are different from previous approaches to learning about issues because they seek to engage students themselves directly with the problem under investigation. When the question of 'what can be done' is posed, then not surprisingly it is students themselves who are expected to be responding. Hence, geography curricula today emphasize participation, service-learning or present geography as a verb. As the authors in McDougal Littell's *World Geography* opine, 'Students are not just learning about geography – they are also learning to *do* geography' (Arreola *et al.* 2005: T29). This might mean changing one's values, attitudes and behaviour, for example recycling waste, changing consumption to reduce one's environmental impact, helping people in less developed countries by supporting the work of

NGOs in developing countries, undertaking local community work, studying abroad or just making connections with people from other cultures. In other words, this means any activity that might conceivably have some small influences on the environment or other people.

In some instances service learning or community-based learning is presented as a way to address global issues, again emphasizing links between geography and citizenship. Dorsey (2001) advocates this approach for undergraduates because it makes direct links between the community and university. It also gives students the opportunity to make links between theory and practice and to experience 'doing citizenship'.

Concluding comments

The first problem with the approach to teaching global issues outlined above is that it is not about learning geography. As noted above, the purpose of learning about global issues is to encourage self-reflection and personal engagement with an issue rather than its exploration in a specific geographical and political setting. The focus has moved from knowledge and understanding about issues to making a connection and empathizing with the people involved. Personal engagement with the issue or doing geography is cited as more meaningful because it gives the lesson some direct relevance to the lives of students and is more likely to lead to political engagement in adult life.

Yet such an approach displays contempt for the value of subject knowledge and underestimates the capacities of young people. It presumes that abstract learning and comprehension of the geographical problems faced by people are not inherently enlightening; that investigating the causes of poverty, famine, desertification or disputes over borders, immigration or water rights will not capture the imagination of students even if they have no immediate relevance to their lives. Yet, why should education be about the student and connected in some way with their everyday life? Shouldn't education seek to show young people about lives and issues that are very different from theirs, taking them beyond the narrow confines of their limited experiences in life? The approach taken to global issues presumes that students will not be motivated by the simple act of learning. However, geography has the potential to enable students to make sense of situations which superficially seem incomprehensible: that people continue to starve when the world has food to feed them, people die from entirely treatable diseases where there is medicine to prevent them or that people blow themselves up without obvious political motivation. For most young people making sense of their world is motivation enough.

Second, there is little evidence to suggest a link between volunteering or helping with a school project and political engagement as an adult.

Both global issues and service-learning reject abstract ideas as a prelude to political thought. Again, how are young people going to act in and shape the world if they do not understand complex contemporary political issues and how systems work? Education is the very thing that has provided people with the tools they need to become active citizens. At least the national model of citizenship education taught students about the political system and the principles and mechanisms of civic engagement. In learning about global issues valuable school time is filled with doing, participating and reflecting on one's feelings. This may help students meet some interesting people and feel good about themselves and to stay in touch with their emotions, but this comes at the cost of geographical knowledge and understanding.

Not only does the approach currently being advocated for teaching about global issues presume that knowledge and understanding do not precede action, but it is sceptical towards objective knowledge itself. It may be the case that in higher education students learn to appreciate that knowledge is complex and open-ended, but in order to appreciate this insight they need to have mastered the very concepts, ideas and theories that are queried later. Think of the teacher who says, 'Well, we told you this was the case in year/grade X, but in year/grade Y we learn that the situation is more complex.' Students of different intellectual maturity are capable of mastering concepts and ideas at sequentially more complex levels. Teachers learn and know this for themselves. If school students are not taught to learn ideas and concepts as solid foundations of knowledge, they will not be able to intellectually build upon these. Their minds will be full of questions and no answers.

Suggested further reading

Balderstone, D. (ed.) (2006) *Secondary Geography Handbook*, Sheffield: Geographical Association.

Lambert, D., Morgan, A., Swift, D. and Brownlie, A. (2004) *Geography: The Global Dimension: Key Stage 3*, London: Development Education Association.

Marshall, H. (2005) 'Developing the Global Gaze in Citizenship Education: Exploring the Perspective of Global Education NGO Workers in England', *International Journal of Citizenship and Teacher Education*, 1 (2): 76–92.

Qualifications and Curriculum Authority (2001) *Citizenship at Key Stage 3*, London: Qualifications and Curriculum Authority, accessed at http://www.standards. dfes.gov.uk/schemes2/citizenship/.

Roberts, M. (2006) 'Geographical Enquiry', in D. Balderstone (ed.) *Secondary Geography Handbook*, Sheffield: Geographical Association.

Chapter 7

Global issues in the geography curriculum

KEY QUESTIONS

1 How are global issues approached in geography curricula today? What are their learning objectives? Are they realized?
2 Are current global issues in the curriculum truly global in nature? How can we tell?
3 How do global issues help students to learn about the problems facing people in a given locality?
4 Can global issues be solved through education?

This chapter will provide some more detailed examples of global issues drawn from textbooks, teaching materials, documentation and interviews with teachers. Because textbooks tend to respond only slowly to changing ideas about a subject, they are not necessarily the best source of identifying some of the most recent curricular shifts in emphasis. While many have incorporated some global issues into their texts, they frequently do so by simply adding on to their existing geography curriculum. In contrast, Web sites with teaching resources, geography magazines and journals or documentation on teaching geography are often where new approaches to teaching are most clearly described. For this reason a variety of sources has been drawn upon for this chapter.

This material comes from both the US and England/Wales as many of the same issues are covered in geography curricula on both sides of the Atlantic. Nevertheless, there are some different emphases and approaches that need to be made apparent. Geography textbooks in both the US and England/Wales include global issues in addition to the more traditional geography curriculum. In England and Wales the emphasis upon the global dimension is more explicit and the centrality of global issues to the geography curriculum has grown dramatically in the twenty-first century, as evidenced by government and geographical associations' publications as well as the writings of prominent geographers. A new pilot geography GCSE has been constructed around the exploration of geographical issues. The latest programme of study for Key Stage 3 (ages eleven to fourteen) also encourages an enquiry approach to issues while simultaneously de-prioritizing learning geographical knowledge. In contrast, the global dimension in US geography curricula tends to be more understated, at least in textbooks, or sometimes is included as well as a national approach. As one textbook author from the south-west explained, she likes to include the themes of global citizenship, but can't call it that because 'people would object' (see Standish 2006). So while most geography standards, documentation and textbooks include global issues, they also discuss issues in more traditional terms along lines of national citizenship.

The chapter will demonstrate that, contrary to the claims of advocates, global issues are neither global in nature nor do they reflect and explain the principal problems people face around the world. Moreover, global issues frequently have little geographical content and do not encourage individuals to explore particularly meaningful moral dilemmas. John Huckle previously expressed concern over 'the political bias inherent in values education', noting that values education 'is the wrong analogy for much decision making' (Huckle 1983: 60). Global issues are selected for the purposes of getting students to consider their personal values. The inherent political bias comes from the selection of these issues for the purposes of exploring a predetermined values position. Simplistic scenarios are presented to students in such a way that most will reach the anticipated values position. This is their objective and it has replaced exploring the issues faced by people in their given location. As discussed in Chapter 6, with global issues a very different question is being asked: not which are the most pertinent issues faced by the people living at a given geographical locality, but how do 'global' issues relate to you? Immediately the issues are being taken out of their social, economic, political and geographic contexts and transposed on to an individual basis, the false assumption being that individual change will have some global effect. However, politics does not operate on the basis of individual values. It is a social affair in which citizens need to consider moral questions about humanity in general, not just about their own lives.

In removing the issues from their social and political context, global issues are being viewed through Western eyes and measured against contemporary Western values. So-called 'global values' include environmental values, respect for cultural diversity, prioritizing human rights over political rights, social justice, empathy and a moral obligation to an

Other. These values are presented as standing above politics and hence something to which all should subscribe. The objective of this chapter is to not only illustrate examples of global issues, but to show that global ethics, informed by liberalism's crisis in the West, represent a partial and individualized version of reality. Instead of offering multiple perspectives, the study of global issues serves to reinforce this new Western perspective.

Environmental issues

The most frequently occurring issues in geography textbooks today are environmental. One 'global' issue often discussed is the loss of rainforest. Yet today the issue is generally presented from a Western perspective and measured against its global ethics. Concerns are usually focused on the importance of the rainforest for all humankind, but rarely is the use of forests such as the Amazon considered the prerogative of indigenous people themselves. In Holt's *World Geography Today* students are informed that in the Amazon basin 'deforestation threatens the region's unique plant and animal life. Development also threatens the ways of life of the Amazonian Indians who have long lived in the forested basin' and also that:

> much of the Amazon forest may disappear within the next 100 years ... large parts of the forest are being cleared for farms and ranches. Other businesses harvest the forest's fine woods. Major mineral deposits attract prospectors and developers to the fragile forests.
> (Helgren and Sager 2005: 269–71)

Students are then given the following question to answer: 'Why is the disappearance of the rainforest a global concern?' They can find the standard answers to this question in the text, which highlights the rainforest as an important resource for species diversity and its supply of oxygen to the atmosphere. However, in depicting the rainforest as a 'global resource' rather than one belonging to the people who live there, the future of the rainforest has been separated from the political will of the South American citizens living there. While it is true that it is in the interest of humanity as a whole to preserve some forest for its species diversity, for example, and presently 11 per cent of total forest is designated for conservation (FAO 2005), deforestation is presented as the most important issue on the continent while more pressing economic, political and social issues for South Americans receive little attention. In most developing countries many people face a daily struggle to feed families, encounter social violence, and have limited political rights and poor access to education and health care. Countries such as Brazil and Bolivia are doing precisely what Western countries did during industrialization and urbanization: they cleared forest for houses, factories and agricultural land. If the millions of Brazilians and Bolivians are to find a way out of poverty then they need to make better use of the natural resources the country has to offer. Then, maybe, they will be in a position to discuss preserving environmental goods for the future of wider humanity.

Schemes to offer economic opportunities to forest communities while preserving the rainforest a little better. The Brazilian government supported the Amazon Reserve and Protected Areas programme that triples the area of forest to be preserved, through ecotourism for example. However, such schemes do not offer a path to larger-scale development and wealth, notes Butcher (2007). No doubt the government was swayed by the $400 million to be invested by Western organizations, including the Global Environment Facility, the World Bank and the conservation organization WWF (*Economist* 2004). Not surprisingly, turning large sections of a foreign country into protected land, frequently to the detriment of the lifestyles of local people who use the forests, has led to accusations of eco-imperialism (Driessen 2003).

Neither are students given facts that place rainforest depletion in a broader setting. Alarmist figures about the area of rainforest being cut down each year leave students with the impression of impending crisis and the imminent need for action. Yet long-term figures produced by the United Nations for global forest coverage from 1950 to 2005 show that forest cover has remained fairly constant at around 4 billion ha or 30 per cent of land coverage, with a net decline of some 7–9 million ha per year since the early 1990s (FAO 2005). Even the Amazon retains some 80 per cent of its original size, an area larger than Western Europe. By comparison the developed world has cleared about half of its forests. Tropical rain forests are sometimes depicted in curricula as the lungs of the world, pumping out oxygen and storing carbon dioxide. Rainforest deforestation then becomes analogous to choking the world. Again, this simplistic presentation is misleading for students. In particular it ignores the role of oceanic plankton, which are by far the largest carbon sink for carbon dioxide on the planet. The elevation of environmental problems such as the preservation of the rainforest into a global issue may fit the eyes and aspirations of the onlooking Western world, but does this really capture the geography of the continent and its people?

A second common environmental issue addressed in geography curricula today is the use of resources. In geography textbooks produced in the 1960s and earlier the ability of humans to transform natural goods into commodities was viewed in positive terms and celebrated. Twenty-first-century curricula downplay the human side of the resource equation and tend to portray many resources as limited in extent. Natural substances become a resource only because people learn how to use them.

In pre-modern times oil or uranium would not have been classified as resources. It is human knowledge and technology that turn natural stuff into a resource.

Rather than expressing faith in society to discover new resources and find new ways to utilize existing resources, some geography curricula encourage young people to reduce consumption or advocate renewable energy sources such as wind and solar power. A popular activity in certain geography lessons today is to get students to measure their 'ecological footprint'. In *Geography: The Global Dimension* teachers are directed to the Global Footprints project Web site, where students can complete a quiz to measure the size of their 'global footprint' (Box 7.1). The quiz is introduced with a child's definition of global footprints: 'Global means the world and footprint means pressing down and we don't want to press down on the world too hard.' The quiz then asks students to respond to a range of questions about their personal values and behaviour.

At the end of the quiz students receive a score indicating their likely environmental impact which they can compare with other people's and are promptly informed of ways they can change their behaviour to reduce it. The Geographical Association document considers this a valuable educational tool because it will 'encourage pupils to consider the impact of their own lifestyle on the possibility of a sustainable future' (Lambert *et al.* 2004: 23).

Clearly there is a strong moral imperative behind 'considering the impact' of one's lifestyle on the environment. The same can be said of the way in which resources are discussed in geography curricula. Most geography textbooks today make the distinction between renewable and non-renewable resources, the implication being that the supply of non-renewable resources is limited and so value is placed on renewable resources and recycling commodities. Holt's *World Geography Today* enlightens its readers:

> Today many products are made from recycled minerals. The advantages of recycling are obvious. For one thing, the more we recycle, the slower we use up non-renewable resources. For another, mines often cut great scars into the landscape. Processing plants belch dust and smoke and consume large amounts of energy. In contrast, using mineral products again can save money and spares damage to the environment.
>
> (Helgren and Sager 2005: 79)

However, because the objective is to educate young people in the virtues of environmentally friendly energy consumption, lessons frequently fail to analyse the issue itself. While geography textbooks highlight some of

---

Box 7.1 Sample questions from the global footprints quiz

(http://www.globalfootprints.org)

Which do you think is the most important for reducing waste?

- Reuse it
- Recycle it
- Make sure it all goes in the bin
- Don't make so much in the first place

Taking action in the local community

- I am involved in a group or club which takes action to help other people or the environment in my community
- I don't take action in my community because there are enough people doing this already
- I am not involved in taking action in my community but would like to find out how I could
- I don't take action because the local environment and the people who live in it aren't important to me

Fair Trade

- Many of the products in our house, like tea, coffee and chocolate, are Fair Trade
- Sometimes my family or myself buy Fair Trade products
- I know what Fair Trade means but I prefer to buy other products
- I don't know what Fair Trade means

(Humanities Education Centre 2007)

---

the benefits of recycling in terms of reusing materials they ignore alternative perspectives. For instance, one study by a Swedish group illustrated that in both economic and environmental terms incineration of waste made more sense than recycling (see Scott 2004). Incinerators may historically have a poor reputation for polluting the air and be viewed negatively in environmental terms. Yet the widespread use of filters and scrubbers in modern plants has enabled them to reduce their emissions of dioxins and other pollutants to levels frequently lower than ambient air. In other words they clean the air. Also, the heat produced in the burning process is a potentially useful energy source and they massively reduce the volume of waste to go into landfills. In contrast, recycling involves a lot of trans-portation and resources to separate and sort waste.

Both of the above examples start from the assumption that resources are finite and are being used up. Yet history shows us that most resources become *more,* not less available as we learn to use them in new and more efficient ways (see Simon, *The Ultimate Resource* 1981). For instance, the quantity of known world oil reserves keeps growing despite increased consumption. In the past decade alone the quantity of world oil reserves has grown 15 per cent (British Petroleum 2007). Why is this? The answer is that new fields are discovered, the ability of contractors to extract more from each field keeps growing and the efficiency of our use of oil rises. There is also the potential to extract oil from Canadian oil sands, Rocky Mountain shale or by converting natural gas into oil. The supply of non-renewable resources is limited only by humanity's potential to find and extract them and our imagination to utilize resources in new ways. These are two perspectives that most geography curricula today don't offer students.

Global warming is another environmental issue that has been covered by geography textbooks for several years, but has become more significant in the twenty-first century. Presently it receives minimal coverage in US geography textbooks, as it is only in the past few years that global warming has been treated seriously as an issue of national concern by mainstream American politicians. National Geographic's Web site has a lesson plan on 'Climate and CO_2: Analyzing their Relationship' which aims to have students 'speculate on the various scenarios of future world climates if the greenhouse effect increases' (Xpeditions Web site, National Geographic Society 2007). In the lesson students examine increasing levels of carbon dioxide, how this relates to population and development, the 1997 Kyoto conference and are informed of possible outcomes related to the green-house effect including 'islands and shorelines could be inundated, climate zones could shift, and weather could grow more turbulent' (*ibid.*).

In England and Wales a concerted and explicit campaign to use the curriculum to change young people's attitudes and behaviour with regard to global warming is well under way. As Education Secretary Alan Johnson stated with regard to global warming, 'Children must think differently' (Johnson 2007). Johnson's attitude here illustrates the authoritarian and anti-intellectual impulse behind some advocates of global issues in the curriculum. He expresses no interest in allowing students to investigate the science behind the issue and decide for themselves how society in the future might address global warming.

Global warming is hence covered in greater detail in textbooks in England and Wales such as *Key Geography for GCSE* and *Global Challenge.* These books provide some very basic atmospheric scientific background to the issue and then discuss possible consequences in a somewhat alarmist fashion: maps showing large areas of the UK under water, the extinction of certain plants and animals, the breakdown of the Gulf Stream and tropical diseases migrating to the country, even though these eventualities factor only into the more extreme warming scenarios. *Global Challenge* suggests research activities for students to learn about the effects of global warming on soil moisture, global biomass, extreme climatic events, human health, sea level and ocean currents. To do this the text includes Web addresses for organizations that study climate change or advocate policy change, such as the Intergovernmental Panel on Climate Change, the Environmental Protection Agency and the Ozone Action Group. In 2007 the UK government announced plans to teach all students about global warming. One initiative towards this end was to send a copy of Al Gore's documentary film *An Inconvenient Truth* to all schools. Not surprisingly, this issue has become an important feature of the geography curriculum and illustrates its links with teaching global citizenship.

Although some curricula do present some basic science behind global warming, most geography curricula emphasize catastrophic scenarios and support the assumption that warming is best reduced by individuals reducing their carbon 'footprint'. This illustrates that the issue is being used to moralize to young people rather than evaluated in scientific and political terms. While the evidence for warming, and its links with anthropocentric activity, is comprehensive, how societies should respond is contested and a political matter. For instance, scientist Mike Hulme comments on how society's present reaction to global warming expresses deeper social anxiety and a discourse of risk:

> The contemporary discourse of climate catastrophe may also be tapping into a deeper and non-negotiable human anxiety about the future, an anxiety which is merely attaching itself at the current time to the portended climates of the future – future climates offered up to society by the predictive claims of science. Science has never before offered such putative knowledge of the far-future, complete with uncertainty ranges, tipping points and probabilities, and so our fragile and nervous human psyche has latched on to such pronouncements with vigour.

> (Hulme in press: 18)

In other words, the contemporary discourse of risk and anxiety is encouraging an alarmist and irrational response to a scientific and technical problem. This helps to explain how global warming has been transposed from the political realm to that of individual morality. Holding children responsible for contributing to global warming is not a very adult way to proceed with the issue, especially when it comes at the expense of geographical education. Again, at issue is not whether global warming is occurring, but rather how society should respond to the problem, and some educators (and politicians) are seeking to deny young people a choice in this matter.

Development issues

Approaches to development have changed drastically over recent decades. There was growing interest in the development of Southern nations in the post-World War II period as the West sought to forge new postcolonial relationships with its former colonies. Early development models were based upon the assumption that the interests of people in the South would best be served by these countries following a similar development path to Western nations or in some cases following the Soviet model. The new emphasis was upon the sovereignty of Southern nations, who could choose their own development path, but whichever avenue was pursued industrialization, economic expansion and advancing technology were all important means to raising the wealth and quality of life of their citizens. Some US geography textbooks still discuss the efforts of countries to industrialize. *World Geography: Building a Global Perspective* highlights the 'Obstacles to development' in the case of Egypt, including the 'limited number of skilled workers' and the 'lack of capital' (Baerwald and Fraser 2005: 529). However, such an approach is today unusual in the West, where the desirability of large-scale development is frequently questioned, let alone whether it is within the reach of Southern nations. Instead, Western anxiety over environmental limits and socio-political unrest, projected on to the developing world, has become the main prism through which development is viewed. The outcome is a restricted view of development in which aid is linked with Western objectives rather than the needs and desires of Southern people.

Despite its ambiguity, sustainable development has become the dominant paradigm through which development is approached and it is presented to students in geography curricula in apolitical and non-contentious terms. Superficially, the term 'sustainable development' appears commonsensical: who would be for unsustainable development? However, sustainable development is a fairly recent Western invention and reflects the collapse of faith in its own modernist project. This is an entirely different model of development from the one described above and one that views development in terms of its environmental impact or is refashioned in psycho-social terms rather than material and societal well-being (Pupavac 2002). The shift to 'Green Development' (Adams 2001) began in the 1980s and was associated with the channelling of aid through NGOs rather than to Southern governments.

The notion of sustainability has only slowly been gaining a foothold in US curricula, now being included in some state standards for social studies.

The term is rare in current geography high-school textbooks. In England and Wales the case is entirely different. Since the mid-1990s geography curricula and textbooks used in England and Wales have adopted sustainability as a concept and model for development. For instance, *New Key Geography for GCSE* instructs students that 'sustainable development involves the sensible use of resources, especially those that are non-renewable, and appropriate technology' (Waugh and Bushell 2002: 270). This, the authors claim, will lead to an improved quality of life and a better standard of living. The use of the term 'appropriate technology' is informative as far as the type of development that is envisaged. The authors clarify that, in contrast to the developed world, in countries that are less economically developed 'alternative forms of technology . . . need to be adopted' (Waugh and Bushell 2002: 270). The textbook includes a photograph (Figure 7.1) of some women surrounding a well and some captions (Box 7.2) describing how the book views appropriate technology for less developed countries.

Figure 7.1 Intermediate technology for developing countries. Members of the Keyo Women's Group at Kisumu, Kenya, unloading the kiln after firing Upesi stoves designed to burn more efficiently than a three-stone fire

(By courtesy of Practical Action, Rugby; photo copyright Neil Cooper)

Box 7.2 Intermediate technology for developing countries

In *New Key Geography for GCSE* the photograph is accompanied by captions including those below. Intermediate technology means:

- Introducing labour-intensive projects, as, with so many people already likely to be seeking work, it is no use replacing existing workers by machines
- Developing projects that are in harmony with the environment
- Encouraging economic development at a pace a country can afford so as to prevent it falling into debt
- Adopting low-cost schemes and technologies that people can afford and manage
- Encouraging technology that uses the existing skills and techniques of local people and which can be handed down to future generations

(Waugh and Bushell 2002: 271)

This section on sustainable development also includes a description of the work of the British development NGO the Intermediate Technology Development Group (ITDG). The text informs students that the group 'helps people to meet their basic needs of food, clothes, housing, energy and jobs' (*ibid.*: 270), although no explanation is given as to why this group has been included in the text over others. Students are then given a number of activities and questions to complete such as 'Why it is important that future development should be sustainable?' and 'Why is support often more valuable' to a developing country 'than large loans given by the World Bank' or a developed country? (*ibid.*: 271). Here, the work of Western NGOs is presented in humanitarian terms and above politics. There is no consideration of the controversy surrounding the work of some development NGOs or alternative perspectives such as the argument put forth by some academics and aid workers that aid does more harm than good (see Vaux 2001).

While sustainable development has become a popular approach to development over recent years few have taken issue with its redefinition of development in personal terms, restricting the possibility of transforming people's social, economic and political circumstances. Its stated objective may well be to improve the quality of life and standard of living of people in less developed countries and no doubt some people welcome the technology and support that go with it. However, this hides the fact that sustainable development and appropriate technology are limited proposals that place industrialization and *real* development off the agenda. Instead of transforming the lives of people in the South through real economic gains, sustainable development encourages rural poor communities to maintain their present economic practices and traditions, *sustaining* the life they have, not *transforming* it. In *New Key Geography* the authors do point out that sustainable development is also appropriate for more economically developed countries, particularly given their higher consumption and pollution levels, but the 'only difference' for those living in developed countries is that 'the appropriate technology is likely to be high-tech' (Waugh and Bushell 2002: 271). In other words people in wealthy countries are allowed high-tech goods such as computers and electronics that save labour, while for people in poor countries these goods are not 'appropriate'. Hence, the emphasis placed in the text on technology that does not replace labour in developing countries, a practice that has produced vast social gains in the West. In the decades after World War II the benefits of a modern, mass consuming society were portrayed as a universal good. Today, in some geography texts, this is evidently good enough only for some people; the rest of the world will have to get by with primitive technology and low levels of consumption.

The limited nature of sustainable development is also apparent in Oxfam's micro-financing programme operating in countries such as Senegal. This example is included in one National Geographic lesson plan. Simply put: micro-financing has replaced macro-financing. In Senegal micro-financing is intended to help women develop their own income through small businesses or savings schemes; for example, enabling women to own some sheep or to pool their finances into a joint savings scheme which provides small loans for women in need. Micro-financing may help some individuals to get by, but again, it rejects industrialization as a model for widespread, long-term development that could raise the standard of living of entire nations to that equivalent in the West. China is the best example in recent times of a country that has raised the wealth of most of its population through industrialization. Between 1981 and 2001 it cut its poverty rate from 53 per cent to 8 per cent, lifting some 400 million people out of poverty (see Ravallion and Chen 2004).

Further, by focusing on the support work of NGOs these lessons reinforce the notion that developing countries are dependent upon Western intergovernmental organizations and NGOs and unable to shape their own futures. A National Geographic lesson covering Oxfam's programme encourages students to value the intervention of Western NGOs and even to promote their work among friends and family without a consideration of the political implications of such intervention, such as the autonomy of indigenous people themselves (this is discussed in greater detail on p. 152). Again, the focus is upon the values that students hold rather than educating them about the causes of poverty, which the lesson plan dismisses as 'complex'.

In many geography curricula, the shift to a stance that is sceptical of industrialization and modernization has been achieved by divorcing the issues from the genuine needs and aspirations of citizens in developing countries. Past approaches to development no doubt also expressed Western interests, but at least they saw industrialization and modernization as keys to a better future for people in the South. Today, many in the West are deaf to the real voices and aspirations of Southern people. In an article discussing the role of Chinese investment in African nations, the author observes that for most citizens in the developing world 'economic rights' and 'rights of subsistence' 'take precedence over personal, individual rights as conceptualised in the West' (Taylor 2007: 11). The article describes how, in contrast to the West, China has frequently respected the sovereignty of developing nations and does not offer aid and investment with strings attached. He Wenping, director of the African Studies Section at the Chinese Academy of Social Sciences in Beijing, is quoted: 'We [China] don't believe that human rights should stand above sovereignty . . . We have a different view on this and African countries share our view' (cited Taylor 2007: 11). Unfortunately, many geography curricula are elevating this Western approach over the real needs and interests of people in developing nations.

Population issues

In the nineteenth century Thomas Malthus raised the prospect that exponential population growth would exceed the arithmetical growth in the land's carrying capacity. Population growth was a topic of concern in geography textbooks with the rise of neo-Malthusianism in the 1960s and 1970s and in recent years has achieved the status of a global issue. Rarely has the topic been dealt with in terms of the labour and resource needs of a given locality or indeed the personal preferences of the people living there. More often, the issue of population reflects Western fears of teeming masses in the developing world or the perception of environmental limits to growth. It has been wrenched from its geographic setting and elevated into a global issue to which all should relate.

During and after decolonization, Western countries were concerned with a 'rising tide of expectations' in Southern nations, which might wreak their revenge on the West for years of colonial exploitation. One way in which this anxiety was expressed was through population (see Furedi 1997). Given that there were vastly more people living in developing countries than developed, the West was concerned about this imbalance, especially given that rates of population growth were also much higher in the South. Hence, local and international schemes to reduce fertility rates were featured in a number of textbooks and generally depicted in positive terms, even though in some instances fertility reduction was achieved through forced sterilization programmes, such as those undertaken in parts of India. Over time the rationale for reducing population has changed and less coercive means proposed for achieving this end are highlighted.

Previous Malthusian apocalyptic predictions have all failed, since they fail to take into account the human potential to transform agricultural production. Since 1961 the global population has doubled, but agricultural production has more than doubled, and has tripled in the developing world (Lomborg 2001). Nevertheless, in the twenty-first century Malthusian arguments are once again abound. Recent advocates of population control surmise that the planet cannot support an ever-growing number of people. Western consumption levels are crassly extrapolated to 6 billion people, ignoring the way in which people continually expand their resource base, the suggestion being once again that resources are a fixed attribute and hence natural resources are being 'used up'.

In Longman's *Global Challenge* population is introduced under the heading 'Shrinking the family' as one of the main 'challenges' humanity faces today. The challenge is 'to lower the fertility rates by voluntary means' (McNaught and Witherick 2001: 91). Quite who is supposed to take up and implement this challenge is not at all clear from the text, although the target population is clearly developing nations. In less economically developed countries 'it is common for women to start bearing children too early and continue for too long. In order to lower fertility rates, education about birth control and more gender equality is required in such countries' (*ibid.*). The text is accompanied by a photograph of a black woman from Burkina Faso breastfeeding a child and a caption asking, 'How many more children will she bear?' (Figure 7.2). But who has decided when it is too early for women to start having children and when is it too late for them to stop? Technology in developed countries is allowing more women to have children much later in life. Why shouldn't women in the South be accorded the same opportunities? And who has the right to tell parents that their family is too large?

That shrinking family sizes in developing countries is considered a worthy objective by the authors of *Global Challenge* is even more surprising, given that they acknowledge that fertility rates are dropping for a variety of reasons across the South, without Western coercion and 'education'. They make note of UN predictions that global population is expected to peak at about 10–11 billion in the mid to late twenty-first century and then *decline*. Even on this level it seems strange that people in the West would be so preoccupied with population growth in the South if the rate of growth is declining of its own accord. Yet *Global Challenge* devotes significant page space to document this issue, including a section detailing the 1994 Cairo conference on Population and Development. The text notes how the conference sought to promote the rights of women

Figure 7.2 A mother breastfeeding her child, Yatenga province, Burkina Faso.
In *Global Challenge* (McNaught and Witherick 2001: 91) the photograph is
accompanied by a caption asking, 'How many more children will she bear?'

(By courtesy of Still Pictures, London; photo copyright Mark Edwards) in developing countries, especially their rights to education and work. Certainly, this is a laudable objective, but upon further reading it becomes clear that a desire to limit reproduction lies behind these goals: 'The thinking behind the Programme was that, with women more in command of their own destinies, the choice of the greater majority would be to have fewer children' (McNaught and Witherick 2001: 112). The text explains this *thinking* of the programme, that if more women have jobs outside the home, have better access to contraception and safe abortion and infant mortality is reduced, then this will reduce the need for and likelihood of larger family sizes. Students are then asked to discuss and write about the conference goals. For example, one activity requires students to research a developing country and 'find out what *progress* has been made in implementing the Cairo conference Programme of Action' (*ibid.*: 113, my italics). But again, in whose eyes is reducing fertility progress? No alternative perspectives being considered on population growth in the South, then!

In fact, especially in the case of most African nations, with the exception of Nigeria, these countries have pretty low population levels, at least by European standards or the density of population across the north-east of the US. Countries with some of the highest population densities in the world include Japan, Singapore, Belgium and Holland. The highest population densities are found in cities such as New York, Mexico City or Mumbai. Yet, in all of these, the living standards are higher than in less densely populated countries and rural parts of the developing world. Hence, there is no direct relationship between population density and wealth. In today's world, if a country cannot feed its people it is not because of the number of people, but the low levels of technology, development and poor political, economic and social organization. India produces enough food to feed its 1.1 billion people; it just fails to adequately organize society in such a way that all have access to this food (de Blij and Muller 2006). In contrast, Manhattan has one of the highest densities in the world accompanied by one of the highest wealth levels. The concept of carrying capacity which supports theories of overpopulation frequently ignores the reality of international trade. Japan and Singapore can support their populations on resource-poor islands because of trade.

National Geographic's Web site also has an example of a lesson examining 'population issues in China and India'. The lesson has students gather population statistics for these two countries using the CIA *Factbook*, read about population issues in both places and decide whether India should adopt a one-child policy, as the Chinese have done. The first part of the lesson focuses on making sure students understand population terms such as birth rate, natural increase and life expectancy. The CIA *Factbook* enables students to compare India's and China's demographic data. Students are told to answer the question 'What do these numbers reveal about China and India?' The suggested assessment activity is to have students write an essay, 'Should India have a one child policy like China's? Why or why not?' Again, there appears to be an underlying assumption that India's population growth is too high. However, the lesson plan does at least consider both sides of the argument. In an extension activity students are asked to consider the economic reasons why people might want to have small families, but also 'Can students think of the reverse scenario, in which it would make more financial sense for a family to have more children?' (Xpeditions Web site, National Geographic Society 2007).

Instead of analysing the geographical setting of its people, population growth as a global issue is viewed through Western ethics of environmental limits. Frequently, geography curricula depict people as polluters, resource consumers and a general burden upon the planet instead of viewing them as a resource. The message given to the up-and-coming generation is that people, and especially those in poor countries, are a part of the problem rather than part of the solution, lending legitimacy to international conferences and organizations to bring pressure to bear on developing countries to lower their population growth.

Trade/industry

Another significant change in the way that geographers are looking at the world today in comparison with the middle decades of the twentieth century is the shift away from a concern with production to that of consumption. As noted above, geography textbooks in the 1950s and 1960s viewed production and its impact upon society in terms of material gain as a positive process. A study of US world geography textbooks from 1950 to 2005 observed the greater consideration given to human consumption of resources in books released in the 1990s or 2000s and less description and analysis of the productive process itself (Standish 2006). How we trade and consume commodities has likewise become a focus of many recent geography curricula in the US and England/Wales. Most textbooks address issues of international trade and the question of national barriers to trade and the regional formation of trade blocs. Most sing the virtues of free trade and its effect on increasing access to markets and enhancing productivity. For instance, Glencoe's *World Geography* includes a quote from Charlene Barshefsky at the National Press Club in Washington, DC: 'an opening world economy has allowed trade to expand fifteen-fold, sparking a six-fold increase in world economic production and a three-fold increase in global per capita incomes' (Boehm 2005: 94).

At the onset of the twenty-first century world trade is portrayed as a global issue in which students themselves can consider their roles as

---

Box 7.3 Sample enquiry questions from the 'People as consumers – the impact of our decisions' theme for the pilot geography GCSE

The questions include:

- What do I buy and why?
- Why do other people buy similar/different things?
- What are some of the spatial consequences of these decisions?
- What are my rights/responsibilities as a consumer? How might they promote a sustainable future?
- What is a product web? Where are the producers/consumers?
- What alternative consumer scenarios are there? Why do different groups prefer different futures? Who gains/loses and where are they located?

(Oxford, Cambridge and RSA 2004: 30–1)

---

consumers. This is the approach taken by the new pilot Oxford, Cambridge and RSA GCSE. One of three themes that students are required to study is entitled 'People as consumers – the impact of our decisions'. The specification document for this examination explains that 'Candidates are asked to see themselves as consumers and to trace the implications of this for places and environments' (Oxford, Cambridge and RSA 2004: 29). To complete this theme, students must follow the production, distribution and marketing of one familiar product, such as Coca-Cola or Nike shoes. The specifications include a number of enquiry questions from which lessons can be developed (Box 7.3).

Clearly there is some interesting geographical knowledge to be pursued here. It is a useful activity to create a detailed product web and learn about the spatial distribution of production and consumption today. This provides some insight into the internationally connected nature of many countries' economies today. However, most of the questions posed for this theme, such as 'What do I buy and why?' have more to do with personal habits, needs and values than geography. Yet in this lesson these questions are being employed to force students to analyse their own consumption and examine the values system upon which it is based. The specifications are quite clear on this matter. They call this process the 'Ethics of Consumption', which means 'examining the consequences of consumers' decisions by analysing the production web' (*ibid*.: 31). Students are expected to find out the spatial, environmental and social implication of purchasing a commodity such as Coca-Cola or Nike shoes. This might include the resources used to make the product as well as the energy consumed and pollution emitted in its transportation, a consideration of the social conditions of the factory/ies that manufactured it, and a breakdown of who gains what income from its sale.

Considering the environmental and cultural impacts of different commodities is also an activity used by some US social studies teachers (see Standish 2006). For example, one teacher at a New Jersey middle school described how she would bring into the classroom a number of products (including an aluminium can, a hamburger container, washing-up liquid and an aerosol can) and talk to the class about the materials used to make them and the different ways they could be disposed of. A lesson plan for this activity can be found on National Geographic's Web site. The lesson 'Where do your possessions come from?' wants students to 'recognize that there are always environmental and human impacts related to the resource extraction process and become more conscious consumers' (Xpeditions Web site, National Geographic Society 2007). The lesson plan suggests that students research the extraction process and environmental and human impacts of producing a favourite possession of theirs. Once their findings have been recorded students are asked to write about their reactions to the things they have learned in the lesson.

Finally, a popular consumption activity explored in some geography lessons today is going on holiday. An activity that used to mean getting away from it all is being presented to students in terms of the ethics of its global consequences in some geography curricula. In *New Key Geography* ecotourism is defined as a sustainable form of tourism, which aims to protect the environment and respect the local culture and customs. The textbook includes a Traveller's Code adapted from a list complied by Friends of Conservation (Box 7.4).

While travel can potentially be an enlightening, refreshing and educational experience, in some geography classes today it has been transformed into a lesson in moral introspection: how students measure up to the latest travel code. Instead of opening the minds of the young to new and unanticipated experiences that challenge the individual traveller, travel codes effectively regulate this experience and seek to control human interaction.

So what are the consequences of the shift from a geographical analysis of a nation's economic resource use and production to the 'geography' of ethical consumption? In modern society, production is usually a social act and one that is active because it seeks to transform natural materials into useful commodities. As such, it has the potential to transform the material and social well-being of a people. Consumption, in contrast, is a generally an individual pursuit and a relatively passive one at that. Despite the claims of ethical consumption, we are relatively powerless as individual

---

Box 7.4 Travellers' code, adapted from a code written by Friends of Conservation

Guidelines for students when travelling abroad:

- When buying holiday souvenirs, remember that local crafts make unusual gifts and help support the local community.
- Resist buying or collecting souvenirs from reefs such as coral, shells and starfish. It contributes to the degradation of the reefs and marine life.
- Buying local clothing, shopping in local outlets and eating local food is a great way of enjoying a country.
- Remember that you are on holiday on someone else's doorstep. Respect the people, culture and the natural surroundings of the countries you visit.
- Leave no litter. As well as being unattractive it can damage fragile environments and have serious consequences on wildlife.

(Waugh and Bushell 2002: 243)

---

consumers to influence either the production process or society more generally. Fair trade goods illustrate the point at hand. In some schools and geography texts, fair trade products are cited as morally superior goods for people to buy. Students are presented with information about the relative costs of buying 'normal' products versus 'fair trade' goods and who gets what in the production supply chain. With fair trade goods the farmer receives an incrementally improved return on their primary product and so presents students with a seemingly positive solution. According to the authors of *Geography: The Global Dimensions*, the advantage of this approach is that it 'encourages pupils to empathise with the producers of agricultural products' (Lambert *et al.* 2004: 25). Yet, in such an activity, there is no evaluation of why a farmer is entirely dependent upon the market value of primary commodities for survival and how that circumstance could be altered through economic development. A few more pennies in the farmer's pocket will not transform their material and social well-being. Again, it avoids the discussion of the need for real development to bring the living standards of farmers and other workers of developing economies up to the levels of those in the West.

Removing the production/consumption process from its broader socio-economic relations prevents students from seeing the bigger picture and understanding the potential of production to raise the material well-being of society in its totality. While ethical consumption probably makes people feel better about what they buy, it also gives the false impression that the world can be changed by shopping.

Responding to disasters

Geography as a discipline that seeks to understand the spatial distribution of human activity and its interaction with the natural world is logically concerned with disasters of both a human and a physical nature. So-called natural disasters provide an opportunity to study the interplay of a challenging natural or political event and how people respond. Disasters and other problems in the developing world became an important feature of geography texts in the postcolonial period as the subject focused on development. In the twenty-first century disasters or crises of various sorts around the globe are presented as important global issues that students need to engage with and respond to, including health issues such as AIDS, malaria or Ebola, civil conflict such as in Sudan, and other natural disasters, including earthquakes, hurricanes, wildfire and landslides. The two examples discussed here are the Asian tsunami of 2004 and malnutrition.

On 26 December 2004 an Asian earthquake and its subsequent tsunami generated a unique response to a natural disaster throughout the developed world. This included historically large donations of financial aid to a single disaster (over $6 billion, according to the BBC), but also a broader sympathetic public response that was to extend into schools themselves. What followed was a flurry of teaching resources and lesson plans designed to educate students about the disaster. While spontaneous expressions of empathy towards fellow human beings in need are to be commended and it is important that schools help young people to make sense of large-scale disasters such as the Asian tsunami, the way that some geographers approached the topic exemplifies some of the problematic aspects of teaching about global issues today. Reviewing some of the geography lessons about the tsunami outlined on Internet Web sites illustrates the point. While some lessons sought to teach students about the tectonic processes that gave rise to the tsunami, the distribution of the waves and their impact on various localities or even about the relief operations and efforts to restore people's lives, others focused on the responses of students themselves, encouraging them to make a personal connection with the disaster even if this wasn't their spontaneous reaction. As Richard Baker explains in a special edition of *Teaching Geography* dedicated to teaching about the tsunami:

> Geography teachers knew they were in a unique position to help students to understand the causes and impacts of the tsunami in terms of tectonic processes, lack of early warning systems and the vulnerability of low-lying coastal communities. But for many . . . this may not have gone far enough. Students and teachers alike found themselves wanting to express their concern, compassion and solidarity across international borders to people they had never met, or known about.
>
> (Baker 2005: 66)

Again, expressing solidarity and compassion towards others is an admirable response to such situations when these emotions are spontaneous and genuine. The problem arises when the emotional responses of students become a pedagogical value and lessons are constructed to manufacture student responses. For instance, Baker proposed some teaching activities (adapted from Oxfam's *Dealing with Disasters*) in relation to the disaster, which he asserts would help students learn about their roles as global citizens. One activity, 'What do we think about disasters?', aims to 'encourage students to consider their own attitudes towards disasters and their causes' (*ibid.*: 67). In the lesson students are given a series of statements on disasters to consider and select one they agree with and one they disagree with. The statements include:

- People who live in regions affected by disasters expect too much from charity. They should do more to help themselves.
- The UK is a rich country. We should help other countries get the things they need.
- There is no such thing as a 'natural disaster'. It is always human causes that turn a natural event into a disaster.
- We should pay as much attention to the disasters of lives lost every day through poverty as we do to natural disasters such as earthquakes and tsunamis.

(ibid.)

The lesson activity then suggests that students share their choices and reasons for them with another group or the whole class. The lesson finishes with some teacher-led questions such as 'Where do our attitudes and opinions about disasters come from?' and 'How can we get other sources of information?' (*ibid.*: 67). A follow-up lesson by Baker looks at 'How we can respond?' Here, students consider a range of suggested responses to the disaster such as donating to NGOs working in the affected regions, making rich countries trade more fairly with poor ones and sending experts from Britain to countries affected by disasters to show people how to solve their problems. Again, they are asked to consider which they think are likely to be more effective and to share their ideas.

A second article by Diane Swift in the same edition of *Teaching Geography* provides lesson activities designed to make a link between students' lives and the tsunami disaster. This, she argues, demands 'ethical teaching approaches' as 'Some students find it challenging to connect their lives with the areas that have been affected by a disaster' (Swift 2005: 78, 80). Swift suggests that teachers discuss the concepts of home and identity on a personal scale using a resource such as the 'Photo journal of a Sri Lankan survivor' from the BBC website; which can be accessed here: http://news. bbc.co.uk/2/shared/spl/hi/picture_gallery/04/south_asia_sri_lankan_ts unami_survivor/html/1.stm. The following tasks are then proposed for the class:

- Students use the images and captions from the photo-journal together with a map showing the location of the images to produce a PowerPoint presentation on the human emotions and concerns.
- In order to tease out the connections between their lives and those of the people affected, students select one image from the journal and use the 'What has this got to do with me?' frame [Figure 7.3].
- A second challenge for the students would be to consider the dilemma faced by tourists in the aftermath of the tsunami – 'Should we go on holiday to Thailand or not?'

(Swift 2005: 80)

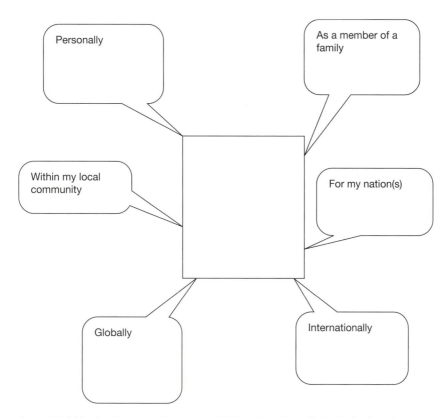

Figure 7.3 'What's this got to do with me?' Worksheet from D. Swift, 'Linking Lives through Disaster and Recovery', *Teaching Geography*, 30 (2), 2005: 78–82

(By courtesy of the Geographical Association, Sheffield)

Clearly, the educational focus is on the relevance of the disaster to students themselves rather than the victims and their locality. They may spend a lot of time thinking about how they feel about the disaster and how they might be able to respond personally, but this raises questions about what they are learning about the spatial and human impact of the tsunami itself.

A further example comes from National Geographic's online lesson plans. The lesson entitled 'Addressing world hunger' is designed for middle-school students (aged eleven to fourteen) and fulfils the national standard 18: How to apply geography to interpret the present and plan for the future. Its purpose is to introduce students to programmes that address world hunger and provide them with 'a few ideas for dealing with the problem and to encourage them to formulate some ideas of their own' (Xpeditions Web site, National Geographic Society 2007). The lesson plan cautions teachers that this is a complex issue and that the lesson does not attempt to provide students with a thorough understanding of world hunger (which is something the students clearly should learn about!).

The suggested opening of the lesson plan is to ask students to name some reasons why they think people go hungry and also why hunger is still a problem in many parts of the world today. The lesson develops with students using the Internet to explore and write about the work of the following NGOs: Future Harvest, Heifer International, Oxfam and the United Nations World Food Program. Next, students are asked to read some articles and Web sites in relations to hunger relief agencies. One of these articles, 'National Geographic News: Agriculture, biodiversity protection must coexist in conservation, study says', informs students of the threat to biodiversity of clearing land for agricultural use. In place of deforestation, the article discusses Conservation International's schemes for farmers to work the land and simultaneously protect species diversity.

One of the teaching resources from Oxfam is its micro-financing schemes in Senegal, discussed in the section on development above. Once the schemes have been introduced it is suggested that the class discuss the benefits of and problems with the schemes proposed in the articles, such as why giving livestock is supposedly superior to giving money. Finally, students are set the following assignment:

> Ask students to imagine that a friend or relative has said to them 'It's such a pity that so many people are hungry in the world, but what can be done? It seems hopeless to me.' Ask students to write statements they would make to this person. Their statements should describe some of the activities that may help to alleviate world hunger.
> (Xpeditions Web site, National Geographic Society 2007)

There are some positives and negatives in this National Geographic lesson. It is certainly important for students to learn about regions where people are malnourished and what is being done to help them. However, the emphasis of this lesson is on the work of NGOs and sustaining rather than transforming lives in the developing world. Giving livestock may or may not help a farmer in the here and now, but it will not raise the productive forces of their society.

There are two main problems with the way geography curricula have elevated disasters into global issues for students to 'relate to'. The first is that the focus of the lesson is on the students, their thoughts, feelings and potential actions towards the disaster instead of learning about how the geography of a locality helps us to understand disasters, from both a physical and a human perspective. Second, it can be argued that it is an invasion of students' privacy to be required to air their personal emotional feelings about a problem that they may or may not care about. What happens to the student who says he feels no emotional response to the Asian tsunami disaster or people starving in a foreign country? In effect, young people's emotions and actions are being managed by teachers who are not trained in such matters and certainly such geography lessons have crossed a line from education to moral instruction.

What do students learn from global issues?

While global issues teach students about some important and interesting events and problems occurring around the world today, they are problematic in terms of their approaches to education and politics. In educational terms global issues turn geography into lessons in self-analysis. As noted in the examples above, frequently global issues have become divorced from the geographical and political context in which they arose. Instead of seeking to understand the problems faced by people in their physical and human settings they are reinterpreted as problems we in the West should have a stake in. In place of trying to understand the lives of individuals *in situ* and the challenges they face, global issues become viewed from a Western perspective. In the classroom students are encouraged to make a connection with these global issues and evaluate their personal values and behaviour according to Western ethics of environment conservation, cultural tolerance, social justice, empathy and human rights instead of political rights. But it is important to recognize that this is not geography. The only insight it provides is into the misanthropic nature of contemporary Western society and how its values are being exported across the world. It teaches students little about the everyday problems and challenges people face in their home regions and countries. Even when the issue touches the everyday lives of citizens, like poverty or a health problem, it is approached in terms of Western aid and intervention rather than how people can transform their own lives for the better.

Not only have global issues been ripped from their geographic settings, but the approach to learning about these issues elevates personal ethics, emotional responses and action over knowledge and understanding. As stated in many geography curricula and texts cited above, the main goal of exploring global issues is to encourage students to examine their own values, attitudes and even behaviour. This in and of itself is a methodological problem. It places the focus of education on what the students in the class think about issues, not an exploration of the issues for the sake of understanding the causes and management of the problem itself. This was clear for example in the National Geographic lesson plan on world hunger and its dismissal of the causes of poverty as 'complex' and beyond the scope of the lesson. Instead, the lesson sought to encourage students to 'make a connection' and find a way to 'make a difference'.

As noted in the previous chapter, the approach to teaching about global issues stresses empathy and participation over intellectual comprehension. Emotional learning has gained credence in schools through the notion of emotional intelligence, popularized by Howard Gardner in *Frames of Mind* (1983) and *Intelligence Reframed* (2000) and Daniel Goldman in *Emotional Intelligence: Why it can matter more than IQ* (1995). Gardner cited eight different intelligences, including bodily-kinaesthetic and interpersonal. Where these ideas have taken hold in schools, mastery of emotions and interpersonal skills are taught alongside or within subjects such as geography. This is problematic for two reasons. First, classrooms are not counselling centres. If emotional responses are becoming part of the curriculum then does this mean that students are evaluated on their feelings? Are young people who choose not to display their emotions penalized? It can be argued that this equates to an invasion of young people's private conscience by teachers who are not trained to teach young people to manage their emotions. Second, it is a mistake to equate being in control of one's emotions with intelligence. The former is a skill we learn as we grow up through everyday experience and is something all adults accomplish to a greater or lesser extent. It is not an intellectual pursuit. In contrast, mastery of subjects such as geography necessitates abstract thought and conceptual comprehension at multiple and sequential levels, as well as mastery of geographical skills and general geographical knowledge. A modicum of geographical knowledge and skills can be acquired through everyday travel, but higher orders of comprehension will never be acquired without methodical study. Geography classes that focus on these global issues may well produce students who are emotionally literate, but they will be geography-shy.

It should also be clear from the examples above that, despite its advocates' claims, global issues do not lead to thorough examination of the ethical possibilities posed by the given issue. While it could be argued that geography is not the place to explore ethics, there are times when the

subject throws up genuine dilemmas, such as development versus conservation, different cultural approaches to problems, intervention versus
sovereignty, land use conflicts, and so forth. In pursuing such ethical
questions geography can make a contribution to the humanities in their
quest to understand the human condition. However, as illustrated above,
the purpose of global issues is not to challenge students to question the
prevailing moral outlook, to seek to understand people in their geographical settings and gain insight into that which makes us human. Instead,
global issues reinforce the very rigid moral mindset predicated upon
contemporary Western ethics of environment responsibility, cultural
tolerance, empathy and social justice.

A second outcome of the psychological approach to solving global
issues is the underlying moral mission. While proponents of global issues
like to think that they are liberating young people by encouraging
them to examine their values systems and they maintain that students are
not coerced into a particular values perspective, there is evidently a strong
moral imperative behind the design of lessons about global issues. In the
lessons about the Asian tsunami there is an underlying assumption that
students should respond and make a connection with survivors. While
this might be a spontaneous response of some students, what about those
that don't feel a connection and just want to get on with learning geography? For all the rhetoric of critical thinking in the geographical education
literature the opposite is in fact the case: classes such as these transform
an educational opportunity into a lesson in morality whereby the student's
emotional and behavioural reactions are being directed by teachers. This
contravenes the idea of a liberal education in which individuals would be
free to determine their own morality.

Can global issues be solved through education?

While global issues have become a feature of international public discourse
in the post-Cold War era, it is worth while interrogating the term and
taking a closer look at what is being accomplished in pursuit of global
solutions. Are global issues really about changing the world or, as will be
argued here, are they more concerned with changing individuals?

Prior to this recent global era, nation states were seen as the main
vehicles through which issues would be addressed, as they were the form
in which the will of citizens could be expressed. This collective will gave
nation states political power and, combined with the apparatus of the
state, governments could effect change domestically and seek to exert
influence internationally. But when issues are viewed in global rather than
national terms, the power of each state to effect change is curtailed. While
some problems, such as global warming, may truly be global in nature
(i.e. necessitating an internationally co-ordinated response), others such

as civil conflict, health issues, poverty, trade, pollution, population, development and even most disasters can be addressed through national policies. Calling them 'global issues' does two things: it makes them into larger issues, which may or may not to be solved, and it blurs the lines of political responsibility for addressing problems. Hence issues become divorced from political responsibility (see Chandler 2004). At times this has opened up the possibility for Western states to intervene in foreign countries. But because this intervention is not tied to political responsibility western nations can escape accountability for their actions.

As noted in Chapter 3, the role of nation states in addressing global issues today is *perceived* as limited, which is not the same thing as *being* limited. International interdependence of economies, for instance, may well reduce the range and effect of national government intervention, but it does not render it impotent. Globalization is as much about a change in how we see the world as it is material change itself (see Chandler 2004). When something like trade becomes viewed in global terms and jobs are lost to outsourcing, governments have been able to claim that they are powerless against the 'forces of globalization'. Similarly, poverty has become a global problem, with many developed nations signing up to meet the Millennium Development Goals or to Make Poverty History. Yet, because these campaigns embrace sustainable development rather than real development, they end up being more self-serving than genuine attempts to raise the productive forces of developing nations and poverty remains at large. The 'End poverty' campaigns keep rolling on and signing people up, but the problem never goes away. Targets go unmet, but without consequence because action was taken without political responsibility.

The international initiatives to slow global warming can also be criticized for being more of a moralistic enterprise than a genuine attempt to reduce temperatures. If its advocates really wanted to slow global warming, then they would put their collective energies into scientific and technical research rather than telling people that they have to change their lifestyles. With global issues, the problem is defined as humanity rather than something out there that we can fix. Hence, the solution is that we need to change ourselves rather than the world around us.

This is why the theme of interdependence has become so popular for geography curricula today. It fits with the contemporary misanthropic mindset that increasingly sees people as the source of the world's problems rather than the resolution or at least that the solution is to fix ourselves. Here, social and political problems have become transposed to the level of the individual psyche. Global inequality can be relieved if we pay a 'fair' price for commodities and support campaigns to end poverty; global warming and environmental damage can be reduced if we buy local, environmentally friendly products, travel less, consume less and undertake only sustainable development; cultural conflict will be alleviated if we all learn to have respect for other cultures and traditions and develop culturally sensitive 'skills'; the impact of disasters can be reduced if we all give a bit more and support relief agencies.

With global issues today there is disregard for the political, economic, social and even environmental contexts that gave rise to these problems. Global issues are seen as too complex or too large to be solved through technical, political or economic means. The only solution proposed is that we change ourselves. For example, simplistic production/consumption scenarios in curricula portray social processes as a matter of individual conscience. This disingenuously leaves young people with the impression that altering their shopping habits can change the world for the better. But of course the world is more complex than this. The sum of individual change does not equate with social change (Habermas 1996). To effect meaningful social change necessitates the collective forces of society to redirect its productive resources towards the designated problem. For example, the physical environments of most developed countries are cleaner than they have been for generations because people decided to clean up much industrial production and waste.

One outcome of reinterpreting social and political issues as problems of individual attitudes is to confuse young people about the nature and mechanisms of social change. To teach students that personal change can result in social change is deceitful about how the world works and severs the link between cause and effect. World hunger, global warming, underdevelopment, cultural conflict, rising population levels or health issues will not just disappear because individuals think differently about them and modify their behaviour. There are social, economic, political and environmental causes for these issues that need to be addressed if meaningful change is to be realized. Several studies make note of how ineffective moral education campaigns are at effecting change (Trenholm *et al.* 2007). The likely outcome of learning about global issues is that young people will become even more disillusioned than they already are with the potential of humanity to change the world for the better.

A further concern with global issues in the curriculum is that political problems from the adult world are being heaped upon the shoulders of children. As noted above, with globalization political leaders have sometimes evaded political responsibility for problems they face by elevating them into global issues beyond the scope of the nation state. As the adult world is shying away from the formal political system with its inherent checks and balances, so 'responsibility' is placed at the feet of all, including children. But of course children are children and not adults because they have yet to reach social, emotional and intellectual maturity and thus are rightly denied political responsibility. Is it not unfair to ask children to shoulder the burden of responsibility for issues they do not fully grasp and without a comprehension of the social and political systems of power?

Concluding comments

The objective of this chapter has been to examine the character of global issues as they appear in geography curricula in the US and England/Wales. Several global issues were selected as examples for this exercise. The chapter concludes that global issues do not enable students to embrace multiple perspectives. In fact, they do the opposite: they impose a new Western perspective upon students and the rest of the world. By removing issues from their political and geographical contexts and turning them into global issues, geography curricula are reinterpreting issues through the prism of the degraded contemporary Western political culture. Here, issues are viewed less in political terms, and more as values which stand above politics, including environmental values, social justice, cultural tolerance, respect for an Other and empathy. These values discourage people from viewing issues in political terms and instead portray a negative vision of the potential of people to solve issues through political frameworks in the face of environmental and cultural constraints. Instead they resolve that global issues are best addressed through individual change. In geography curricula the goal is thus to encourage students to examine their own values with respect to global ethics and internalize its value system. This is an authoritarian and dehumanizing trend in that the state is seeking to direct the values of students and deny them a liberal education.

Suggested further reading

Students should read some contrasting opinions on contemporary issues, so that they are aware of the contested nature of global issues and values.

Baker, R. (2005) 'Global Catastrophe, Global Response', *Teaching Geography*, 30 (2): 66–9.

Butcher, J. (2003) *The Moralisation of Tourism: Sun, Sand and . . . Saving the World*, London: Routledge.

Chandler, D. (2004) *Constructing Global Civil Society: Morality and Power in International Relations*, Basingstoke: Palgrave Macmillan.

Lomborg, B. (2001) *The Skeptical Environmentalist: Measuring the Real State of the World*, Cambridge: Cambridge University Press.

National Geographic (2007) Geography Standards in Your Classroom: Lesson Plans. http://www.nationalgeographic.com/xpeditions/lessons/18/g68/tghunger. html (visited 18 July 2007).

Simon, J. (1981) *The Ultimate Resource*, Princeton, NJ: Princeton University Press.

Swift, D. (2005) 'Linking Lives through Disaster and Recovery', *Teaching Geography*, 30 (2): 78–81.

Taylor, I. (2007) 'Unpacking China's Resource Diplomacy in Africa', in H. Melber (ed.) *China in Africa*, Current African Issues, 33: Uppsala, Nordiska Africainstitute.

Vaux, T. (2001) *The Selfish Altruist*. London: Earthscan.

Chapter 8

Global advocacy and the cosmopolitan citizen in the curriculum

Contributing material from Vanessa Pupavac

KEY QUESTIONS

1 Can children act as citizens with political responsibility before they have achieved intellectual and emotional maturity?
2 How do global citizens effect social and political change without a political framework and relationship to centres of power?
3 What are the intellectual and emotional consequences for children of blurring the lines between politics and education?

In order to understand how the introduction of global perspectives has changed the geography curriculum it is necessary to examine the political background to the transition from the national perspective, which informed the evolution of the discipline as described in Chapter 1. Such an analysis of the political framework behind global issues is all too absent in most texts that have embraced this approach. Again, this is not to say that global perspectives or global citizenship inform the teaching of geography in all classrooms of the US and England/Wales. Many well-trained geography teachers continue to approach the study of culture and issues in their geographical contexts. However, global perspectives have become the main approach to the subject adopted by leading organizations such as the National Geographic Society and the Geographical Association, as well as many teachers and textbook publishers. As such, its model of education and conception of the embryonic citizen need to be addressed.

This chapter will show how, in addition to a change of scale, a more fundamental transition is taking place than the shift from national to global citizenship concerns. In modern global citizenship the educational focus has changed from the acquisition of subject knowledge to learning about social issues that inform the values and attitudes of students themselves.

In fact, the promotion of global citizenship education is premised on the notion of a cosmopolitan political subject and challenges many of the traditional assumptions held about the nature and purpose of education in a liberal democracy. In many ways, it is about its replacement with a new model of education, based upon a different notion of the individual. While the democratic model was premised upon the development of a politically autonomous individual, the cosmopolitan citizen needs 'guidance' to negotiate 'complex' moral issues like sustainability (Wood 2005).

It is also important to further critique the assumptions behind the global approach to solving issues. Do all global citizens play an equal part in both setting and solving the issues agenda or are some more influential than others? Who are the main actors in addressing global issues and how do problems get resolved? If children are being viewed as actors in global issues then what is their role and how is that different from the role of adults?

From national politics to global advocacy

The growing popularity of global citizenship and global ethics has mirrored declining attachment to the nation state, traditional political parties and the nation framework for civic engagement (see Sassens 2002). As should be clear from Chapter 2, this is a long-term trend, which contributed to the anti-establishment politics and the crisis of citizenship education in the 1960s and 1970s. In this section the transition from national politics to global advocacy will be explored.

While the characteristics of a state include a land territory, permanent resident population, government, organized economy, a circulation system, sovereignty and recognition (Glassner and de Blij, cited in Knight 1982: 517), Knight noted that territory by itself is passive; that it is human actions and ideas that give the territory meaning. He observed, 'Clearly, common territory by itself is not enough, for there must also be a complex set of other factors that physically, socially, and especially psychologically link the people who live in different parts of that territory' (Knight 1982: 520). These factors that link people to the nation state are frequently called centripetal forces in geography texts. Similarly, Hartshorne (1950) argued that the state must have a *raison d'être* and that this is the most basic centripetal force. Ladis Kistoff developed this idea further, suggesting that the *raison d'être* was supported at two levels: a *spiritus movens* or national idea, which is 'a semi-conscious tendency rooted in the collective psychology of national tradition and inhibitions', the other being the state idea, which is 'a philosophical and moral conception of the state's destiny and mission in terms of human teleology' (Kistoff, cited in Knight, 1982: 522). Kistoff suggested that the state idea was generated by the political and intellectual elite while the national idea pertained more to the masses, was more amorphous, and not necessarily political.

There are certainly many material and social changes in the post-World War II period that illustrate the rise of transnationalism. These include the growth of supranational organizations and transnational bodies, increased international migration, greater international economic integration and trade, improved global communications systems, social models of pluralism and multiculturalism, the growing importance of non-governmental organizations as political actors, secessionist movements, and new social movements promoting alternative theories of identity and citizenship. Yet perhaps the most significant change is that nation states have become increasingly redundant as a system of leadership for the national elites who invented them. Declining levels of participation in traditional political life and attachment to the public life of the nation by the vast majority of US and UK citizens in the latter decades of the twentieth century are an implicit recognition that the public view the political system as less able to advance their lot in society (Furedi 2004).

At first glance it appears paradoxical that Western liberalism should be in political crisis in the wake of its triumph against its Cold War enemy and the demise of rival ideologies. Here liberalism is being broadly interpreted to mean the West's core political philosophy, founded upon the individual and individual freedoms, and the privatization of beliefs and conscience. Liberalism's crisis emerges from the intrinsic contradictions in a civic ethos elevating the individual (Hunter 2001). Its success depends upon individuals taking their private ideas into the public realm. Liberalism's demise has been analysed in terms of 'the fall of public man' (Sennett 1976), 'the culture of narcissism' (Lasch 1984), 'the end of history' (Fukuyama 1992), 'demoralization' (Ferve 2000), 'the emotivist ethos' (Nolan 1998) and 'therapy culture' (Furedi 2004).

How does a civic ethos revolving around individual realization guard against citizens turning inward and disengaging from the public sphere? Historically the risks of liberalism's civic ethos imploding have been deferred in its crusade against tradition and rival political ideologies or in its defensive restitution of tradition along with liberalism's international mission. Political contestation at the state and national levels was intimately tied to foreign policy, which in turn helped shape a sense of national coherence and identity. As Alexander Gourevitch notes, 'The idea of national interest is dependent upon domestic conflict. It is only when the fundamental organizing institutions of society are challenged that the question of national interest poses itself in a consistent way' (Gourevitch 2007: 64). In other words, problems in the international arena provoke a discussion about how to respond to them. Conflicting viewpoints on such matters help to clarify what the nation stands for both domestically and in its international vision. Thus, considering foreign policy objectives in the name of national interest 'mediates a broader, political conflict over what it is that must be preserved' (ibid.), while the state functions as an arbiter between competing political camps and acts in the interest of society as a whole. Here, Gourevitch is emphasizing that foreign policy also plays a constitutive role with regard to domestic politics and that it is also constituted by it.

In the post-World War II period Cold War ideology played an important role in legitimizing national elites, sustaining the political framework of liberal democracy, including people's engagement in the public sphere. Zaki Laïdi (1998) describes how both communism and capitalism sustained *meaning* for people, both through their claims to be a potentially universal system and through material and social advance for their citizens (although this was increasingly difficult for the Soviet Union to sustain with time). He explains:

> The will and capacity of the two Timons to provide meaning indisputably added to their respective power. To 'provide meaning' was to convey explicitly their claims to be able to decode, advance and disseminate – to decode the word; to advance beyond present reality, 'neither halting nor resting' (Hegel), seeking an end that is deemed better, and to disseminate it to others, not because of plain simple national ambition, but because of a claim to universalism.
>
> (Laïdi 1998: 18)

Laïdi identifies three aspects to meaning in the political context. It encompasses:

> the triple notion of foundation, unity and final goal: 'foundation' meaning the basic principle on which a collective project depends; 'unity' meaning that 'world images' are collected into a coherent plan of the whole; and 'end' or 'final goal', meaning projection towards an elsewhere that is deemed better.'
>
> (ibid.: 1).

Laïdi's significant point is to explain how political ideology, as channelled though the state, provided a sense of purpose and meaning to the everyday lives of individuals. Most citizens collectively shared in a vision of a better tomorrow and had faith in their political system to deliver it. This gave broader meaning to everyday acts of life like work, parenting, education, worship and even cultural activities like sport. These acts existed within a wider social and ideological framework of understanding, bridging the gap between the self and society. The legitimacy of states in both the East and the West was founded upon their claim to advance modernity in every sphere. Despite its destructive tendencies, Cold War politics instilled in Western societies a sense of purpose, invigorated progressive politics and checked cultural tendencies towards disenchantment, trivialization and meaninglessness, which have come to the fore since its end (Hammond 2007). These observations help to account for the magnitude of perceived change and the crisis of meaning, precipitated by the end of the Cold War, not only for former communist countries but states in the West have also lost their central rationale and their primary means of uniting their citizens.

In the post-Cold War era, what is to prevent liberalism's descent from the public into the personal in the wake of de-traditionalism and secularization and its triumph over alternative ideologies? If there are no longer big competing political visions to struggle over in political life, then contestation between parties becomes narrowed to more technical discussions as to who are better professional managers and political involvement for the mass of the population becomes redundant. Political fragmentation and disorientation are evident across the political spectrum, as old ties and allegiances, fostered by the previous political divisions, have crumbled. When domestic political conflict has receded it can no longer play a constitutive role with regard to foreign policy. The result is international policy lacking attachment to any vision of social advancement, a loss of *telos* (Laïdi 1998).

Global advocacy has represented an important way of trying to counter liberalism's demoralization at home by maintaining a sense of mission through liberalizing the South. While for most of the World War II period the Western world was highly defensive about political intervention in developing nations, this began to change in the 1980s as humanitarian organizations perceived the need to make their work more political and long-term in order for it to have a more lasting effect (Duffield 2001). The rise in the number of NGOs since the early 1980s has been remarkable. While there were only a few hundred NGOs in the 1970s, by the mid-1990s there were an estimated 29,000 (Duffield 2001). However, Duffield also notes that some twenty American and European NGOs accounted for 75 per cent of all relief expenditure. The political clout and niche these NGOs have carved for themselves in the post-Cold War international framework should not be underestimated. As politics becomes increasingly conducted above and below the nation state, the term 'government' has not surprisingly been replaced with 'governance' in both national and international discourse.

Western governments have found it nearly impossible to bring about a renewed feeling of national purpose since the end of the Cold War and frequently have recoiled from doing so. The reaction to the attacks on the World Trade Center and the Pentagon at first glance appears as an anomaly, yet any renewed sense of national purpose in the US was short-lived (Brooks 2000). It wasn't long before President Bush went to great lengths to emphasize the 'international' constitution of the interventions in Afghanistan and Iraq and any talk of defending national self-interest was replaced with that of winning freedom and democracy for the Iraqi people. Samuel Huntington suggests that in the US business and political leaders have been busy 'Merging America with the World' (Huntington, 2004). By this he means that they no longer identify what they do in relation to a national project or mission. Instead, they view their roles globally. In 1996 Ralph Nader wrote to the chief executive officers of 100 top American corporations to urge them to show their support for 'the country that bred them, built them, subsidized them, and defended them', only to find that many were dismissive of the suggestion (Huntington 2004: 7). As the representative from Ford explained: 'As a multinational . . . Ford in its largest sense is an Australian company in Australia, a British company in the United Kingdom, a German company in Germany' (*ibid.*). In effect, the answer to the crisis of national identity has been to devise a new 'global' mission, albeit one born of contemporary Western crisis.

The expansion and political importance of intergovernmental bodies such as the United Nations and the European Union exemplify this process. Today, the term the 'international community' is frequently cited to lend legitimacy to causes and initiatives. Where once international relations meant the representation of national self-interest, today collective interests are increasingly identified at the international level, constituting the very subjectivity of national leaders in the absence of a connection with a mass political base (Chandler 2005).

Whereas humanitarian work was becoming politicized in the 1990s, Western politicians moved into the space of humanitarianism, leading to the merging of development and security (Chandler 2002; Duffield 2007a). It is striking how Western policy makers or would-be policy makers have been drawn to global advocacy in the last decade, from Bill Clinton to Carl Bildt to Tony Blair. Now military interventions into countries such as Rwanda, Bosnia, Somalia and Kosovo were being cast in terms of human rights and protecting minorities as opposed to self-interest. Where Western leaders appeared impotent to change the political face of their nation states in the international arena, they have found new purpose and the possibility of appearing to 'do good' in the world.

A main attraction of global citizenship education is its elevation of the individual over states inherent in the notion of universal human rights (see Pupavac 2005). While national citizenship is seen as promoting division, global citizenship portrays all as equal, thus enhancing unity. Exponents of global citizenship attack the traditional geopolitical conception of international society founded on the principle of national sovereignty and states as the only legitimate actors. They have condemned the traditional geopolitical paradigm as lacking in morality for giving paramountcy to national politics over global morality (Allott 2001; Held 2002; Midgely 1999) and treating 'the survival and prospering of each human individual and all-humanity' as 'secondary, in practice and theory' (Allott 2001: 77). Global ethicists assert a common humanity and universal moral claims in opposition to the particularist morality in the traditional state-centric model, which has no place for non-state actors or ethical claims transcending national interest (Allott 2001; Falk 1995; Held 2002). Instead of geopolitics, advocates have called for humane governance in which the voices of individuals and non-state actors may be heard in international relations and human rights claims may challenge assertions of national sovereignty and non-interference in the internal affairs of states (Falk 1995; Roth 1999). This new system of governance has been labelled a global civil society by some (Kaldor 2001) and is heralded as a more progressive approach to international relations. Global citizenship is envisaged as creating a new, more inclusive space for political action beyond traditional electoral politics for marginalized voices and social movements. A key theme has been the entrenchment of international human rights to which those lacking rights nationally can appeal.

However, despite its claims to offer a new and progressive era, global advocacy grows out of the demoralized Western political culture identified above. Globalization's promise of a New World Order fails to live up to expectations because it lacks a vision, a leader, a final goal and belief in collective action for change. Because grand schemes for social transformation have been discredited through the end of ideology, this global era is characterized by a 'total absence of perspective' and thus has little direct meaning for people's lives (Laïdi 1998: 11). Hence, it is not the first stage in a new political project, 'rather its negation' (*ibid.*). Global advocacy then is focused not on creating a better future, but on sustaining the present, in which citizens become 'slaves of emergency' (*ibid.*). Nevertheless, this can be achieved only by further undermining the democratic foundations of its system.

For instance, one consequence of global advocacy and global political intervention is to undermine the right of national sovereignty and erode further the legitimacy of the nation state. Today, global politics has all but killed the right of nation states to determine what takes place within their national boundaries. Further, liberalism's demoralization domestically impacts on the character of its global mission: inhibiting its aspirations for the South and the capacity of its global advocacy to counter liberalism's crisis at home (Pupavac 2005). The demoralized character of liberalism's global mission likewise informs 'global perspectives' in the geography curriculum and its vision of global justice and political subjectivity. These concerns will be addressed below.

The foundations of national citizenship

It order to make apparent how the global approach to citizenship is different from that under the nation state it is necessary to recall the origins and principles upon which the latter was founded. The origins of modern citizenship date back to Ancient Greece and Rome and particularly the writings of Aristotle. The Latin words *civitas* or *civis* denote membership of a city-state. In turn, *civitas* was derived from the Greek concept of *polites*, meaning a person who rules and is ruled. In Aristotle's conception of a citizen there was no distinction between citizens and the state: the state was the aggregate of citizens. It was political engagement that gave meaning to citizenship in Aristotle's eyes. Aristotle argued that what distinguishes the citizen proper from all others is his 'administration of justice and in the holding office' (Aristotle III, see Barker 1958: 92). Holding office here does not necessarily mean an office of state, but some form of public duty, such as service on juries. For Aristotle the origins of citizenship lie in human nature and the need to associate in order to effect social change: 'men have a desire for life together, even when they have no need for each other's help . . . The good life is indeed a chief end, both communally and individually; but they form and continue to maintain a political association for the sake of life itself' (Aristotle III, see Harrington 2005: 187).

Essential to Aristotle's view of the citizens and their political role were the capacities of citizens themselves. In order to pass judgement on matters of ethics, economics, virtue and so forth, a citizen was expected to be educated and wise:

> The citizen is not merely an inhabitant of the state, nor simply a member of a politically privileged class; he is the essence of the state's ability to achieve the greatest measure of happiness and virtue as a community. For this, the citizen must have the leisure to devote himself to the educative cultural pursuits which facilitate his understanding of virtue.
>
> (cited in Harrington 2005, *Politics* VII: 415)

Of course this meant that most city dwellers, especially slaves, the poor and women, could not be citizens in Aristotle's time, because they had neither the time nor the resources for 'educative cultural pursuits'. As Ralph Harrington observes, this meant that 'Those who are incapable of sharing a perception of justice, good and evil, those who cannot participate in the processes of discussion, deliberation and decision which lie at the heart of the human political association, cannot be admitted to the citizen body' (Harrington 2005).

The key points to take from Aristotle's theory of politics are that citizenship was an integral part of membership and participation in a larger political body, that to be a citizen one had to possess a certain degree of education and cultural appreciation and finally that the state or 'civic body in every *polis* is sovereign' (Aristotle III, see Barker 1958: 114).

The expansion of the Roman Empire led to new ideas about citizenship as the rule of Rome was extended across Europe. Augustine talked of a City of God that extended across the Roman Empire (Isin and Turner 2002). Augustine may well have been the first person to conceptualize global citizenship, albeit of an incomplete globe.

Aristotle's concept of citizenship weighed heavily upon the thinking of modern scholars during the evolution of European nation states from the sixteenth century onwards. Of course in large nation states citizens could not practically run the state in the same way Aristotle conceived of it, but otherwise the modern notion of the nation state was founded upon the idea that it was constituted through its citizen body. In particular that citizenship was an esteemed position carrying responsibilities for the political and moral direction of the nation.

With the rise of capitalism and with it civil society in seventeenth-century Europe a clearer concept of citizenship was articulated by writers such as John Locke and Thomas Hobbes. Locke saw citizenship as a liberal tradition, which elevated the role of the individual. Here, the individual was depicted as endowed with reason (usually understood as the voice of God at that time) and generally acting as a rational being. Hobbes emphasized the bond between the individual as a political subject and the nation state as a sovereign expression of that political will (Burchell 2002). Thus citizenship in modern times came to be understood by many as a relationship between the individual in society and the governing body. These ideas, derived from Aristotle, informed the English Bill of Rights (1689) which set out the civil and political rights of Englishmen and restricted the power of the monarchy *vis-à-vis* Parliament.

During the Enlightenment period the idea of rights as naturally endowed, and hence independent of a political authority, grew in popularity. All humans were regarded as possessing rights simply by way of their existence as human beings. This mirrored the trend towards recognition of formal equality between all men, which in turn informed the movement to abolish slavery. Nevertheless, the American and French revolutions at the end of the eighteenth century reinforced the notion of citizenship as a contractual relationship between members of society and the state. Two historic documents illustrate this point: the US Declaration of Independence, which drew heavy from the English Bill of Rights, and, in France, the Declaration of the Rights of Man.

In the nineteenth century a strong tradition of citizenship and political participation continued to develop in Western societies. Tocqueville noted the benefits of public engagement for both the community and the individual. He asserted that republican citizenship was both integrative and educative (Dagger 2002). Through public engagement Tocqueville saw individuals being integrated into the community and learning personal virtue and integrity through the habits of participation. Hence, in some contexts, citizenship means more than simply political and legal rights. The term is also used to denote membership of some organization, such as a church or school, and in relation to a standard of moral conduct (Smith 2002). This republican model of citizenship became dominant in the US whereby a strong common ethos prevailed. This tradition is perhaps best epitomized by the town meeting, in which a community came together to make collective decisions. The European model of citizenship followed a stronger liberal tradition. John Stuart Mill advocated individuality and self-interest as the source of social progress and well-being. 'Mill insisted that untrammelled freedom of individual thought, inquiry, worship, and expression is the surest path to truth and social improvement,' reports Schuck (2002: 131).

In both the American and the French republics the idea of educating young people to become active citizens began to take hold. Education was seen as fundamental for individuals to be able to hold the office of citizen. With a degree of separation between most citizens and the state, Thomas Jefferson spoke of the need for citizens to keep the state in check, given the concentration of power at its disposal. Hence, he saw education as a tool to arm citizens with 'knowledge and literature' to protect themselves from the tyranny of the state (Ravitch and Viteritti 2001). In the second half of the nineteenth century public education was expanded to all sections of society in the US and UK. During this period, education was seen as an essential part of inducting each new generation into the national culture. In practice this meant instilling a sense of patriotism, discipline and a basic level of education for all members of society to be able to participate in a liberal democracy both economically and politically, although it wasn't until the twentieth century that women were given suffrage and the civil rights movement led to equal political rights for minorities. Schools in both the US and England/Wales taught students to respect the values upon which the nation was based: freedom, democracy, capitalism, Christian virtues, patriotism, some of which clashed with its libertarian ethos. In the US, citizenship education was the explicit goal of social studies education, while in England and Wales the more libertarian approach meant that in only some schools was citizenship directly taught. However, subjects such as history and English played a similar role, conveying a sense of nationalism and cultural heritage for students. The modern curriculum was the instrument devised for this task and in both the US and England/Wales a dual education system operated with very different aspirations for the working and ruling classes.

In the twentieth century the meaning of citizenship expanded beyond political rights. Marshall (1950) provided a frequently cited categorization of rights into political, economic and social rights. Rights are an important vehicle for citizens to play a full and active role in civil society, voicing political concerns, participating in social life, ensuring legal protection and contributing to production.

The concept of natural rights, articulated during the Enlightenment, morphed into a discussion of human rights during the twentieth century. While the principle of equal rights for all people is an attractive one to uphold, the history of the modern period has demonstrated that in practice rights are gained in a political struggle with a governing authority. Janoski and Gran maintain that 'At a foundational level, all citizenship rights are legal and political because citizenship rights are legislated by governmental decision-making bodies, promulgated by executive orders, or enacted and later enforced by legal decisions' (Janoski and Gran 2002: 13). Hence, the authors suggest, that legal and political rights undergird other citizenship rights. If this is the case, it raises some questions that inform the contemporary discussion of citizenship: what happens to social rights if citizens do not exercise their formal political rights? What does it mean if citizenship becomes more about social activity and personal conduct without the political dimension?

As discussed above, central to national citizenship is the idea of the nation embodied by its state. Membership of a nation, of a political body, carries meaning only if there is some project or direction that is being advanced through the collective will. It is the crisis of belief in national projects and liberalism more generally that has led political and business leaders to reconfigure a new political project along global lines, presently being reflected in the curriculum. However, this has been achieved only by undermining some of the foundations upon which liberal democracies were fashioned. The conception of global citizenship is not premised upon a central political body directed by autonomous moral subjects. In fact, global citizenship starts from a critique of national citizenship, rejecting the political authority derived from national systems of representation. Instead, it locates morality outside the individual and their society. It finds morality in a set of 'Others': the natural environment, non-Western cultures, victims. This new morality is presented as a basis for education in subjects such as geography. Yet, in rejecting the national lines of political action and responsibility, the parameters of global advocacy are blurred. Who holds political power and responsibility in the global model of citizenship? Who has set this new moral agenda and how do we know whether it is agreed upon? Indeed, its vision of a cosmopolitan individual is decidedly apolitical in nature, where 'political' actions have been re-articulated from a social context to the level of individual identity and behaviour.

What is different about global citizenship?

In global citizenship education, the national citizen has been replaced by a cosmopolitan one. Under normal circumstances, a cosmopolitan perspective would be considered more virtuous than a national one, as its definition suggests: 'having worldwide rather than limited or provincial scope or bearing' or 'having wide international sophistication' (Merriam-Webster 2002: 261). Hence, global citizenship appeals to those seeking to surpass national divisions. However, the contemporary version of cosmopolitan citizenship in geography and other curricula is far from enlightened. Upon closer inspection, its vision of a global citizen has been achieved only through the redefinition of previously held norms of rights, political action, acquisition of knowledge, the privacy of individual conscience and the standing of the political subject itself (see Table 8.1). The outcome is to challenge the very meaning of citizenship itself and in the process empty it of political responsibility and individual moral autonomy.

In the US, and to a lesser extent England/Wales, many of the ideas that inform the rise of global citizenship were already prevalent in school curricula in the 1980s and were radically changing the American social studies and English/Welsh curriculum, although of course they were not labelled as such. That the revision of the traditional liberal model of education preceded the rise of global advocacy in the 1990s illustrates that a more fundamental educational shift is afoot than the scale at which we identify our citizenship. The origin of many of the ideas that inform global citizenship can be found in postmodern social theory, which has grown in influence since the 1970s and was introduced in Chapter 2.

Gilbert proposes a series of questions to help educators identify whether their practice addresses the new issues for citizenship in the postmodern age:

> Do citizenship education programs integrate the social and economic with the political and civil elements? Is the practice of consumption seen as an arena for citizen action? How will citizens' education empower people in their dealings with the media, and does it develop competence in using media forms to express and promote the practice of citizenship? Do programs recognize the importance of a sense of place in the construction of identity, and is this connected with concern for our common future on earth and for the quality of its environment? Does the consideration of the rights and obligations of citizens include their personal welfare in the private sphere as well as their formal status in the public sphere?
>
> (Gilbert 1997: 81)

The starting point for cosmopolitan citizenship is its critique of traditional citizenship, alluded to above. Its advocates decry national citizenship as

Table 8.1 Schematic outline of citizenship models

	National	Cosmopolitan
Geographic focus	Nation	Local and global
Government	State and federal government	Transnational and non-governmental governance
Identity	Nationally determined	Multiple levels, more individual choice
Content of citizenship education	National and/or state: principles, foundations, heritage, structures and mechanisms of government, symbols and traditions	Emphasis on local actions tied to global issues of health, environment, culture, trade and development
Form of citizenship education	Acquisition of disciplinary knowledge, especially history and civics	Acquisition of knowledge about socio-political issues through which values and attitudes are clarified
Civic and political participation	Traditional political issues with state/federal model for political action. Community service	New political issues with new forms of protest/action, e.g. new social movements or consumption
International affairs	Extension of national interest	Nation states have shared interests to solve global problems
Conception of the citizen	Public role contributing to progress of the community and nation	Awareness of contemporary social issues and using them as a guide to personal and social actions
Rights	Defined nationally	All have human rights
Definition of membership	Exclusive	Inclusive
Period	Modernity to 1980s	1980s onwards

exclusivist, elitist, and privileging of Western ideals and history, into which others must be assimilated (see Ong 2004). As was noted in Chapter 2, even knowledge itself has been deconstructed. Western notions of knowledge as potentially universal and objective are dismissed as elitist and not representative of the real world. Instead, knowledge has come to be seen as culturally situated, which inhibits the possibility of finding truths that apply across cultural lines. All knowledge then becomes a moral battleground and the door to a homogeneous culture and shared understanding of history has been closed, for now at least. With social constructivism, knowledge has come to be viewed as not just influenced by the social values of its creators but rooted to them and hence is not truly social in nature.

Thus, global or cosmopolitan citizenship values the contributions of non-Western cultures, including previously alienated minorities and their alternative versions of knowledge, irrespective of the nature of the contribution or the accuracy of their knowledge. In a multicultural approach to citizenship 'The common rights of citizenship, originally defined by and for white, able-bodied, Christian men, cannot accommodate the special needs of these groups. Instead, a fully integrative citizenship must take these differences into account' (Kymlicka, cited in Janoski and Gran 2002: 22). By 'these groups', the author is referring to groups previously excluded from citizenship rights such as minority ethnic groups. Western and national models of citizenship have been dismissed by some for their dualistic approach which elevates the role of the 'Other'. Engin Isin (2002) asserts that Western citizenship is premised upon ideas of Orientalism (that the world is divided into two civilized blocs: one rational, secular and modern, the other 'irrational', religious and traditional) and synoecism (that the polity embodies spatial and political unity). Both of these premises have been challenged by some of the transnational trends described above, especially the transition from a culturally homogeneous nation state to one that promotes pluralism or multiculturalism, and also by post-modernist thought.

However, multiculturalism has meant more than including minorities in the political process; it has led to a new interpretation of politics altogether. Isin explains the role of postmodernism in this process:

> If we define post-modernization as both a process of fragmentation through which various group identities have been formed and discourses through which 'difference' has become a dominant strategy, its effect on citizenship has been twofold. On the one hand, various groups that have been marginalized and excluded from *modern* citizenship have been able to seek recognition . . . On the other hand, these various claims have strained the boundaries of citizenship and pitted group against group in the search for identity and recognition.
>
> (Isin 2002: 122–3)

The shift that Isin describes here is the transition from traditional politics to the politics of identity and recognition. When the focus of citizenship has shifted to recognition of different group identities or claims, then the very meaning of citizenship and politics itself has changed. The modern political system constructed around nation states was premised upon the notion of moral citizens capable of shaping the political course of that nation state, either as individuals or more likely as part of a collective. Individuals may have acquired particular identities, through membership of a political party or trade union, but this was a means to an end: furthering the lot of individuals and society. In cosmopolitan citizenship, identity has become 'a primary ground for the operation of politics' (Rasmussen and Brown 2002: 182). For many, identity is now the ends of politics as much as the means.

The focus on identity is also a consequence of the absence of a collective vision of a better tomorrow, a horizon of expectation (Laïdi 1998). In place of an identity generated by participation in a broad project of social advancement, people increasingly look to the past or present to obtain their sense of identity, finding cultural differences which previously seemed irrelevant, notes Laïdi. For many, the quest for identity has become politics, sometimes to the detriment of the material circumstances of the people themselves. Laïdi cites the break-up of the former Czechoslovakia as one example and the civil war in Iraq is perhaps another. Sustaining the present or fixating on small cultural differences takes the place of social advance; preservation of culture or lifestyles takes precedence over their trans-formation.

This has led many social theorists to reconceptualize the very meaning of politics and the nature of human actions that can be viewed as political in nature. Political action is now interpreted as anything you do as an individual to enact social or personal change, no matter how small. With the politics of identity the goal of political action is to shape identity rather than effect social and material change (Kincheloe 2001). Hence, the realm of the individual psyche has become part of the world of politics. Indeed, academics such as Laclau have drawn upon psychoanalytical and post-structural theory to investigate individual identity formation. Similarly, Mitchell (2003) suggests that nurturing cosmopolitan citizens is about 'the constitution of subjects orientated to individual survival and/or success in the global economy' (Mitchell 2003: 387). Here, the constitution of subjects has been equated with forging identity; subjectivity has been reinterpreted as *who you are* rather than *what you do*.

Therefore, individual acts are now endowed with wider political mean-ing. Hence, one's personal acts of consumption are frequently politicized today; witness the rise of environmentally friendly and socially conscious products, such as organic produce and fair trade coffee, or the moralization of travel (Butcher 2003). Citizens of the nation state were concerned with advancing the productive forces of society. In contrast, a cosmopolitan subject is keenly aware of their consumption choices. In a book describing the rise of the post-material economy, James Heartfield explains, 'Today, the fact that the arena of production is not up for debate means that consumption seems to be the only avenue for self-expression' (Heartfield 1998: 23).

When citizenship actions are reinterpreted in individualized terms, then they become divorced from broader social change. Even social acts are no longer viewed in 'political' terms by many. A study of the attitudes of young Americans towards citizenship revealed that most actions, such as volunteering to help at a hospital or cleaning trash from a river valley, are viewed in personal terms, as philanthropic acts, rather than tied to a broader project of social change (Chiodo and Martin 2005). This contrasts with the attitude of national citizens, who viewed their actions as contributing to the betterment of society. In American schools the development of civic competence was seen as 'the knowledge, skills, and attitudes required of students to be able to assume "the office of citizen" (as Thomas Jefferson called it) in our democratic republic' (National Council for Social Studies 2003). The expectation was that upon reaching adulthood young people would assume the 'office of citizen' in order to effect social change either through upholding moral standards of conduct or directly influencing the political process at state and/or federal scales.

That citizenship actions are today viewed by many young people in individualized or apolitical terms is a reflection of the crisis of liberalism and the delegitimization of social transformation outlined above. When there is no project for social advancement with which citizens can identify, be it at the national scale or otherwise, then they no longer see themselves as 'in the same boat'. Here, the state has lost its ability to offer its citizens a sense of *telos*. It fails to decode the world and place people's lives within a bigger picture of social transformation. Thus, citizenship as a relationship between the individual and the state has become less meaningful and so people do not look to effect social change through the state in the way that they used to. This does not make young people uninterested in social change. Indeed, several studies have shown relatively high rates of volunteering among the current generation (see Lopez 2003). However, they lack a framework for understanding how social change takes place and access to social institutions that seek to transform society in a meaningful way. This has undermined the moral legitimacy of the state to act on people's behalf, as without meaning 'power is nothing' (Laïdi 1998: 16). Instead of viewing power as concentrated in the hands of the state, social theorists have come to view power as socially diffuse and not necessarily the prerogative of the state. This development is reflected in Foucault's theory of power as socially constituted and no longer concentrated in the hands of the centralized state. Instead, he saw power as everywhere embedded in many social institutions and discourses (McHoul and Grace 1993).

Accepting Foucault's thesis involves removing the subject–state relationship from the citizenship equation: 'As politics in Foucauldian and post-modern theory has come to see power everywhere, theories of citizenship have expanded from state–citizen relationship to everything citizens might do to change their circumstances whether or not the state is involved' (Janoski and Gran 2002: 13). Likewise, Ichilov has argued: 'Because societies are equally fragmented, the grounds for the contractual relation individual–society (on which citizenship is said to depend) no longer exists' (Ichilov 1997: 22). One of the consequences of removing citizenship action from a relationship with the state is to divorce the concept of citizenship from power. 'Power is everywhere' is another way of saying it is nowhere or at least that citizens shouldn't focus their attention on where it is concentrated. Instead, cosmopolitan citizenship today is about changing individual attitudes and values, effecting a gradual change in how people see the world and their role in it. In effect, it moves the focus of citizenship on to individual rather than societal change. With globalization and the decline of the state, individuals have to find their own 'horizon of expectation'. However, without a sense of collective possibilities for change, individual transformation is limited in scope. Laïdi surmises that too often citizens find themselves seeking to 'guard against exclusion from the anonymous game' of globalization (Laïdi 1998: 11).

One consequence of relocating the definition of political action from the social and public realm to the personal is that it is now open to anybody. If politics is now about personal action and the construction of identity, then individuals do not necessarily need adult maturity or worldly knowledge to become active citizens. At first glance, conferring rights to those previously excluded from national citizenship appears egalitarian. However, this has been achieved not by raising all to a high level of intellectual and political understanding such that they are equipped to hold the 'office of citizen', but instead by hollowing out the political responsibility from citizenship. Many personal actions that today are interpreted as political, such as recycling, reducing one's carbon footprint, buying local products and so forth are carried out outside of a framework for social progress. Without a vision of how society could advance, the objective of such action is simply to sustain the present. However, these environmental and multicultural projects are even limited in this objective, as they avoid a discussion of power and the mechanisms for social transformation. In the end, individual 'political' acts are celebrated for shaping one's identity, as they are not tied to observable outcomes and hence are devoid of political responsibility. While the rhetoric of individual identity formation appears radical and progressive in that it elevates the role of the individual in shaping identity, it downplays the purposeful social actions from which identity is derived, avoiding the issue of collective action for political change. As Chandler observes, 'Without a prior relationship of collective aspirations and engagement individual activism loses any sense of collective meaning' (Chandler 2004). Political action that can result in meaningful social change comes from citizens who express a common purpose and exercise their political right to bring that change about, by focusing their collective energies on institutions with social and/or political power. Personal actions that are detached from a collective movement for change and avoid the question of power are better understood as moral acts, since whether or not an individual carries them out will not lead to widespread social and political change. They are devoid of larger political repercussions.

This apolitical definition of politics has thus expanded the notion of citizenship to individuals previously deemed unfit for political responsibility, including children. Instead of viewing children as embryonic citizens or citizens in the making, the cosmopolitan model of citizenship treats children as fully competent citizens on a par with adults. The idea of children as active citizens has grown in significance since the 1989 United Nations Convention on the Rights of the Child asserted that the child is 'no longer the passive recipient of benefits, the child has become the subject or holder of rights' (United Nations Convention on the Rights of the Child 1989). There is an expanding literature on 'children's geographies' including a new journal dedicated to the topic that explores the lives of children, their understanding of the world and seeks to empower them as 'active citizens' (see Holloway and Valentine 2000). Students' inclusion in developing their own curriculum has been suggested by some geographers, including Oxford Brookes professor Simon Catling (2003). Writing in the journal *Geography*, Catling has argued for a student-centred curriculum which advocates 'working with children as participants, partners and responsible members of the local and global community' (Catling 2003: 190). However, children can be viewed as 'responsible members of the global community' only if membership does not come with political responsibility. Significantly, 'empowering' children is linked with their participation in a discussion of global ethics in which they reflect on their personal values and actions. This is all that is demanded of citizens in the cosmopolitan model, which is likewise applied to adults, and is the only way that children can be viewed as on a par with adult citizens.

While the attempt to extend rights to previously excluded groups is no doubt well intentioned, it has been achieved only by a hollowing out of the meaning of political responsibility and rights to the detriment of adult citizens themselves. Hannah Arendt has criticized the notion of human rights for failing to take account of the institutions which uphold them. In a discussion about the plight of refugees during World War II she observed:

> If a human being loses his political status, he should, according to the implications of the inborn and inalienable rights of man, come under exactly the situation for which the declarations of such general rights provided. Actually the opposite is the case.
>
> (Arendt 1985: 300)

She continued: 'it turned out that the moment human beings lacked their own government and had to fall back upon their minimum rights, no authority was left to protect them and no institution was willing to guarantee them' (Arendt 1985: 292). Hence, our rights have meaning because they have been gained by citizens with respect to a given political authority. Outside of this political context, for instance in a foreign country, an individual does not have the same rights. Today, human rights violations are upheld to justify Western intervention in situations such as Darfur, Sudan or Kosovo, but whether or not someone acts on these so-called violations of rights is entirely dependent upon the whim of powerful nations or external advocates. This points towards a further problem with the current notion of cosmopolitan citizenship, the separation of the rights holder and the rights advocate (see Table 8.2).

In modern nation states, citizens were both the holders and the advocates of rights. People fought for and defended their own rights. In the new cosmopolitan model, the holder of rights and the advocate of rights are frequently separated. The previous chapter on global issues showed that global citizenship sometimes calls for unaccountable advocates to champion the rights of others. This is a dangerous precedent, since, without legal appointment, who has the right to speak on behalf of another? And what happens when the advocates misrepresent the rights and interests of the rights holders? This approach to rights is predicated on an assumption of the incapacity of rights holders, elevating the role of external advocates.

This is certainly true in the case of education and children. As noted above, the inclusion of children as global citizens is not tied to any elevated faith in their moral capacities. In fact the opposite is the case. Proponents of global citizenship education presume that people are not evolving into political subjects through the acquisition of knowledge and skills alone. This leaves them potentially detached from public life and a meaningful relationship to the state. As noted by political theorist Vanessa Pupavac, 'the children's rights discourse, premised on the incompetency of the child, challenges the assumption that the rights-bearing individual is competent' and 'calls into question the existence of the rational, autonomous individual' (Pupavac 2000: 146). The very idea of children's incompetence and detachment from contemporary social issues has raised the possibility for the state to play a constituting role with respect to individual morality and identity. The presumption is that this is not coming from the parents, otherwise why would intervention be necessary? That the state and professionals are promoting global citizenship education calls into question the legitimacy and capacity of parents to undertake such a task: 'Children's rights empower professionals to act in the name of the child and undermine the right of the individual citizens to decide how to bring up their children' (Pupavac 2000: 146).

In an attempt to establish new meaningful connections between itself and citizens, the state is seeking to ensure the psychological and moral well-being of children through its schools (Nolan 1998; Furedi 2004). The

Table 8.2 Conceptions of national and human rights

	National right	*Human rights*
Geographic scale	National	Global
Type	Exclusive	Inclusive
Subject holder	Individual self	Individual self
Advocate/originator	Individual self	External other
Guarantor	State/federal government	?

Source Pupavac (2005).

new emphasis upon the positive emotional and moral well-being of the individual is not just some new fad. Indeed, it has become the new organizing principle of education in both the US and England and Wales. Nurturing a positive self-concept or self-esteem in children is today seen as essential both to moral growth and to learning in general. The reorganization of education to promote self-esteem has been well documented (Hewitt 1998; Ecclestone 2004). It informs lessons on sex education (which includes all relationships), drugs education, physical education, health education, but also mathematics, science, languages and geography. The previous chapter illustrated how geography's ethical turn has led to a combined focus on moral and psychological objectives for students in the geography curriculum.

With the conflation of politics and identity liberalism's separation of private conscience and the public realm, which acted as a defence against the politicization of the curriculum, no longer makes sense. Instead, the realm of the individual psyche has come to be seen as an essential element of citizenship education. Again, this happened first in the US, with psychological and emotional objectives being imported into the curriculum in the 1980s (Hunter 2001). At a time when traditional citizenship and education were being questioned, Hunter suggests, psychology appealed as a scientific and neutral way to 'understand and cultivate the best qualities of the human person' (Hunter 2001: 82). While theocracy and ideology were being undermined as sources of moral authority, social theorists began to articulate an emotional side to morality. Hunter suggests that in the late 1970s 'the idea of mental and emotional well-being has become established as the foundation for positive social behaviour and moral conduct' (Hunter 2001: 84): for instance, that empathy was necessary for justice, fear a prerequisite to courage and experiencing threats to one's livelihood would breed caution.

In this therapeutic model of education students are encouraged to look inwards into their own personalities and lives rather than outwards to gain an understanding of the real world. 'Supporters of a therapeutic approach to education do not look outwards to social change and genuine political consciousness but inwards to explore or repair damaged identities,' notes educational theorist Kathryn Ecclestone (2004: 131). However, such introspection is more likely to lead to self-obsession than to a basis for political action. With the cosmopolitan model of citizenship, identity takes on 'an individualized, emotional and introspective form', rather than being seen as 'a foundation for a politicised or social understanding' (Ecclestone 2004: 123).

Concluding comments

The crisis of education and citizenship identified above has been precipitated by liberalism's decline and a loss of faith in the potential for social transformation. This is not to argue that nation states have some unique claim on human progress and emancipation. They do not. In the modern era, nation states encouraged a divisive view of the world and led millions of citizens to undertake personal sacrifice for some questionable political causes. There is also no way back to the national model of citizenship and neither should there be. However, in moving to a post-national view of citizenship and society, there are certain ideas and principles inherent in the national model that are worth maintaining as foundational to any movement for social progress. These include faith in the individual and collective capacities of people, including future citizens, to shape the world as they see fit. For young people to assume their 'office of citizenship' they need access to a broad and rigorous liberal education, including subjects such as geography, so that they can comprehend and interpret the world they inherit.

Yet global advocacy, expressed in the geography curriculum as global perspectives, is none of these things. On the contrary, it lacks a vision of social progress, a final goal, leadership and faith in collective action. Global advocacy is premised upon a so-called 'cosmopolitan' citizenship model, which lacks faith in the moral capacity of autonomous individuals. Without a framework for social change, the cosmopolitan model removes citizenship from its social and political context, sidestepping questions of power and social change, and recasts it as a project in individual transformation. This reinvention of the meaning of citizenship has refocused education on to the values, attitudes and psychological well-being of students, instead of their intellectual development. The state and professional educators have been recast as guardians of the emotions and values, the very identity, of young people. Tellingly, lessons on global citizenship seek to explore the ethics of students, encouraging them to look inwards to their personalities, rather than outwards to engage with knowledge, literature and political understanding so that they might one day shape their own world. Thus, global advocacy is not the starting point of social transformation, but rather its very negation.

Suggested further reading

Catling, S. (2003) 'Curriculum Contested: Primary Geography and Social Justice', *Geography* 88 (3): 164–210.

Chandler, D. (2002) *From Kosovo to Kabul: Human Rights and International Intervention*, London: Pluto Press.

Duffield, M. (2007) *Development, Security and Enending War: Governing the World of Peoples*, Cambridge: Wiley.

Ecclestone, K. (2004) 'Learning or Therapy? The Demoralisation of Education', *British Journal of Educational Studies*, 52 (2): 112–37.

Isin, E. and Turner, B. (eds) (2002) *Handbook of Citizenship Studies*, Thousand Oaks, CA: Sage.

Laïdi, Z. (1998) *A World without Meaning*, London: Routledge.

Mitchell, K. (2003) 'Educating the National Citizen in Neo-liberal Times: From the Multicultural Self to the Strategic Cosmopolitan', *Transactions of the Institute of British Geographers*, 28: 387–403.

Pupavac, V. (2000) 'From Statehood to Childhood: Changing Approaches to International Order', in M. Pugh (ed.) *Regeneration of Wartorn Societies*, London: Macmillan.

Pupavac, V. (2005) 'The Demoralised Subject of Global Civil Society', in B. Gideon and D. Chandler (eds) *Global Civil Society: Contested Futures*, London: Routledge.

Conclusion

Global perspective in the curriculum: demoralized geography, demoralized citizenship

This conclusion will show that *Global Perspectives in the Geography Curriculum* amounts to much more than a reflection on a post-national world. Indeed, its deconstruction of the nation state, its political system and perspective on the world is simultaneously a deconstruction of social progress, expressed in the form of liberal democracy, its education system, built upon the intellectual foundations of subjects such as geography, and the individual moral being. To the extent that it offers any perspective on the world, it is one that devalues these human achievements.

For geography, global perspectives have served to further undermine its inherent qualities, leading to a growth of instrumental aims for the subject, including social, economic, political and moral objectives. The inherent qualities of geography have been eroded by cultural relativism, its contextually rooted view of knowledge and a therapeutic ethos, culminating in the subject's embrace of 'cosmopolitan' or global citizenship education. Geography as a universal discipline that helps young people to visualize, to understand and to make sense of the world around them has been undermined, in some educational settings, by policy makers and social theorists who see knowledge and identity as culturally rooted. In these instances the subject of geography has been demoralized: emptied of its moral content.

In place of a scientific and/or humanistic geography, a new rationale has emerged for the subject in many curricula. Students are told that geography can offer them global or multiple perspectives on the world. Yet, despite this apparently progressive aim, this book has shown how precisely the opposite is the case. Global advocacy is characterized by an absence of social perspectives because it lacks a vision of social progress and faith in the individual and collective moral capacities of citizens. Reflecting liberalism's contemporary crisis, it encompasses decidedly illiberal and ultimately dehumanizing tendencies, which are imported into the geography curriculum in the form of global perspectives.

As Marsden (2001a) observes, education *for* citizenship is an inherently authoritarian practice in that it counters one of the foundations of liberalism: *the freedom of the individual* to determine their own moral values. Instructing students in how they should live their lives and the values to which they should conform is tantamount to denying them the possibility to shape their own future. As Arendt noted, 'It is in the very nature of the human condition that each new generation grows into an old world, so that to prepare a new generation for a new world can only mean that one wishes to strike from the newcomers' hands their own chance at the new' (Arendt 1968: 174). One of the cornerstones of liberal democracies was that each generation was free to change the world as it saw fit.

Of course, nation states also did not always live up to the ideals of liberal democracy. National citizenship education itself contained an inherent illiberal tendency, in that it sought to mould the value system of young people to serve national interests. However, in seeking to find a new post-national basis for citizenship, there are certain principles worth preserving from the national model; in particular, its notion of an individual autonomous moral being who, through political association, could shape their society. And, in order to assume the 'office of citizen', young people need to learn something about the world, so that they have ideas and opinions to put forth.

In the twenty-first century, the conception of the individual 'cosmopolitan' citizen in some geography curricula is fundamentally at odds with these democratic foundations. Unlike national citizens, the current cosmopolitan citizen is conceived as an individual who will not develop into a moral being by virtue of education, political knowledge and adult maturity. Its starting point is an individual of diminished human capacity. Hence, the moral self of cosmopolitan citizens needs to be *guided* or *directed* through values education. While national citizenship education sought to influence the value system of young people as they developed into autonomous moral subjects through education and life experiences, with global citizenship education moulding the moral individual to fit predetermined ethics and personality traits has become a central focus of lessons, devaluing the importance of geographical knowledge and skills. In the absence of a political community to provide meaning to individuals' lives, so-called cosmopolitan citizens are expected to conform to contemporary Western ethics (environmental values, cultural diversity, social justice, empathy and respect for an Other), dispositions and behaviours. As noted in Chapter 7, global issues in geography curricula have frequently been extracted from their geographical and political setting and instead presented through the eyes of contemporary Western ethics. As such, this inhibits the ability of students to explore the *real* issues people face in their given locality, gain an understanding of their lives and maybe achieve *genuine* respect and empathy for them. With a global perspective these values, as curricular objectives, are foisted upon students, not something they are allowed to realize for themselves. This imposed view of the world can only lead to values that are superficial and insincere. Therefore, while the national liberal model of education sought to create moral citizens, global citizenship undermines the moral self, in that the state and professionals have taken responsibility for fundamental aspects of personality, such as values and emotional responses, away from the individual.

With global perspectives, geographical education is being redefined as inculcation into a mindset and model of behaviour determined by the state, NGOs or professional educators. For students, embracing 'global perspectives' equates with conforming to this model of identity, which confers membership of its 'global community'. While the state can no longer provide meaning to the lives of its future citizens as stakeholders in a project for social advancement, it is seeking to play a new therapeutic role by influencing the psycho-social development of individuals (Nolan 1998; Furedi 2004).

If adopting global perspectives confers membership of a 'community', it is a community that holds an antisocial and dehumanizing view of the world. The loss of faith in the individual moral selves of students parallels a more widespread loss of faith in *social progress*. Under national citizenship, individuals were provided with a positive vision, albeit a limited one, of society and the role of people in effecting social change. Competing Left and Right wing ideologies of how society might progress shared a common belief in the potential for human emancipation. In nation states morality was derived from its potential to advance the lives of its citizens and their society. This morality was informed by a vision of nations capable of utilizing their productive forces to shape the landscape in beneficial ways, to advance material wealth and human capital, to resolve natural and social problems as they arose, albeit from differing ideological standpoints. These competing ideologies were also founded upon a belief in the universal potential of knowledge, values and the economic and political systems they upheld. Despite their shortcomings, they expressed faith in human potential to comprehend the world and pool collective human resources to change it for the betterment of humankind. Whichever ideology one clung to, it provided meaning for the lives of citizens through connections with a project for improving society for tomorrow (see Laïdi 1998). Conversely, the message carried by global perspectives in the curriculum is precisely the opposite: that people cannot accurately know their world and that attempts to change it have negative outcomes.

In the twenty-first century, Western society has lost its faith in the potential of humanity to change the world for the better and hence seeks to regulate and restrict people's freedom instead of expressing faith in it. This is the political context that informs the character of global perspectives. As this book has illustrated, some geography curricula have adopted aspects of this misanthropic outlook and communicate these to students by portraying environmental limits to production, consumption, development and growth; by presenting people as destructive and polluting of the natural environment; through its pluralistic interpretation of culture, in which people's identity is ruled by who they are rather than what they do; and, also, by instructing students in the limited potential of disciplines such as geography to accurately describe and explain the world.

This demoralized view of humanity likewise informs the presentation and interpretation of social progress for the developing world, in some geography curricula. In ways reminiscent of the colonial past, Western intervention in the South today takes the form of 'educating' people in the ways of sustainable development, respecting cultural differences and human rights. In doing so, global perspectives generate a new division between the morally superior West and the supposedly immoral South. However, the likely outcome of this moral divide is to maintain a relationship of dependency, sustaining the underdeveloped status of the South and enhancing global injustice (Duffield 2007b). Real social justice for the South will only come about when its people can determine their own future, rather than the one that fits the West's 'global' values (Pupavac 2006).

While in liberal democracies morality and meaning were derived from the potential of nation states to advance the lives of their citizens individually and collectively, cosmopolitan citizenship situates morality and meaning outside of the individual and their society. Each of the global values described above is external to the self and/or our current society. Hence, with global perspectives, there is no place to advance the lives of young people or society in general. The only vision offered in global perspectives is that we should all be subservient to an Other: the natural environment, people of other cultures, minorities or victims. Here, the global dimension is about 'decreasing pupils' egocentricity' (Lambert *et al.* 2004). In effect, this means teaching them to respect differences of opinion rather than challenge them. But of course this removes the possibility for any collective advancement in understanding the world or social improvement.

Despite national bias, the liberal model of education was premised upon the idea that young people needed to know something about the world in order that they could participate in political projects to change it for the better. With global perspectives the process has been reversed. Global issues convey to students a negative interpretation of humanity's role in the world. They are explored in some geography curricula with the expectation that students will internalize the anti-human values that inform global issues. While a liberal education encouraged students to open their eyes to the world around them and see possibilities of social progress, global perspectives teach them to gaze inwards at themselves and internalize limited human aspirations. In other words, it seeks to deny them their humanity.

Reclaiming the moral case for geography

There are two essential steps that need to be taken for geography to re-establish its intrinsic worth in the education of students. First, a clear separation needs to be made between the world of politics and the lives of children. As Hannah Arendt cautioned, a 'destruction of the real living space occurs wherever the attempt is made to turn children themselves into a kind of real world' (Arendt 1968: 183). In effect, this demands that all political, social and economic extrinsic aims for geography are expelled from the discipline. Schools need to be recognized as institutions of education, not a place to fix social and political problems which arise in the adult political sphere. Children need 'a place of security where they can grow' (Arendt 1968: 183). They need the sanctuary from the real world that schools can offer them while simultaneously providing insight into the adult world. Only by shielding children from the real world of political responsibility and public attention will they be able to focus on the task of education and be given the space to act as children, not adults. Such a space is essential for young people to experiment, to learn, to enquire, to hypothesize and find their feet in the world, without political conse-quences. This is why many skilled teachers frequently mimic real-life scenarios in lessons, but without real-life consequences.

Creating such a space for children to develop is not lowering our expectations of them. In fact it is the opposite. It is raising them. Expect-ing children to assume political responsibility as citizens before they have reached adult intellectual and emotional maturity demonstrates the absence of moral autonomy expected of individuals implicit in the cosmopolitan model of citizenship currently being promoted in some geography curricula. The focus on the values, identity and emotional state of students, directing the moral self, in the teaching of global perspectives illustrates the low expectations professionals hold towards the capa-bilities of young people to develop their own moral compass and identity. The danger with this approach is that it can become a self-fulfilling prophecy, as noted by Ecclestone: 'A therapeutic ethos erodes optimism that education should enable people to transform their own and others' lives and embeds psychological deficiency in educational beliefs about people' (Ecclestone 2004: 131). Young people take their lead from adults. The more you tell young people that they need moral guidance and psychological support, the more they are likely to believe it. Nevertheless, this means that it is adults who are in a position to turn the situation round. By raising their expectations of students, teachers can communicate a belief in their personal and intellectual capabilities and an expectation that young people must assume responsibility for the world upon reaching adulthood. By providing students with a space separate from the real world they can develop intellectually and emotionally to a degree adequate to assume the 'office of citizen'. Through their instruction, teachers will communicate to young people that there is much learning to be done before they are ready to take on board this responsibility.

The second step for geography to reclaim its moral worth is that educators must take responsibility themselves both for the world around them and for how their discipline enlightens students about this world. Again, the insights of Arendt are helpful here. She notes that teachers occupy a position at the gateway *Between Past and Future*. It is they who must stand before children and show them the world, and implicitly take responsibility for that world, even though they may 'secretly wish it were different':

> The teacher's qualification consists in knowing the world and being able to instruct others about it, but his authority rests upon his assumption of responsibility for that world. *Vis-à-vis* the child it is as though he were a representative of all adult inhabitants, pointing out the details and saying to the child: This is our world.
>
> (Arendt 1968: 186)

The teacher's authority derives from the perceived responsibility for the world because it shows the up-and-coming generation the nature of political responsibility they are soon to inherit.

For geography teachers this means being clear about how the subject helps students to make sense of the world. They need to know the inherent educational qualities that geography has to offer. Here, it is not necessary to reinvent the wheel. As noted in Chapter 1, the discipline evolved into a science over hundreds of years, with some clarity about its purpose emerging in the middle to late twentieth century. No doubt the curriculum needs updating to incorporate recent geographical change, but its underlying qualities should remain relatively constant. The following list of educational qualities draws heavily from Phil Gersmehl's text *Teaching Geography*, to which geography students are referred for a more detailed account of geography's underlying qualities and principles.

Geography is the discipline that deals with knowledge of location. Gersmehl (2005) identifies four foundational ideas that underpin geographical enquiry: location, place, links and region. Through an exploration of these four linked concepts, geography helps students to:

1 *Know where things are (location).* You have to know where something is before you can study it (Gersmehl 2005). This might include an absolute and relative location of a *site* as well as knowledge of its *situation*, what is around the location. To describe locations requires mastery of some spatial concepts, including distance, direction, adjacency and enclosure.

2   *Understand different places (place)*. Included here are knowledge of a location's characteristics that give it a unique character (climate, vegetation, geology, population, culture, land use, economic activities, etc.) as well as the reasons behind them. Students then need to understand some of the causes and effects behind the characteristics of places, including natural and human causes and historical legacies. This involves both a recognition that each location has a 'distinctive mix of forces that interact to produce unique features' as well as 'dominant forces that in turn have a number of predictable consequences' (Gersmehl 2005: 66).

3   *Understand connections between different locations (links)*. Locations are not spatially isolated. They have natural and human connections to other locations both near and far. The shape of the landscape can bring some locations in proximity to one another or throw up geographic boundaries between them. Rivers and climate can connect different locations. Political boundaries determine which locations are governed by which state and which set of social norms and laws. Today, economic activity connects numerous localities that otherwise have no obvious relationship.

4   *Identify and comprehend spatial patterns (region)*. Regionalization is a form of classification which helps students to make sense of otherwise incomprehensible amounts of data. Regions can be either formal (groups of places with similar characteristics) or functional (places linked through some connecting activity or feature).

A fifth core idea that could be added is that geography also helps students view and understand the human condition. (Gersmehl might argue that this is achieved through his four foundational cornerstones.) However, it has been highlighted here as many teachers see geography as part of the humanities as well as a science. Of course this objective is not unique to geography, but is accomplished by all the disciplines that contribute towards the humanities. It does this through:

1   Identifying and describing cultural practices that arise in different social and natural circumstances.
2   Identifying and describing different landscapes shaped by human ideas and actions.
3   Exploring the issues faced by people in different localities and under different physical conditions.

Geography realizes all of the above aims through the teaching of facts, theories and issues. Gersmehl rightly notes that geography teachers need to discriminate between different facts, theories and issues, since not all are equally important for students to learn. Also, he cautions against the tendency for textbooks to seek to cover the whole world and all geographical topics. This is not necessary to grasp the underlying principles and ideas behind geography. However, curriculum leaders must decide upon the most important facts that students should learn. This might include facts that help students to identify geographical features at different geographical scales as well as facts that help them to observe the range of geographical features on offer at a given locality. Curricula should also specify which locations are the most important ones for students to learn about. This list will be location-specific but might also include the most influential countries, some rapidly developing countries and locations that vary geographically, economically, culturally and politically.

However, geographers are going to be able to teach students about the importance of location only if they seek to describe accurately and explain the world. While many geography teachers already do this, others present truth as relative and seek to avoid making judgements about how the world is. As Kronman observes, 'there can be no coherent discussion of any subject without an implicit belief in the possibility of discovering the truth about it' (Kronman 2007: 133). Geography is a medium for understanding the world, and without a direct connection with reality it ceases to fulfil this task: geographical knowledge loses its explanatory power and becomes meaningless to the student.

With regard to selecting causal traits and theories that students need to learn, hypothesis testing is a scientifically rigorous method of approach (Gersmehl 2005). Gersmehl suggests three questions for evaluating their intellectual credibility:

1   Does the theory explain the observed data?
2   If the theory explains the data, does it also fit with other generally accepted theories?
3   If several theories explain the data, which one has the fewest undesirable side-effects?

(ibid.: 68)

The formulation of hypotheses, theories and laws enables geographers to model and predict real-world phenomena. In the classroom these abstract models help students to identify and understand spatial differences and patterns.

In order to acquire the insights of geography, students must also learn the tools and skills of geographers. This includes:

1   Asking geographical questions about what can be found where and why.
2   Gathering geographical information, including fieldwork, maps, spatial data or other data/theories needed to help answer the question.

3 Organizing geographical information into a coherent form that can be analysed.
4 Displaying geographical information on maps, cartograms, graphs, Geographical Information Systems etc.
5 Answering geographical questions through interpretation of results and drawing appropriate conclusions.

This list is analogous to the research skills identified by Roberts (2006). These skills need to be intimately tied to the foundational knowledge and ideas students need to acquire to become competent geographers. Some of the above skills are by no means unique to geography, such as data handling and analysis, but others such as spatial analysis and map construction are.

As noted in Chapter 1, there are generally two approaches that geography teachers take towards the subject, the regional or the thematic. The regional approach involves learning about the many features of one area or region, while the thematic approach addresses spatial patterns on a broad scale. Frequently, teachers and textbooks try to combine the two by inserting regional case studies into a thematic approach or inserting themes into the regional approach. Gersmehl suggests that learning is enhanced when the two are not separated, rather the teacher moves from one to the other. Such an approach enables students to comprehend an important part of the geographical perspective: 'awareness that the world has forces that operate on a global scale but interact with other forces on a local scale' (Gersmehl 2005: 18). From this brief account of the unique qualities of the discipline it is possible to gain some insight into the real meaning of gaining a 'geographical perspective'. In short, this means learning to see what is around us beyond superficial appearances, to place facts and information into a wider framework of knowledge, to identify and comprehend how things are spatially related and to identify the interaction of spatial phenomena at large and small scales.

To date, *Geography for Life: The National Standards*, as compiled by the Association of American Geographers, the National Geographic Society and the National Council for Geographic Education, is probably the most comprehensive document outlining the content of geographical education for students at secondary/high-school level. This document was the outcome of a decade's work involving some 350 geographers. That said, some find its eighteen standards rather cumbersome and prefer to work with the five themes identified by the 1984 *Guidelines for Geographic Education*. Gersmehl thinks that the inclusion of the theme 'human–environment relations' was a defensive move on the part of the authors, who were reacting to the rise of environmental education. He sees this theme as implicit within his four foundational concepts and he probably has a point.

For many geography's strength is its ability to engender in students a sense of wonder at the world around them. Initially, students, like all people, are motivated by an inner 'curiosity about the reasons and causes for the world's being as it is' which is characterized by an absence of understanding (Kronman 2007: 216). This leads to a quest for knowledge or the process of education at the end of which lies a second sense of wonder. Here, our wonder *about* things has been transformed into wonder *at* them, 'to amazement at the structures of things and our capacity to grasp this structure ourselves' (*ibid.*: 217). In essence, education is a thing of beauty in and of itself, regardless of its utility. It is also unique to the human world and thus contributes to our humanity. When geography classes can both present students with the complexity of the world and then reveal order in this complexity, this learning experience is motivation enough for most students. The curriculum does not need to be made 'relevant' to the lives of students or to be about them. Rather, it should lead them into an existence beyond their own, giving them a truly geographical perspective on the world.

Suggested further reading

Arendt, H. (1968) *Between Past and Future*, with an introduction by J. Kohn (2006), New York: Penguin.
Gersmehl, P. (2005) *Teaching Geography*, New York: Guilford Press.

Bibliography

Adams, W. M. (2001) *Green Development: Environment and Sustainability in the Third World*, 2nd edition, London: Routledge.

Advisory Group on Citizenship (1998) *Education for Citizenship and the Teaching of Democracy in Schools: Final Report of the Advisory Group on Citizenship*, London: Qualifications and Curriculum Authority.

Agnew, J. (2003) 'Contemporary Political Geography: Intellectual Heterodoxy and its Dilemmas', *Political Geography*, 22: 603–6.

Ainsley, F., Elbow, G. and Greenow, L. (1992) *World Geography: People in Time and Place*, Morristown, NJ: Silver Burdett & Ginn.

Allen, R., Bettis, B., Kurfman, D., McDonald, W., Mullins, I. and Salter, C. (1990) *The Geography of High School Seniors*, Washington, DC: Office of Educational Research and Improvement, US Department of Education.

Allott, P. (2001) 'Globalization from Above: Actualizing the Ideal through Law', in K. Booth, T. Dunne and M. Cox (eds) *How Might We Live? Global Ethics in the New Century*, Cambridge: Cambridge University Press.

Anderson, R. (1983) 'Geography's Role in Promoting Global Citizenship', *NASSP Bulletin*, 67: 138–9.

Arendt, H. (1968) *Between Past and Future*, with an introduction by J. Kohn (2006), New York: Penguin.

Arendt, H. (1985) *The Origins of Totalitarianism*, San Diego, CA: Harcourt.

Arreola, D., Deal, M., Petersen, J. and Sanders, R. (2005) *McDougal Littell World Geography*, Boston, MA: Houghton Mifflin.

Asia Society (2007) *International Education: What are the Goals?*, accessed at http://www.internationaled.org/goals.htm (visited 24 June 2007).

Asia Society (2008) *Directory of State Initiatives*, accessed at http://www.internationaled.org/directory.htm (visited 28 January 2008).

Assessment and Qualifications Alliance (2002) *GCSE Geography Specification A*, accessed at http://www.aqa.org.uk/qual/pdf/AQA-3031-3036-W-SP-04 (visited 30 May 2003).

Association of American Geographers (2006) 'AP Human Geography Testing Surges', *AAG Newsletter*, 41 (11), December 2006.

Bacon, P. (1989) *World Geography: The Earth and its People*, Orlando, FL: Harcourt Brace Jovanovich.

Baerwald, T. and Fraser, C. (2005) *World Geography: Building a Global Perspective*. Upper Saddle River, NJ: Prentice Hall.

Baker, R. (2005) 'Global Catastrophe, Global Response', *Teaching Geography*, 30 (2): 66–9.

Barker, E. (1958) *The Politics of Aristotle*, London: Oxford University Press.

BBC (2005) *Photo Journal: A Sri Lankan Survivor*, accessed at http://news.bbc.co.uk/ 2/shared/spl/hi/picture_gallery/04/south_asia_sri_lankan_tsunami_survivor /html/1.stm (visited 18 July 2007).

Bednarz, S. (2003) 'Citizenship in the Post-9/11 United States: A Role for Geography Education?' *International Research in Geographical and Environmental Education*, 12 (1): 72–80.

Bednarz, S. (2004) 'US World Geography Textbooks: Their Role in Education Reform', *International Research in Geographical and Environmental Education*, 13 (3): 16–31.

Boehm, R. (2005) *Glencoe World Geography*, New York: Glencoe.

Bohan, C. H. (2004) 'Early Vanguards of Progressive Education: The Committee of Ten, the Committee of Seven, and Social Education', in C. Woyshner, J. Watras and M. S. Crocco (eds) *Social Education in the Twentieth Century*, New York: Peter Lang.

Bowen, J. (1981) *A History of Western Education* III, London: Methuen.

Braungart, R. and Braungart, M. (1998) 'Citizenship Education in the United States in the 1990s', in O. Ichilov (ed.) *Citizenship and Citizenship Education in a Changing World*, Portland, OR: Woburn.

British Petroleum (2007) *Statistical Review of World Energy 2007*, accessed at http://www.bp.com/sectiongenericarticle.do?categoryId=9017902&contented= 7033474 (visited 1 January 2008).

Brooks, D. (2000) *Bobos in Paradise: the New Upper Class and How They Got There*, New York: Simon & Schuster.

Bruner, J. (1960) *The Process of Education*, Cambridge, MA: Harvard University Press.

Bruner, J. (1966) *The Culture of Education*, Cambridge, MA: Harvard University Press.

Burack, J. (2003) 'The Student, the World, and the Global Education Ideology', in J. Leming, L. Ellington and K. Porter-Magee (eds) *Where Did the Social Studies Go Wrong?* Washington, DC: Thomas B. Fordham Institute.

Burchell, D. (2002) 'Ancient Citizenship and its Inheritors', in E. Isin and B. Turner (eds) *Handbook of Citizenship Studies*, Thousand Oaks, CA: Sage.

Butcher, J. (2003) *The Moralisation of Tourism: Sun, Sand and . . . Saving the World*, London: Routledge.

Butcher, J. (2007) *Ecotourism, NGOs and Development*, London: Routledge.

Catling, S. (2003) 'Curriculum Contested: Primary Geography and Social Justice', *Geography*, 88 (3): 164–210.

Central Bureau/Development Education Association (2000) *A Framework for the International Dimension for Schools in England*, London: Central Bureau/ Development Education Association.

Chandler, D. (2002) *From Kosovo to Kabul: Human Rights and International Intervention*, London: Pluto Press.

Chandler, D. (2004) *Constructing Global Civil Society: Morality and Power in International Relations*, Basingstoke: Palgrave Macmillan.

Chandler, D. (2005) 'Constructing Global Civil Society', in G. Baker and D. Chandler (eds) *Global Civil Society: Contested Futures*, Abingdon: Routledge.

Chiodo, J. and Martin, L. (2005) 'What do Students Have to Say about Citizenship? An Analysis of the Concept of Citizenship among Secondary Education Students', *Journal of Social Studies Research*, 26 (2): 3–9.

Chorley, R. and Haggett, P. (eds) (1965) *Frontiers in Geographical Teaching*, London: Methuen.

Chorley, R. and Haggett, P. (1967) *Models in Geography*, London: Methuen.

Cotton, K. (1996) 'Educating for Citizenship', *School Improvement Research Series*, accessed at www.nwrel.org/scpd/sirs/10/c019.html (visited 4 January 2004).

Dagger, R. (2002) 'Republican Citizenship', in E. Isin and B. Turner (eds) *Handbook of Citizenship Studies*, Thousand Oaks, CA: Sage.

Danzer, G. and Larson, A. (1982) *Land and People: A World Geography*, Glenview, IL: Scott Foresman.

De Blij, H. and Muller, P. (2006) *Geography: Realms, Regions and Concepts*, 12th edn, Hoboken, NJ: Wiley.

Department for Education and Employment/Qualifications and Curriculum Authority (1999) *The National Curriculum for England: Geography*, London: Department for Education and Employment/Qualifications and Curriculum Authority.

Department for Education and Employment (1999) *Preparing Young People for Adult Life*, London: Department for Education and Employment.

Department for Education and Science (1967) *Children and their Primary Schools: A Report of the Central Advisory Council for Education*, London: HMSO.

Department for Education and Science (1991) *Geography in the National Curriculum*, London: HMSO.

Department for Education and Skills/Department for International Development (2000, updated 2005) *Developing a Global Dimension in the School Curriculum*, London: Department for Education and Employment/Department for International Development/ Qualifications and Curriculum Authority *et al.*

De Roche, E. and Williams, M. (2001) *Educating Hearts and Minds: A Comprehensive Character Education Framework*, Thousand Oaks, CA: Corwin Press.

Development Education Association (2001) *Citizenship and Education: The Global Dimension*, London: Development Education Association.

Disinger, J. (2001) 'Tensions In Environmental Education: Yesterday, Today, and Tomorrow', in J. Disinger, E. McCrea and D. Wicks, *The North American Association for Environmental Education: Thirty Years of History, 1971–2001*, accessed at http://naaee.org/aboutnaaee/naaeehistory2001.pdf (visited 20 July 2003).

Dorsey, B. (2001) 'Linking Theories of Service Learning and Undergraduate Geography Education', *Journal of Geography*, 100: 124–32.

Douglas, L. (2001) 'Valuing Global Citizenship', *Teaching Geography*, 26 (2): 89–90.

Dowler, L. (2002) 'The Uncomfortable Classroom: Incorporating Feminist Pedagogy and Political Practice into World Regional Geography', *Journal of Geography*, 101: 68–72.

Driessen, P. (2003) *Eco Imperialism: Green Power, Black Death*, Bellevue, WA: Merril.

Duffield, M. (2001) *Global Governance and the New Wars: The Merger of Development and Security*, New York: Zed Books.

Duffield, M. (2007a) *Development, Security and Unending War: Governing the World of Peoples*, Chichester: Wiley.

Duffield, M. (2007b) 'Development, Territories, and People: Consolidating the External Sovereign Frontier', *Alternatives: Global, Local, Political*, 32: 225–46.

Dunn, R. (2002) 'Growing Good Citizens with a World-Centred Curriculum', *Educational Leadership*, 60 (2): 10–13.

Ecclestone, K. (2004) 'Learning or Therapy? The Demoralisation of Education', *British Journal of Educational Studies*, 57 (3): 127–41.

Economist (2004) 'Saving the Rainforest', *Economist*, 24 July, 372: 12.

Edexcel (2000) *Specifications for GCSE in Geography A: First Examination 2003*, London: Edexcel Foundation.

Edwards, G. (2002) 'Geography, Culture, Values and Education', in R. Gerber and W. Williams (eds) *Geography, Culture and Education*, London: Kluwer Academic Publications.

Ellington, L. and Eaton, J. (2003) 'Multiculturalism and the Social Studies', in J. Leming, L. Ellington and K. Porter-Magee (eds) *Where did the Social Studies Go Wrong?* Washington, DC: Thomas B. Fordham Foundation.

English, P. (1995) *Geography: People and Places in a Changing World*, St Paul, MN: West.

Falk, R. (1995) *On Humane Governance: Towards a New Global Politics*, Cambridge: Polity Press.

FAO (2005) *Global Forest Resource Assessment*, accessed at http://www.fao.org/forestry/foris/data/fra2005/kf/common/GlobalForestA4-ENsmall.pdf (visited 15 January 2008)

Ferve, R.W. (2000) *The Demoralization of Western Culture: Social Theory and the Dilemmas of Modern Living*, New York: Continuum.

Fien, J. and Gerber, R. (1988) *Teaching Geography for a Better World*, Edinburgh: Oliver & Boyd.

Finn, C. and Ravitch, D. (2004) *The Mad, Mad World of Textbook Adoption*, Washington, DC: Thomas B. Fordham Institute.

Flemming, D. (1981) 'The Impact of Nationalism on World Geography Textbooks in the United States', *International Journal of Political Education*, 4: 373–81.

Frymier, J., Cunningham, L., Duckett, W., Gansneder, B., Link, F., Rimmer, J. and Schulz, J. (1996) 'Values and the Schools: Sixty Years Ago and Now', *Research Bulletin*, 17: 4–5, Bloomington, IN: Phi Delta Kappa, Center for Evaluation, Development and Research.

Fukuyama, F. (1992) *The End of History and the Last Man*, London: Hamish Hamilton.

Furedi, F. (1997) *Population and Development: A Critical Introduction*, Cambridge: Polity Press.

Furedi, F. (2004) *Therapy Culture: Cultivating Vulnerability in an Uncertain Age*, London: Routledge.

Furedi, F. (2007) 'Introduction: Politics, Politics, Politics', in R. Whelan (ed.) *The Corruption of the Curriculum*, London: Civitas.

Gardner, H. (1983) *Frames of Mind: The theory of multiple intelligences*. New York: Basic Books.

Gardner, H. (2000) *Intelligence Reframed: Multiple Intelligences for the Twenty-First Century*, New York: Basic Books.

Geographical Association (1998) 'Geography and History in the 14–19 Curriculum', *Teaching Geography*, 23 (3): 125–8.

Geographical Association (1999) 'Geography in the Curriculum: A Position Statement', *Teaching Geography*, 24 (2): 57–9.

GeoVisions GCSE Working Party (undated) *A Planning Guide to Support the OCR Pilot Short Course in Geography (Geography 21)*, accessed at http://www. geography.org.uk/download/PRGCSEpilotGCSE.doc (visited 22 June 2007).

Gerber, R. and Williams, M. (eds) (2002) *Geography, Culture and Education*, London: Kluwer Academic Publications.

Gersmehl, P. (2005) *Teaching Geography*, New York: Guilford Press.

Gilbert, R. (1997) 'Issues for Citizenship in a Postmodern World', in K. Kennedy (ed.) *Citizenship and the Modern State*, Washington, DC: Falmer Press.

Goldman, D. (1995) *Emotional Intelligence: Why it can Matter more than IQ*, New York: Bantam Books.

Goodman, J. and Lesnick, H. (2001) *The Moral Stake in Education: Contested Premises and Practices*, New York: Longman.

Gordon, D. (ed.) (2003) *A Nation Reformed? American Education Twenty Years After: A Nation at Risk*, Cambridge, MA: Harvard Education Press.

Gore, A. (1990) *Earth in the Balance: Ecology and the Human Spirit*, Boston, MA: Houghton Mifflin.

Goss, H. (1985) *World Geography*, Rockleigh, NJ: Allyn.

Gourevitch, A. (2007) 'National Insecurities: The New Politics of American National Self-Interest', in J. Bickerton, P. Cuncliffe and A. Gourevitch (eds) *Politics without Sovereignty: A Critique of Contemporary International Relations*, London: University College of London Press.

Greene, J. (1984) *American Science in the Age of Jefferson*, Ames, IA: Iowa State University Press.

Grimwade, K., Reid, A. and Thompson, L. (2000) *Geography and the New Agenda*, Sheffield: Geographical Association.

Gritzner, C. (1985) *Heath World Geography*, Lexington, MA: Heath.

Habermas, J. (1996) *Between Facts and Norms: Contributions to a Discourse Theory of Law and Democracy*, Cambridge, MA: MIT Press.

Hall, D. (1991) *Charney Revisited: Twenty-five Years of Geography Education'*, in R. Walford (ed.) *Viewpoints on Teaching Geography: The Charney Manor Conference Papers*, Harlow: Longman.

Hammond, P. (2007) *Media, War and Postmodernity*, London: Routledge.

Harrington, R. (2005) *Aristotle and Citizenship: The Responsibilities of Citizenship in Politics*, accessed at http://www.greycat.org/papers/aristotl.html (visited 29 December 2007).

Hartshorne, R. (1939) *The Nature of Geography*, Lancaster, PA: Association of American Geographers.

Hartshorne, R. (1950) 'The Functional Approach in Political Geography', *Annals of the Association of American Geographers*, 40: 95–130.

Harvey, D. (1973) *Social Justice and the City*, London: Edward Arnold.

Harvey, D. (1982) *The Limits to Capital*, Chicago: University of Chicago Press.

Hayl, J. and McCarty, J. (2003) 'International Education and Teacher Preparation in the US', paper presented at the conference on *Global Challenges and US Higher Education: National Needs and Policy Implications*, 24 January.

Heartfield, J. (1998) *Need and Desire in a Post-Material Economy*, Sheffield: Sheffield Hallam University Press.

Held, D. (2002) 'Globalization, Corporate Practice and Cosmopolitan Social Standards', *Contemporary Political Theory*, 1: 59–78.

Helgren, D. and Sager, R. (2005) *World Geography Today*, Austin, TX: Holt, Rinehart & Winston.

Hewitt, J. (1998) *The Myth of Self-Esteem: Finding Happiness and Solving Problems in America*, New York: St Martin's Press.

Hewlett Packard (2007) *HP Global Citizenship*, accessed at http://www.hp.com/hpinfo/globalcitizenship/ (visited 9 June 2007).

Hicks, D. (2001) 'Envisioning a Better World', *Teaching Geography*, 26 (2): 57–60.

Hicks, D. (2003) 'Thirty Years of Global Education: A Reminder of the Key Principles and Precedents', *Education Review*, 55: 265–75.

Hirst, P. (1974) *Knowledge and the Curriculum*, London: Routledge and Kegan Paul.

Holloway, S. and Valentine, G. (2000) *Children's Geographies: Playing, Living, Learning*, London: Routledge.

Holt, T. (1991) 'Growing up Green: Are Schools turning Kids into Eco-activists?' *Reason*, 38–40.

Huckle, J. (1983) 'Values Education through Geography: A Radical Critique', *Journal of Geography*, 82 (2): 59–63.

Huckle, J. (2002) 'Reconstructing Nature: Towards a Geographical Education for Sustainable Development', *Geography*, 87 (1): 64–72.

Hulme, M. (in press) 'The Conquering of Climate: Discourses of Fear and their Dissolution', *Geographical Journal*.

Humanities Education Centre (2007) *Global Footprints Quiz*, accessed at http://www.globalfootprints.org/issues/kidsquiz/kidsquizl.htm (visited 10 October 2007).

Hunter, J. (2001) *The Death of Character: Moral Education in an Age without Good or Evil*, New York: Basic Books.

Huntington, S. (2004) *Who Are We? Challenges to America's National Identity*, New York: Simon & Schuster.

Ichilov, O. (1997) 'Patterns of Citizenship in a Changing World', in K. Kennedy (ed.) *Citizenship and the Modern State*, Washington, DC: Falmer Press.

Independent Commission on Environmental Education (1997) *Are We Building Environmental Literacy?* Washington, DC: George C. Marshall Institute.

International Geographic Union/Commission on Geographic Education (1992) *International Charter on Geographic Education*, Brisbane: International Geographic Union/Commission on Geographic Education.

Isin, E. (2002) 'Citizenship after Orientalism', in E. Isin and B. Turner (eds) *Handbook of Citizenship Studies*, Thousand Oaks, CA: Sage.

Isin, E. and Turner, B. (eds) (2002) *Handbook of Citizenship Studies*, Thousand Oaks, CA: Sage.

Israel, S., Roemer, N. and Durand, L. (1976) *World Geography Today*, Holt, Reinhart & Winston.

Jackson, R. (1976) 'The Persistence of Outmoded Ideas in High School Geography Texts', *Journal of Geography*, 75: 399–408.

James, P. and Davis, N. (1967) *Wide World: A Geography*, New York: Macmillan.

Janoski, T. and Gran, B. (2002) 'Political Citizenship: Foundations of Rights,' in E. Isin and B. Turner (eds) *Handbook of Citizenship Studies*, Thousand Oaks, CA: Sage.

Jarolimek, J. (1990) 'The Knowledge Base of Democratic Citizens', *Social Studies*, 81 (5): 194–7.

Jickling, B. and Spork, H. (1998) 'Education for the Environment: A Critique', *Environmental Education Research*, 4 (3): 309–27.

Johnsen, E. (1993) *Textbooks in Kaleidoscope: A Critical Survey of the Literature and Research on Educational Texts*, New York: Oxford University Press.

Johnson, A. (2007) 'Children Must Think Differently', *Independent*, 13 June.

Johnston, R. (2000) 'Authors, Editors, and Authority in the Postmodern Academy', *Antiopode*, 32 (3): 271.

Johnston, R., Gregory, D., Pratt, G. and Watts, M. (2000) 'Cultural Geography', in *The Dictionary of Human Geography*, 4th edn, Oxford: Blackwell.

Jones, S. and Murphy, M. (1962) *Geography and World Affairs*, Chicago: Rand McNally.

Kaldor, M. (2001) *New and Old Wars: Organized Violence in a Global Era*, Stanford, CA: Stanford University Press.

Kaufhold, T. (2004) 'Geography Education: Where is Geography's Location in our Schools' Curriculum?' *Middle States Geography*, 37: 90–9.

Keith, S. (1991) 'The Determinants of Textbook Content', in P. Altbach, G. Kelly, H. Petrie and L. Weis (eds) *Textbooks in American Society*, Albany, NY: State University of New York Press.

Kincheloe, J. (1991) *Curriculum as Social Psychoanalysis: The Significance of Place*, New York: State University of New York Press.

Kincheloe, J. (2001) *Getting beyond the Facts: Teaching Social Studies/Social Sciences in the Twenty-First Century*, New York: Peter Lang.

Kirman, J. (2003) 'Transformative Geography: Ethics and Action in Elementary and Secondary Geography Education', *Journal of Geography*, 102: 93–8.

Knight, D. (1982) 'Identity and Territory: Geographical Perspectives on Nationalism and Regionalism', *Annals of the Association of American Geographers*, 72 (4): 514–31.

Knox, P. and Marston, S. (2004) *Human Geography: Places and Regions in a Global Context*, 3rd edn, Upper Saddle River, NJ: Person/Prentice Hall.

Kohn, C. and Drummond, D. (1971) *World Today: Its Patterns and Cultures*, New York: McGraw-Hill.

Kronman, A. (2007) *Education's End: Why our Colleges and Universities have Given up on the Meaning of Life*, New Haven, CT: Yale University Press.

Laïdi, Z. (1998) *A World without Meaning*, London: Routledge.

Lambert, D. and Machon, P. (2001) *Citizenship through Secondary Geography*, London: RoutledgeFalmer.

Lambert, D., Morgan, A., Swift, D. and Brownlie, A. (2004) *Geography: The Global Dimension: Key Stage 3*, London: Development Education Association.

Lasch, C. (1984) *The Minimal Self: Psychic Survival in Troubled Times*, New York: Norton.

Lasch-Quinn, E. (2001) *Race Experts: How Racial Etiquette, Sensitivity, Training and New Age Therapy Hijacked the Civil Rights Revolution*, New York: Rowman & Littlefield.

Lawes, S. (2007) 'Foreign Languages without Tears', in R. Whelan (ed.) *The Corruption of the Curriculum*, London: Civitas.

Livingstone, D. (1992) *The Geographical Tradition: Episodes in the History of a Contested Enterprise*, Oxford: Blackwell.

Lomborg, B. (2001) *The Skeptical Environmentalist: Measuring the Real State of the World*, Cambridge: Cambridge University Press.

Lopez, M. H. (2003) *Volunteering among Young People*, Centre for Information and Research on Civic Learning and Engagement, accessed at http://www.civicyouth.org/PopUps/FactSheets/FS_Volunteering2.pdf (visited 6 January 2008).

McEachron, G. (2001) *Self in the World: Elementary and Middle School Social Studies*, Boston, MA: McGraw-Hill.

McGovern, C. (2007) 'The New History Boys', in R. Whelan (ed.) *The Corruption of the Curriculum*, London: Civitas.

Machon, P. (1998) 'Citizenship and Geographical Education', *Teaching Geography*, 23 (3): 115–17.

Machon, P. and Walkington, H. (2000) 'Citizenship: The Role of Geography?' in A. Kent (ed.) *Reflective Practice in Geography Teaching*, London: Paul Chapman.

McHoul, A. and Grace, W. (1993) *A Foucault Primer: Discourse, Power and the Subject*, New York: New York University Press.

McKeown, R. and Hopkins, C. (2003) 'EE Does Not Equal ESD: Defusing the Worry', *Environmental Education Research*, 9 (1): 117–28.

Mackinder, H. (1887) 'On the Scope and Methods of Geography', paper given at the *Proceedings of the Royal Geographical Society and Monthly Record of Geography*, London, 31 January.

Makler, A. (2004) '"Problems of Democracy" and the Social Studies Curriculum', in C. Woyshner, J. Watras and M. S. Crocco (eds) *Social Education in the Twentieth Century*, New York: Peter Lang.

McNaught, A. and Witherick, M. (2001) *Global Challenge: A2 Level Geography for Edexcel B*, Harlow: Longman.

Marsden, W. (1997) 'On Taking the Geography out of Geographical Education: Some Historical Pointers in Geography', *Geography*, 82 (3): 241–52.

Marsden, W. (2001a) 'Citizenship Education: Permeation or Pervasion? Some Historical Pointers', in D. Lambert and P. Machon (eds) *Citizenship through Secondary Geography*, London: RoutledgeFalmer.

Marsden, W. (2001b) *The School Textbook: Geography, History and Social Studies*, London: Woburn Press.

Marshall, H. (2005) 'Developing the Global Gaze in Citizenship Education: Exploring the Perspective of Global Education NGO Workers in England', *International Journal of Citizenship and Teacher Education*, 1 (2): 76–92.

Marshall, T. (1950) *Citizenship and Social Class and other Essays*, Cambridge: Cambridge University Press.

Mayhew, R. (2000) *Enlightenment Geography: The Political Languages of British Geography, 1650–1850*, New York: St Martin's Press.

Meadows, D. H., Meadows, D. L., Randers, J. and Behrens, W. III (1972) *The Limits to Growth: A Report for the Club of Rome's Project on the Predicament of Mankind*, New York: Universe Books.

Merrett, C. (2000) 'Teaching Social Justice: Reviving Geography's Neglected Tradition', *Journal of Geography*, 99 (2): 207–18.

Merriam-Webster (2002) *Merriam-Webster's Collegiate Dictionary*, 10th edn, Springfield, MA: Merriam-Webster.

Midgely, M. (1999) 'Towards an Ethic of Global Responsibility', in T. Dunne and N. Wheeler (eds) *Human Rights in Global Politics*, 195–213, Cambridge: Cambridge University Press.

Mitchell, K. (2003) 'Educating the National Citizen in Neo-liberal Times: From the Multicultural Self to the Strategic Cosmopolitan', *Transactions of the Institute of British Geographers*, 28: 387–403.

Mortensen, L. (2000) 'Global Change Education: Education Resources for Sustainability', in K. Wheeler and A. Bijur (eds) *Education for a Sustainable Future: A Paradigm of Hope for the Twenty-First Century*, New York: Kluwer Academic/ Plenum Publishers.

Mullen, (2004) '"Some Sort of Revolution": Reforming the Social Studies Curriculum, 1957–1972', in C. Woyshner, J. Watras and M. S. Crocco (eds) *Social Education in the Twentieth Century*, New York: Peter Lang.

National Council for the Accreditation of Teacher Education (2006) *Professional Standards for the Accreditation of Schools, Colleges and Departments of Education*, Washington, DC: NCATE, accessed at http://www.ncate.org/institutions/ unitStandardsRubrics.asp?ch=4 (visited 10 October 2007).

National Council for Geographic Education (1994) *Geography National Standards: Geography for Life*, Washington, DC: Committee for Research and Exploration, National Geographic Society.

National Council for Geographic Education (2003) *The Eighteen National Geography Standards* accessed at http://www.ncge.org/publications/tutorial/standards (visited 10 April 2003).

National Council for Social Studies (2003) *Expectations of Excellence: Curriculum Standards for Social Studies* http://www.socialstudies.org/standards/strands/ (visited 21 April 2004).

National Curriculum Council (1993) *Spiritual and Moral Development: A Discussion Paper*, York: National Curriculum Council.

National Geographic Society (2006) *My Wonderful World: For Educators*, accessed at nttp://www.mywonderfulworld.org/educators_welcome.html (visited 7 July 2007).

National Geographic Society (2007) *Geography Standards in your Classroom: Lesson Plans*, accessed at http://www.nationalgeographic.com/xpeditions/lessons/ 18/g68/tghunger.html (visited 18 July 2007).

New Jersey Department of Education (2006) *New Jersey Core Curriculum Content Standards for Social Studies*, Trenton, NJ: Department of Education.

Nolan, J. (1998) *The Therapeutic State: Justifying Government at Century's End*, New York: New York University Press.

North American Association for Environmental Education (2003) *Perspectives: Foundations of EE*, accessed at http://eelink.net/perspectives-foundationsofee. html (visited 21 July 2008).

Nuffield Foundation (2006) *Citizenship through Geography*, accessed at http:// www.citizenship.org.uk/resources/citizenship-through-geography,68,NA. html (visited 12 June 2006).

Ong, A. (2004) 'Higher Learning: Educational Availability and Flexible Citizenship in Global Space', in J. Banks (ed.) *Diversity and Citizenship Education*, San Francisco, CA: Jossey-Bass.

Orr, D. W. (1992) *Ecological Literacy: Education and the Transition to a Postmodern World*, Albany, NY: State University of New York Press.

Orrell, K. (1990) 'The Schools Council Geography 14–18 Project', in R. Walford (ed.) *Viewpoints on Teaching Geography: The Charney Manor Conference Papers*, Harlow: Longman.

Oxfam (1997) *Curriculum for Global Citizenship, Oxfam Development Educational Programme*, Oxford: Oxfam.

Oxford, Cambridge and RSA Examinations (2004) *OCR GCSE in Geography (Pilot) Specifications*, Cambridge: Oxford, Cambridge and RSA.

Palmer, J. and Neal, P. (1994) *The Handbook of Environmental Education*, London: Routledge.

Packard, L., Overton, B. and Wood, B. (1953) *Geography of the World*, New York: Macmillan.

Pak, Y. K. (2004) 'Teaching for Intercultural Understanding in the Social Studies: A Teacher's Perspective in the 1940s', in C. Woyshner, J. Watras and M. S. Crocco (eds) *Social Education in the Twentieth Century*, New York: Peter Lang.

Pattison, W. D. (1961) 'The Four Traditions of Geography', *Journal of Geography*, 63 (5): 211–16.

Peet, R. (1998) *Modern Geographical Thought*, Malden, MA: Blackwell.

Perks, D. (2006) *What is Science Education For?* London: Institute of Ideas.

Pounds, N. and Cooper, E. (1957) *World Geography: Economic, Political, Regional*, Cincinnati, OH: Southwestern Publishing.

Proctor, J. D. and Smith, D. M. (1999) *Geography and Ethics: Journeys in a Moral Terrain*, London: Routledge.

Project Wild (2003) *About Project Wild*, accessed at http://www.projectwild.org/aboutPW/about.htm (visited 17 July 2003).

Pupavac, V. (2000) 'From Statehood to Childhood: Changing Approaches to International Order', in M. Pugh (ed.) *Regeneration of Wartorn Societies*, London: Macmillan.

Pupavac, V. (2002) 'Afghanistan: The Risks of International Psychosocial Risk Management', *Heath in Emergencies* (WHO), 12, accessed at http://www.who.int/hac/about/7735.pdf (visited 1 October 2008).

Pupavac, V. (2005) 'The Demoralised Subject of Global Civil Society', in B. Gideon and D. Chandler (eds) *Global Civil Society: Contested Futures*, London: Routledge.

Pupavac, V. (2006) 'The Politics of Emergency and the Demise of the Developing State: Problems for Humanitarian Advocacy', *Development in Practice*, 16 (3–4): 255–69.

Qualifications and Curriculum Authority (1998) *Areas of Cross-Curricular Concern within Citizenship Education*, London: Qualifications and Curriculum Authority.

Qualifications and Curriculum Authority (2001) *Citizenship at Key Stage 3*, London: Qualifications and Curriculum Authority, accessed at http://standards.dfes.gov.uk/schemes2/citizenship/.

Qualifications and Curriculum Authority (2002a) *Citizenship at Key Stages 1 and 2*, London: Qualifications and Curriculum Authority, accessed at http://www.standards.dfes.gov.uk/schemes2/ks1–2citizenship/.

Qualifications and Curriculum Authority (2002b) *Citizenship at Key Stage 4*, accessed at http://www.standards.dfes.gov.uk/schemes2/ks4citizenship/?view=get.

Qualifications and Curriculum Authority (2002c) *GCE AS and A-level Specifications: Subject Criteria for Geography*, accessed at http://www.qca.org.uk/nq/subjects/geography.asp (visited 22 June 2002).

Qualifications and Curriculum Authority (2007) *Draft GCSE Subject Criteria for Geography*, London: Qualifications and Curriculum Authority.

Rasmussen, C. and Brown, B. (2002) 'Radical Democratic Citizenship: Amidst Political Theory and Geography', in E. Isin and B. Turner (eds) *Handbook of Citizenship Studies*, Thousand Oaks, CA: Sage.

Ravallion, M. and Chen, S. (2004) *Understanding China's (Uneven) Progress against Poverty, Finance and Development*, December, accessed at http://www.imf.org/external/pubs/ft/fandd/2004/12/pdf/ravallio.pdf (visited 10 January 2008).

Ravitch, D. (2003) *The Language Police: How Pressure Groups Restrict What Students Learn*, New York: Knopf.

Ravitch, D. and Viteritti, J. (2001) *Making Good Citizens: Education and Civil Society*, New Haven, CT: Yale University Press.

Rawling, E. M. (1991) 'Innovations in the Geography Curriculum, 1970–1990: A Personal View', in R. Walford (ed.) *Viewpoints on Teaching Geography: The Charney Manor Conference Papers, 1990*, York: Longman.

Rawling, E. M. (2001) *Changing the Subject: The Impact of National Policy on School Geography, 1980–2000*, Sheffield: Geographical Association.

Reid, A. (2001) 'Environmental Change, Sustainable Development and Citizenship', *Teaching Geography*, 26 (2): 72–6.

Roberts, M. (2003) *Learning through Enquiry: Making Sense of Geography in the Key Stage 3 Classroom*, Sheffield: Geographical Association.

Roberts, M. (2006) 'Geographical Enquiry', in D. Balderstone (ed.) *Secondary Geography Handbook*, Sheffield: Geographical Association.

Robinson, L. (2001) 'Leaving More than Just Footprints', *Teaching Geography*, 26 (2), 56.

Roth, K. (1999) 'Human Rights Trump Sovereignty in 1999', *Human Rights Watch*, 9 December, accessed at: http://www.hrw.org/press/1999/dec/wr2keng.htm (visited 10 June 2005).

Ruskey, A., Wilke, R. and Beasley, T. (2001) 'A Survey of the Status of State-Level Environmental Education in the United States – 1998 Update', *Journal of Environmental Education*, 32 (3): 4–14.

Sager, R. and Helgren, D. (2005) *World Geography Today*, Austin, TX: Holt, Reinhart & Winston.

Sanera, M. and Shaw, J. (1999) *Facts, Not Fear: Teaching Children about the Environment*, Washington, DC: Regnery Publishing.

Sassens, S. (2002) 'Towards Post-National and Denationalized Citizenship', in E. Isin and B. Turner (eds) *Handbook of Citizenship Studies*, Thousand Oaks, CA: Sage.

Schools Curriculum Assessment Authority (1997) 'Geography Position Statement' (internal Geography Team paper for National Curriculum Review Conference), London: Schools Curriculum Assessment Authority.

Schuck, P. (2002) 'Liberal Citizenship,' in E. Isin and B. Turner (eds) *Handbook of Citizenship Studies*, Thousand Oaks, CA: Sage.

Scott, P. (2004) 'Quick, Hide, the Bin Police are Coming', *The Times*, 27 March, accessed at http://www.timesonline.co.uk/tol/comment/columnists/guest_contributors/article1052217.ece (visited 10 January 2008).

Sennett, R. (1976) *The Fall of Public Man*, New York: Norton.

Shanker, A. (1996) 'The Importance of Civic Education', *Issues in Democracy*, 1 (8), accessed at http://usinfo.state.gov/journals/itdhr/0796/ijde/shanker.htm (visited 10 December 2006).

Shaver, J. (1977) *Building a Rationale for Citizenship Education*, Bulletin No. 52, Arlington, VA: National Council for Social Studies.

Simon, J. (1981) *The Ultimate Resource*, Princeton, NJ: Princeton University Press.

Sinclair, S. (1997) 'Going Global?' *Teaching Geography*, 22 (4): 160–4.

Sitarz, D. (1993) *Agenda 21: The Earth Summit Strategy to Save our Planet*, Boulder, CO: Earthpress.

Sitarz, D. (ed.) (1998) *Sustainable America: America's Environment, Economy and Society in the Twenty-First Century*, President's Council on Sustainable Development, Carbondale, IL: Earthpress.

Smith, D. (1997) 'Geography and Ethics: A Moral Turn?' *Progress in Human Geography*, 21 (4): 583–90.

Smith, D. (2000) *Moral Geographies: Ethics in a World of Difference*, Edinburgh: Edinburgh University Press.

Smith, R. (2002) 'Modern Citizenship', in E. Isin and B. Turner (eds) *Handbook of Citizenship Studies*, Thousand Oaks, CA: Sage.

Standish, A. (2002) 'Curriculum Change in Geography at the Turn of the Twentieth Century', unpublished master's thesis, Department of Education, Canterbury Christchurch University College.

Standish, A. (2006) 'Geographic Education, Globalization, and Changing Conceptions of Citizenship in American Schools, 1950–2005', unpublished doctoral thesis, Department of Geography, Rutgers, the State University of New Jersey.

Steinberg, P. (1997) 'Political Geography and the Environment', *Journal of Geography*, 96 (2): 113–18.

Stoltman, J. (1990) *Geography Education for Citizenship*, Bloomington, IN: Social Studies Development Center, Education Research Index Center, Social Studies Education Consortium.

Stoltman, J. and DeChano, L. (2002) 'Political Geography, Geographic Education, and Citizenship', in R. Gerber and M. Williams (eds) *Geography, Culture and Education*, Boston, MA: Kluwer Academic Publishers.

Stromquist, N. (2002) *Education in a Globalized World: The Connectivity of Economic Power, Technology, and Knowledge*, New York: Rowman & Littlefield.

Strouse, J. (2001) *Exploring Socio-cultural Themes in Education: Readings in Social Foundations*, Upper Saddle River, NJ: Merrill Prentice Hall.

Surface, G. (1909) 'Thomas Jefferson: A Pioneer of American Geography', *Bulletin of the American Geographical Society*, 41: 743–50.

Swift, D. (2005) 'Linking Lives through Disaster and Recovery', *Teaching Geography*, 30 (2): 78–81.

Tatham, G. (1951) 'Geography in the Nineteenth Century', in G. Taylor (ed.) *Geography in the Twentieth Century*, London: Methuen.

Taylor, I. (2007) 'Unpacking China's Resource Diplomacy in Africa', in H. Melber (ed.) *China in Africa*, Current African Issues, 33: Uppsala, Nordiska Africainstitut.

Trenholm, C., Devenay, B., Fortson, K., Quay, L., Wheeler, J. and Clark, M. (2007) *Impacts of Four Title V, Section 510 Abstinence Education Programs*, Princeton, NJ: Mathematica Policy Research.

Tuan, Y. F. (1977) *Space and Place: The Perspective of Experience*, Minneapolis, MN: University of Minnesota Press.

Tye, B. B. and Tye, K. A. (1992). *Global Education: A Study of School Change*. Albany, NY: State University of New York Press.

UNESCO–UNEP (1978) *Final Report: Intergovermental Conference on Environmental Education*, Tbilisi: United Nations Scientific and Cultural Organization/United Nations Environment Programme.

United Nations Convention on the Rights of the Child (1989) *Convention on the Rights of the Child*, Geneva: Office of the High Commissioner for Human Rights.

Van Matre, S. (1990) *Earth Education: A New Beginning*, Greenville, WV: Institute for Earth Education.

Vaux, T. (2001) *The Selfish Altruist*, Earthscan, London.

Veck, W. (2002) 'What Are the Proper Ends of Educational Inquiry: Research for Justice, for Truth, or Both?' Paper presented to biennial conference of the International Network of Philosophers of Education, Oslo, 9 August.

Walford, R. (1995) 'Geography in the National Curriculum of England and Wales: Rise and Fall?' *Geographical Journal*, 166 (2): 192–8.

Walford, R. (2001) *Geography in British Schools, 1850–2000: Making a World of Difference*, London: Woburn Press.

Wagner, P. and Mikesell, M. (eds) (1962) *Readings in Cultural Geography*, Chicago: University of Chicago Press.

Waugh, D. and Bushell, T. (2002) *New Key Geography for GCSE*, Cheltenham: Nelson Thornes.

Wellington, J. (ed.) (1993) *The Work Related Curriculum: Challenging the Vocational Imperative*, London: Kogan Page.

Westaway, J. and Rawling, E. (2003) 'A New Look for GCSE Geography?' *Teaching Geography*, 28 (1): 60–2.

Wheeler, K. (2000) 'Introduction', in K. Wheeler and A. Bijur (eds) *Education for a Sustainable Future: A Paradigm of Hope for the Twenty-First Century*, New York/London: Kluwer Academic/Plenum Publishers.

Wilbanks, T. (1994) 'Sustainable Development in Geographic Context', *Annals of the Association of American Geographers*, 84: 541–57.

Wood, P. (2005) 'In Defence of the "New Agenda"', *Geography*, 90 (1): 84–9.

Woodward, A., Elliot, D. and Nagel, K. (1988) *Textbooks in Schools and Society: An Annotated Bibliography and Guide*, New York: Garland Publications.

World Commission on Environment and Development (1987) *Our Common Future*, Oxford: Oxford University Press.

Woyshner, C., Watras, J. and Crocco, M. S. (eds) (2004) *Social Education in the Twentieth Century*, New York: Peter Lang.

Yoon Pak (2004) , in C. Woyshner, J. Watras and M. S. Crocco (eds) *Social Education in the Twentieth Century*, New York: Peter Lang.

Zhang, H. and Foskett, N. (2003) 'Changes in the Subject Matter of Geography Textbooks, 1907–1993', *International Research in Geographical and Environmental Education*, 12 (4): 312–29.

Zimmerman, J. (2002) *Whose America? Culture Wars in the Public Schools*, Cambridge, MA: Harvard University Press.

Index